Taking Local Control

PUBLISHED IN ASSOCIATION WITH THE
CENTER FOR COMPARATIVE IMMIGRATION STUDIES
UNIVERSITY OF CALIFORNIA, SAN DIEGO

Taking Local Control

Immigration Policy Activism in U.S. Cities and States

Monica W. Varsanyi, editor

STANFORD UNIVERSITY PRESS • STANFORD, CALIFORNIA

Stanford University Press
Stanford, California

Printed in the United States of America on acid-free, archival-quality paper

Library of Congress Cataloging-in-Publication Data

Taking local control: immigration policy activism in U.S. cities and states / edited by
Monica Varsanyi.
      p. cm.
Includes bibliographical references and index.
ISBN 978-0-8047-7026-2 (casebound: alk. paper)
ISBN 978-0-8047-7027-9 (pbk.: alk. paper)
1. United States—Emigration and immigration—Government policy. 2. Emigration
and immigration law—United States. 3. Local government—United States. 4. State
governments—United States. I. Varsanyi, Monica, 1971–
   JV6483.T33 2010
   325.73—dc22

                         2010018827

Typeset by Jonathan Parker in 9/13.5 Palatino

CONTENTS

SECTION THREE: TRACING THE EVOLUTION OF LOCAL POLICY ACTIVISM

SECTION FOUR: EXPLORING TENSIONS AT THE LOCAL SCALE

PREFACE

When the U.S. Congress failed to enact comprehensive immigration reform in 2006 and again in 2007, this failure—and the political paralysis that it signified—opened a veritable Pandora's Box of state and local immigration control initiatives seeking to fill the policy void. While there had been some significant attempts by the states in the 1990s to legislate by ballot box in this area (California's Proposition 187 in 1994 was the most prominent), there was a quantum leap in such policy activism in 2006 and 2007.

To find a similar period of state- and local-level immigration policy making, we must go back to the early twentieth century, when a series of *pro-immigrant* measures were implemented in various states and cities. For example, in some cities noncitizen immigrants were granted the right to vote and bilingual education was introduced in public schools. In recent years, state- and local-level immigration policy making has taken a decidedly *anti-immigration* direction, particularly in politically conservative areas of the South and Southwest but even along the East Coast. Such activism has taken the form of attempts to restrict unauthorized immigrants' access to public services (including driver's licenses), penalize employers who knowingly hire the undocumented, and increase local police collaboration with federal authorities for immigration law enforcement, among other initiatives.

Why do states and localities pursue such policies? Most commonly, they are justified as responses to federal policy failures and inaction: the executive branch's failure to control the border, gridlock in Congress on immigration reform legislation, the federal government's refusal to reimburse states and localities for social service costs resulting from the presence of unauthorized immigrants in their jurisdictions. But states and localities often have engaged in policy activism not with any real expectation of solving the problems that they attribute to immigration. Rather, they engage in symbolic political acts designed to "send a message" to Washington that tougher action on immigration control is needed. California's Proposition 187 is the classic example. Exit polls found that a large majority of Californians who voted for this measure, aimed at denying public education and nearly all other public services to the undocumented, never expected it to be implemented; rather, they expected the federal courts to strike it down, as indeed occurred.

Sometimes anti-immigrant measures, such as crackdowns on migrant day laborers and landlords who rent to the undocumented, have been portrayed by local governments as appropriate responses to constituent complaints about the "illegals" in their midst. But these types of measures have also proven effective in vote getting, used by politicians from California Governor Pete Wilson to Hazleton, Pennsylvania Mayor Lou Barletta to win reelection or solidify their political base for higher office. In short, states and localities can—and usually do—have mixed motives for pursuing their own immigration policies.

The contemporary United States offers a wide range of such policies for comparative analysis. As a field of study, subnational immigration policy making is important for several reasons. First, state and local policies can affect the outcomes of national-level immigration policies—their efficacy and the uniformity of their effects. Second, state and local measures may go farther than federal laws, one way or another, and thus are substantively important. Third, the collision of state and local government policies with the federal judiciary creates new tensions, often resolved by court rulings that block or attenuate the implementation of such policies. Finally, subnational policies can have significant human impacts. What happens in states and localities can affect immigrants' conditions of employment, housing, education, health, and the life chances of immigrants' U.S.-born children more than can federal laws and policies.

This subject lends itself well to interdisciplinary treatment, and the present volume draws upon the expertise of a broadly multidisciplinary group of scholars, including political scientists, sociologists, anthropologists, geographers, and legal studies practitioners. They provide the first truly comprehensive overview of state and local immigration policy making in the United States, using detailed case study evidence from across the country. The contributors document the determinants, politics, jurisprudence, and consequences of subnational immigration policies and suggest promising new lines of research.

This book grew out of a research workshop held on May 9, 2008, under the auspices of the Center for Comparative Immigration Studies (CCIS) at the University of California, San Diego. Monica Varsanyi, at that time a Visiting Research Fellow of CCIS, proposed the workshop and provided essential intellectual leadership throughout the project. CCIS is delighted to have partnered with Stanford University Press in bringing this important and timely body of work to publication.

Wayne A. Cornelius, Director Emeritus, CCIS
La Jolla, California
23 March 2010

ACKNOWLEDGEMENTS

This book could not have been possible without the support of Wayne Cornelius and the Center for Comparative Immigration Studies (CCIS) at the University of California, San Diego. The ideas presented here first took shape when I was at UC San Diego in 2005 and 2006 and crystallized during the May 2008 conference. And finally, Wayne, along with the new Director and Associate Director of CCIS, John Skrentny and David FitzGerald, provided the financial support for the coproduction of the volume with Stanford University Press. I can't thank them enough.

I would also like to thank the staff of CCIS for their hard work throughout the duration of this project. In particular, I thank Ana Minvielle for her excellent coordination of the May 2008 conference, and Sandra del Castillo, editor extraordinaire, for her careful attention to detail, hard and speedy work, and patience as the final manuscript was whipped into shape.

Thank you, too, to Stacy Wagner, my editor at Stanford, for her good advice as this volume came together.

Colleagues and friends have talked with me about these ideas, offered constructive criticism, and provided much-needed encouragement and assistance. In addition to the contributors to the volume, a big thank you to Marisa Abrajano, Madeline Adelman, Janet Benton, Piers and Sally Blaikie, Sarah Blue, Mat Coleman, Scott Decker, Eileen Diaz-McConnell, Dora Fisher, David FitzGerald, Vanna Gonzales, LaDawn Haglund, María Inclán, Tomás Jiménez, Paul Lewis, April Linton, Alison Lee, Torin Monahan, Lorraine Phillips, Marie Provine, Gaku Tsuda, Eiko Thielemann, and Theresa Thorn. I extend a special thank you to Joe Nevins, who has been a wonderfully supportive colleague, friend, and coauthor, and who has always, despite his own busy schedule, offered help and advice when I most needed it.

And finally, I offer my deepest gratitude to my family, particularly to Luke, whose arrival nearly delayed the completion of the final manuscript; to my mother, whose love and support has always been crucial; and, of course, to Joshua, long my Number One Fan, without whose love, support, enthusiasm, and encouragement none of this would be possible.

For Joshua

1 Immigration Policy Activism in U.S. States and Cities: Interdisciplinary Perspectives

MONICA W. VARSANYI

On November 8, 1994, the California electorate passed Proposition 187, also known as the Save our State initiative, by a two-to-one margin. The proposition was designed to prevent undocumented immigrants living in the state from accessing a variety of publicly funded social services, including health care and education (K–12 as well as postsecondary). It also required all local law enforcement agencies in the state to cooperate with federal authorities in the enforcement of federal immigration law. The campaign leading up to passage of the proposition was full of political rancor. It pitted supporters, who conjured images of illegal immigrants flooding across the U.S.-Mexico border to take advantage of California taxpayers, against opponents, who argued that the proposition would do little to stop illegal immigration and would instead drive a crucial sector of the state's workforce further under ground, where they would pull their children out of school, be afraid to contact the police when victimized by crime, and avoid medical treatment for life-threatening conditions or potentially communicable diseases.

Campaign politics aside, the supporters of Prop. 187 were fighting an uphill legal battle. Though states and cities in the United States are permitted to develop policies that affect immigrants living within their jurisdictions, for the most part they have been excluded from making immigration policy—policy that affects "the entry of noncitizens and their continued stay" (Motomura 1999, 1361)—since the late 1800s, when a series of Supreme Court cases established the federal government's sole authority, or "plenary power," over immigration policy making and enforcement (Aleinikoff 2002; Varsanyi 2008a).

Indeed, in the case that ultimately invalidated much of Prop. 187, *League of United Latin American Citizens (LULAC) v. Wilson* (1995), U.S. District Court Judge Mariana Pfaelzer first reaffirmed the plenary power of the federal government over immigration and naturalization matters, and then invalidated much of the proposition, citing its reliance on a state-level "comprehensive scheme to detect and report the presence and effect the removal of illegal aliens" (769), even though "state agents are unqualified—and also unauthorized—to make independent determinations of immigration status" (770).

Although Judge Pfaelzer's decision shut down California's attempt to get into the immigration enforcement business, echoes of Proposition 187 were heard in Washington, DC. Two years later, as part of the "Republican Revolution," the 104th Congress passed a suite of laws that, among other things, reflected the themes of the proposition. The Personal Responsibility and Work Opportunity Reconciliation Act, the act that (in)famously "[ended] welfare as we know it" (Clinton 1993), dramatically scaled back legal immigrants' access to publicly funded social services, including Food Stamps, Medicaid, Supplemental Security Income, and Temporary Assistance to Needy Families,[1] and devolved authority over select social services to the states. The Antiterrorism and Effective Death Penalty Act gave local police the authority to arrest previously deported noncitizen felons, and the Illegal Immigration Reform and Immigrant Responsibility Act (IIRIRA) created a program whereby local and state police could be trained to enforce federal immigration laws. California voters had spoken and the U.S. Congress had listened.

Over the next few years, states grappled with their newfound authority over welfare programs, but in other realms it seemed that state and local attempts to create immigration policy had come to an end.

In 2002, however, state and local immigration policy activism returned. That year, Arizona state voters passed Proposition 200, "Protect Arizona Now," with 56 percent of the vote. Proposition 200 was modeled after Prop. 187, but was drafted in such a way as to prevent legal challenges of the sort that invalidated the California effort: it required individuals to show proof of citizenship before voting and applying for state-funded public benefit programs. The same year, the Florida Department of Law Enforcement became the first state or local law enforcement agency to sign a memorandum of understanding (MOU) with federal immigration authorities under the 287(g) section of IIRIRA. The MOU agreement enabled thirty-five Florida state troopers to receive training and locally enforce certain aspects of civil immigration law.

---

1. Unauthorized residents were already barred from receiving these benefits.

Not all state and local policy activism was exclusionary: in 2002, the Austin, Texas, Police Department became the first local law enforcement agency to accept the Mexican government–issued *matrícula consular*, or consular ID card, as a valid form of identification for the city's undocumented residents, in response to growing concerns that these residents were fearful of contacting the police when victims of or witnesses to crime (Varsanyi 2007).

This trickle of state and local immigration policy activism soon turned into a flood. In 2005, according to the Immigration Policy Project of the National Conference of State Legislators, state legislatures considered approximately 300 immigration- and immigrant-related bills and passed around fifty. In 2006, 500 bills were considered, 84 of which became law. In 2007, 1,562 immigration- and immigrant-related pieces of legislation were introduced, and 240 became law. And most recently, in 2009, approximately 1,500 laws and resolutions were considered in all 50 state legislatures, and 353 were ultimately enacted.[2] These laws address a wide range of immigrant- and immigration-related issues. They include state-level employer sanctions laws that penalize employers who knowingly employ illegal immigrants, laws preventing undocumented residents from receiving driver's and business licenses, and laws excluding undocumented students from in-state tuition benefits at public colleges and universities. State legislatures have also actively sought to promote the integration of immigrants, and have passed laws increasing legal immigrant eligibility for state-funded health insurance and creating opportunities for immigrants to learn English.

Immigration policy activism has also increased exponentially in cities across the United States. Starting with the decision of the Austin Police Department in 2002, by late 2005 approximately four million *matrículas consulares* had been issued to Mexican nationals living in the United States, and the cards are now accepted by 1,204 police agencies as well as 393 city and 168 county governments.[3] Sixty-four cities—including Los Angeles, Houston, Minneapolis, Seattle, Washington, DC, Philadelphia, and San Francisco—have passed "sanctuary" ordinances declaring their noncooperation with federal immigration authorities except in cases involving felony crimes.[4] And

---

2. http://www.ncsl.org/default.aspx?tabid=19232.

3. Mexican consulate in San Diego, personal communication, December 14, 2005.

4. Sanctuary ordinances have their roots in the Central American refugee flows of the 1980s. The current increase in "limited cooperation" ordinances builds upon policies first developed at that time (Wells 2004; Ridgley 2008; National Immigration Law Center Web site, http://www.nilc.org/immlawpolicy/LocalLaw/locallaw-limiting-tbl-2008-12-03.pdf).

on the exclusionary end of the spectrum, 133 cities have passed or considered Illegal Immigration Relief Acts (IIRAs), ordinances that penalize local employers for hiring undocumented workers and local landlords for renting to undocumented residents,[5] and 67 jurisdictions have signed 287(g) agreements with federal immigration authorities, authorizing over a thousand local law enforcement officers to enforce civil immigration laws (Immigration and Customs Enforcement 2009).

Given the federal government's long-standing plenary power over immigration and the relegation of state and local governments to the realm of immi*grant* policy making, the recent (re)emergence of state and local immigration policy activism raises interesting questions regarding not only the constitutionality of these policies but also the shifting and appropriate role of subnational governments in immigration policy formation. While some policies, such as the acceptance of *matrículas consulares*, can be interpreted as policies of local immigrant *integration*, other policies—such as IIRAs, state and local employer sanctions laws, and local-federal law enforcement cooperation emerging from 287(g) agreements—can more readily be interpreted as influencing immigration—not only into the nation-state, *but in states and localities*. Therefore, these policies, contentious as they are, can be interpreted as *local immigration policy*, something that since the late nineteenth century in the United States has been a constitutional impossibility. These policies blur and cross the line between a politics of immigrant integration—public policy—and a politics of immigration control—technically considered foreign policy in the United States (Coleman 2008), dealing, as they do, with relationships between the United States and foreign powers. And indeed, a number of these policies have been challenged in courts on these grounds.

Just as these emerging policies cross and blur long-held constitutional boundaries, the study of these policies necessitates a multidisciplinary perspective that crosses and blurs conventional disciplinary boundaries. There is a long and venerable tradition, particularly in sociology, of studies exploring the local integration (or assimilation) of immigrants, particularly in "traditional gateways" such as Chicago, Boston, and New York (Park and Burgess 1925; Gans 1962; Portes and Zhou 1993; Foner 2002; Kasinitz, Mollenkopf, and Waters 2006; Kasinitz et al. 2008).[6] More recently, scholars

---

5. Puerto Rican Legal Defense and Education Fund database of cities considering local anti-immigrant ordinances, http://www.prldef.org/Civil/LATINO%20JUSTICE%20 CAMPAIGN.xls.

6. See Rogers and Tillie 2001; Penninx et al. 2004; Alexander 2007; and García 2007 for discussions of urban immigrant integration policies in the European context; Tsuda

have turned their attention to the shifting settlement patterns and integration of immigrants into nontraditional "new destinations" in the American South and Midwest and in suburbs and rural towns throughout the United States (Zúñiga and Hernández-León 2005; Smith and Furuseth 2006; Massey 2008; Singer, Hardwick, and Brettell 2008; Nelson and Hiemstra 2008). Other studies have explored the political incorporation of immigrants as voters and active citizens in urban America (DeSipio 1996; Jones-Correa 1998; Varsanyi 2005). And political scientists and others who study immigration politics and policy (as opposed to immigrant integration) have, on the whole, studied a *national* "politics of control," in other words, policies that influence the entry, exclusion, and expulsion of migrants into and out of the territory of the nation-state (Cornelius et al. 2004; Torpey 2000; Andreas 2000; Aleinikoff 2002; Tichenor 2002; Nevins 2002; Ngai 2003; Zolberg 2006; Hollifield 2008).

However, one of the unique and challenging characteristics of state and local immigration politics and policy is that they blur the conventional boundary between, for instance, political scientists' focus on a politics of control—a focus on immi*gration*, which is generally approached from the perspective of the nation-state and federal politics—and sociologists' or anthropologists' focus on (a politics of) integration, with a focus on immi*grants*, more often from a local or urban perspective. Therefore, this volume approaches the phenomenon from both multidisciplinary and interdisciplinary perspectives, including as it does chapters by an anthropologist, demographers, geographers, legal scholars, political scientists, and sociologists. Each author writes both from the perspective of her or his discipline and necessarily reaches beyond conventionally understood disciplinary boundaries to address this emerging phenomenon, blurring analyses of control with those of integration and engaging with the multiscalar dynamics—local, state, and national—of these policies.

What explains the recent explosion in state and local immigration policy activism? What policies have been considered and passed, and what are the justifications given? What tensions have emerged as a result of these policies within communities and between different levels of government? Does this wave of grassroots policy activism point to cracks in the foundation of the federal government's plenary power over immigration? What role are state and local governments playing in the creation and enforcement of immigration policy, and what role *should* they play? These are the questions, among

---

2006 for coverage of Japan; and Kemp and Raijman 2004 and Alexander 2007 for looks at similar policies in Israel.

others, that the contributors to this volume seek to answer. While state and local immigration policy activism in the United States has received widespread attention in the popular media, this phenomenon has yet to receive sustained coverage in the scholarly literature, and as such, detailed description, analysis, and explanation of this phenomenon are in short supply.[7] This volume aims to fill this gap.

In this introductory chapter, I first present the historical context in which the federal government's plenary power developed and discuss the legal decisions that restricted the participation of states and localities in immigration policy making. I then discuss three types of factors—economic, demographic, and political—that have combined to create the context in which state and local immigration policy activism is currently emerging. Lastly, I provide an overview of the themes and chapters in the volume, concluding with some thoughts outlining possible, much-needed future research trajectories.

HISTORICAL CONTEXT

For the first hundred years of American history, during what legal scholar Gerald Neuman (1996) calls the "lost century of American immigration law," states and cities—not the federal government—maintained a significant degree of power, in both law and practice, over immigration policy. As Neuman details, during this century cities and states formulated and enforced varying statutes that barred the immigration of convicts, paupers, and those with contagious or other diseases (1996, 19–43; see also Filindra and Tichenor 2008).

During the latter decades of the nineteenth century, however, the federal government's supreme authority, or "plenary power," over immigration and naturalization policy was firmly established through a series of Supreme Court cases. The case that most clearly articulated the plenary power doctrine is *Chae Chan Ping v. United States* (1889), in which the justices upheld the exclusion of a long-term Chinese resident on the basis of the recently passed Chinese Exclusion Acts. In the case, the justices first emphasized the "inherent sovereign powers" of the federal government over determining membership, that is, the fact that the exclusion of noncitizens was

---

7. For some notable exceptions, see Body-Gendrot and Schain 1992; Skerry 1995; Lahav 1998; Spiro 2001; Wells 2004; Light 2006; Ellis 2006; Hayduk 2006; Coleman 2007; Varsanyi 2008a, 2008b; Newton and Adams 2009. There is also an expanding discussion of these policies in the legal literature: Spiro 1994; Johnson 1995; Wishnie 2001, 2004; Romero 2002; Pham 2004; Hethmon 2004; *Harvard Law Review* 2005; Olivas 2007; Schuck 2007; Motomura 2008; Rodríguez 2008.

a fundamental right of any sovereign government: "[The Chinese] laborers are not citizens of the United States; they are aliens. That the government of the United States, through the action of the legislative department, can exclude aliens from its territory is a proposition which we do not think is open to controversy" (603). Second, as control over immigration was defined as an element of foreign policy and in the interest of the federal government to control, the Court considered it a legislative and political concern, thus removing it from judicial review: "This court is not a censor of the morals of other departments of the government; it is not invested with any authority to pass judgment upon the motives of their conduct" (628). Finally, and crucially, the Court made clear that local governments did not have power over immigration: "[The federal government] is invested with power over all the foreign relations of the country, war, peace, and negotiations and intercourse with other nations; all of which are forbidden to the state governments.... For local interests the several states of the Union exist, but for national purposes, embracing our relations with foreign nations, we are but one people, one nation, one power" (629).

In the century since, the federal government's plenary powers over immigration have been tested and upheld through a series of cases setting the limits of state and local governments' abilities to create immigration policy. First, local policies regarding immigrants that mirror federal policies have generally been struck down in courts on "preemption" grounds: the basis that the federal government fully "occupies the field" of immigration and naturalization policy.[8] For example, in *Hines v. Davidowitz* (1941), a Pennsylvania state law that included alien registration provisions was struck down as it was preempted by the Federal Alien Registration Act. And more recently, as discussed above, California's Proposition 187 was invalidated on preemption grounds in *LULAC v. Wilson* (1995).

Second, with a few interesting exceptions, states and localities have generally been held to an "equal protection standard" when passing laws affecting their noncitizen residents (see particularly *Plyler v. Doe*, 1982). The federal government's plenary power over immigration authorizes the treatment of "people as immigrants"—in other words, individuals as "aliens"—essentially "nonpersons" beyond the protections of the Constitution. In a famous statement, Supreme Court Justice John Paul Stevens admitted that plenary power effectively upholds a double standard: "in the exercise of

---

8. For a thorough discussion of this issue, see the chapter by Rodríguez, Chishti, and Nortman, this volume.

its broad power over naturalization and immigration, Congress regularly makes rules that would be unacceptable if applied to citizens" (*Mathews v. Diaz*, 1976, 1891; see also *De Canas v. Bica*, 1976). In stark contrast, until the mid-1990s local and state governments were almost wholly excluded from this policy realm and relegated instead to the formulation of immigrant policy: laws that govern the "treatment of noncitizens in the United States with respect to matters other than entry and expulsion" (Motomura 1999, 1361). As a result, state and local laws affecting noncitizens are judged against constitutional norms such as the Fifth Amendment's Due Process Clause and the Fourteenth Amendment's Equal Protection Clause. As such, state and local governments are held by the courts to a "personhood" standard: they are required to treat "immigrants as people," that is, as persons protected by the Constitution (Varsanyi 2008a).[9]

Despite this restriction, there has also been ad hoc and informal participation of local authorities in immigration enforcement at various times throughout the last hundred years (McDonald 1999; Filindra and Tichenor 2008). For example, during the Great Depression, over 400,000 Mexicans in the U.S. Southwest and Midwest (approximately 60 percent of whom were U.S. citizens by birth) were "repatriated" to Mexico by the federal Immigration and Naturalization Service (INS), with the cooperation of city and county welfare relief agencies (Ngai 2004, 71–73; see also Balderrama and Rodriguez 1995). Miriam Wells also details the way in which "effective enforcement [of immigration laws] depends on local actors" (2004, 1315). She explores three aspects of this local dynamic: how the disjuncture between government levels in the United States has enabled a proliferation of limited cooperation (sanctuary) ordinances, how the decentralized nature of the INS had provided regional and district administrators a great deal of autonomy in developing operating agreements with local governments, and how the disjuncture between government agencies (in her example, the Department of Labor and INS) has allowed for regional disparities in the enforcement of immigration laws.

---

9. Even with plenary power, there are several ways in which states and localities have been directly involved in immigration matters. For example, under the "political function exception," states and local governments are able to treat people-as-immigrants and discriminate on the basis of noncitizen status when the constitution of their political communities is in question. For example, in *Cabell v. Chavez-Salido* (1982), California was permitted to require citizenship as a qualification for state employment as a peace officer (see also *Sugarman v. Dougall*, 1973).

CONTEMPORARY CONTEXT

Given 120 years of plenary power, what is the context in which contemporary state and local immigration policy activism has exploded in recent years? As I discuss in this section, shifting economics, demographics, and politics have all played an important role. None of these factors is causal. They do not explain, for instance, why some states and cities have passed or considered laws while others have not,[10] but they do provide an important backdrop against which these policies have emerged.

Economics and the Labor Market

Over the last several decades, the number of undocumented immigrants living and working in the United States has increased fourfold, from approximately three million in the early 1990s to approximately twelve million today (Passel and Cohn 2008). The reasons for this increase are complex but can be explained partially as a result of economic factors. In 1994 the governments of Mexico, Canada, and the United States signed the North American Free Trade Agreement (NAFTA), liberalizing trade between the signatory nations. Among other things, NAFTA and similar commodity-specific free trade agreements significantly decreased tariffs on agricultural goods such as corn and coffee. Being passed on the heels of a decade of neoliberal structural readjustment and economic crisis, these free trade agreements further fostered circumstances in which millions of rural farmers in Mexico and Latin America were no longer able to make a living on the land, and migration—either domestic (rural-to-urban) or international—quickly became one of their few viable livelihood options (Nevins 2007). Some supporters were aware that NAFTA would create (in their minds, a short- and medium term) pressure for migration from Mexico to the United States. As a consequence, continued expansion of border enforcement and militarization were made simultaneous priorities.[11]

At the same time as migration "push" factors have increased in Mexico and elsewhere, "pull" factors have simultaneously increased in the United States. With the exception of periodic economic downturns (Papademetriou and Terrazas 2009) over the past decades, and building upon decades of sustained labor migration networks between the United States, Mexico, and elsewhere (Calavita 1992), there has been a continued and increasing demand by

---

10. For more on this question, see Ramakrishnan and Wong, this volume.
11. For more on the militarization of the U.S.-Mexico border, see Andreas 2000; Dunn 1996; Nevins 2002.

business and corporate interests for low-wage, flexible, relatively unregulated labor in the United States (Cornelius 1998; Massey, Durand, and Malone 2002), particularly in the construction, hospitality, home care, and service industries. At the same time as the federal government has privileged border militarization and enforcement, there has been spotty and declining internal enforcement of employer sanctions throughout much of the decade (Brownell 2005),[12] creating a situation in which migrants are guaranteed access to a relatively free labor market *within* the United States as long as they can get past the increasingly deadly obstacle course at the border (Cornelius 2005; Nevins 2008).

Demographic Factors

As the numbers of undocumented immigrants living in the United States have increased, there has been a significant concomitant shift in the settlement patterns of contemporary migrants, particularly migrants from Mexico, who make up approximately 57 percent of the unauthorized population (Passel 2006). Migrants are increasingly settling away from traditional gateway destinations such as Los Angeles, Houston, and Chicago, choosing instead to settle in "new gateways" in rural, suburban, and urban areas throughout the U.S. South, Midwest, and Northeast (Zúñiga and Hernández-León 2005; Massey 2008; Singer, Hardwick, and Brettell 2008). Between 1990 and 2000, the Mexican-origin population in the states of New York, Pennsylvania, Washington, and Wisconsin increased by 200 to 400 percent, in Utah by 645 percent, in Arkansas and Minnesota by 1,000 percent, and in North Carolina, Tennessee, and Alabama by over 1,800 percent (Zúñiga and Hernández-León 2005, xiv). Importantly, however, because Mexican-origin populations in many of these states were very small in 1990, an increase of 1,800 percent does not reflect a large *absolute* increase in the number of migrants from Mexico. In North Carolina, for example, the Mexican-origin population in 2000 was 376,000 out of a total state population of eight million. Nonetheless, this settlement shift has brought the phenomenon of immigration—particularly undocumented immigration—to cities and states that have never before grappled to any significant extent with the challenges and costs—both real and perceived—of large-scale immigrant settlement.[13]

---

12. There has been a renewed emphasis on enforcing employer sanctions under the Obama administration (Meyer and Gorman 2009), though results of this directive are still unclear.

13. For a discussion of why this settlement shift has occurred, see Zúñiga and Hernández-León 2005.

Political Factors

Several political factors have also played an important role in the recent emergence of state and local immigration policy activism. First, it is important to note that the upswing began shortly after the events of September 11, 2001. The IIRIRA, passed in 1996, authorized state and local law enforcement agencies to partner with the federal government and enforce civil immigration laws, but before 9/11 there were no agencies that had signed 287(g) MOUs. Shortly after 9/11, however, Attorney General John Ashcroft issued a classified memo affirming the authority of state and local police to enforce civil immigration law, overturning a prior memo issued by former Attorney General Janet Reno stating exactly the opposite. Ashcroft's memo thus opened the door to the devolution of immigration policing powers, and as discussed above, there are now a growing number of sub-federal governments that have operating agreements with the federal government to enforce immigration law at the state and local level.

After 9/11, energy for policy activism was also generated at the grassroots. As national security trumped all other political priorities and "immigrant" and "noncitizen" were frequently understood as synonyms for "terrorist" (Cole 2003), many cities and states responded to the "War on Terror" with local initiatives with widely divergent strategies for enhancing national security at the local scale. Some took an enforcement path and sought ways to serve as a "multiplier force," while others sought to further integrate and develop connections with their immigrant communities (Thacher 2005).

Other political factors have also been key in the recent explosion of state and local immigration policy activism, most specifically Congress's failure to pass comprehensive immigration reform legislation in 2006 and 2007, as well as the politics surrounding the congressional midterm elections in 2006. Starting in 2005, the House and Senate laboriously crafted and ultimately passed immigration reform bills: the Border Protection, Antiterrorism, and Illegal Immigration Control Act of 2005 (H.R. 4437) and the Comprehensive Immigration Reform Act of 2006 (S. 2611), respectively. However, given glaring differences between the bills, as evidenced by their titles, the House and Senate were unable to pass compromise legislation, and efforts at immigration reform failed. In the competitive midterm elections, however, a number of candidates hitched their political wagons to the immigration reform train, and as congressional reform collapsed, state and local governments and candidates sought to "take matters into their own hands" and earn political capital on the issue of immigration reform.

THEMES AND ORGANIZATION OF THE VOLUME

The volume is divided into four sections. The chapters in the first section provide an overview of state and local immigration policy activism by exploring the phenomenon from a broadly thematic perspective. The second section includes three chapters, each of which explores a different facet of the state and local immigration policy phenomenon: policies arising from devolution, immigration-specific grassroots policies, and immigration policy making "through the back door." The chapters in the third section delve more deeply into the evolution of anti-immigrant activism and policy making in particular localities: Hazleton, Pennsylvania; Charlotte, North Carolina; Prince William County, Virginia; Phoenix, Arizona; and Vancouver, British Columbia. And finally, the authors in section four provide a close reading of the politics and discourse of local immigration policy activism in a number of high-profile cases, including Vista, California; Hazleton, Pennsylvania; Prince William County, Virginia; Farmers Branch, Texas; and Escondido, California.

The contributing authors take as their primary focus the *what, how,* and *why* of contemporary state and local immigration politics and policy activism in the United States.[14] Though the authors did not utilize a uniform set of questions to frame their investigations, their chapters make (at least) three important contributions to a broader understanding of the phenomenon. First, the chapters offer rich empirical description (the *what* and *how*) of the circumstances and contexts in which particular policies and strategies have arisen, as well as the content of these policies. Second, a number of the chapters seek to understand—both implicitly and explicitly—the reasons for which this policy activism has exploded onto the scene in recent years. In other words, these authors explore the *why* of state and local immigration policy activism. Finally, a number of the contributors explore the tensions arising out of this moment: between different groups within particular localities and between different levels of government, most specifically, between the federal government and states and cities.

Section 1: National Overview

The three chapters in section 1 approach the phenomenon of state and local immigration policy activism from a broadly thematic perspective. Rather

---

14. This volume does not focus on immigration outcomes of these policies. In other words, it does not document how they do or do not influence immigrant settlement at the local level. Though there is anecdotal evidence indicating that immigrants may leave or choose to settle away from states and localities with restrictive policies, reliable data are not yet available to substantiate this claim. For a preliminary analysis of the issue, however, see Papademetriou and Terrazas 2009, 11.

than delving into the way in which these policies have emerged in particular places (the task of later chapters), these introductory chapters explore the phenomenon itself, one examining the legality of measures falling on the exclusionary end of the spectrum, another detailing the wide range of measures falling on the integrationist end of the spectrum, and a third whose authors seek to explain why certain localities across the United States have passed exclusionary measures and others have not.

Legal uncertainty is at the core of growing tensions surrounding the explosion of state and local immigration policy activism. Though sub-federal jurisdictions are prohibited by plenary power from regulating immigration, legal ambiguity has arisen over what exactly it means to "regulate immigration." Using this question as a starting point, the chapter by legal scholars Cristina Rodríguez, Muzaffar Chishti, and Kimberly Nortman offers a solid foundation for the volume by presenting a framework for assessing the constitutionality of these emerging policies. These coauthors offer a warning that certain state and local immigration measures have the potential to threaten individual rights and long-established constitutional protections, such as due process, free speech, and equal protection. More specifically, they explain how two of the most controversial policies—state and local employer sanctions laws and the growing involvement of state and local police in civil immigration enforcement (via 287(g) agreements)—may be preempted by federal law.

The lion's share of popular media coverage of state and local immigration policy activism has focused on exclusionary—anti-immigrant—measures. Chapter 3, by sociologists Pablo A. Mitnik and Jessica Halpern-Finnerty, offers a welcome antidote to this popular media coverage as the authors systematically survey the wide range of policies designed to *integrate immigrants*—legal and undocumented—into local communities. The prevalence of these integrative policies is not insignificant. As noted in a recent report by the Progressive States Network (2008), integrative policies are far more common than exclusionary policies, and a large proportion of the immigrant population in the United States lives in states that have passed integrative policies (see also NCSL 2008). Mitnik and Halpern-Finnerty provide a comprehensive overview of these policies, including limited cooperation ordinances (sometimes called "sanctuary" ordinances) and measures that regulate employment, wages, and access to health care. Offering a clue as to the success of these measures, they note that many of these policies are not geared specifically toward immigrants, even though in some locales they disproportionately benefit immigrants.

As discussed above, while we may understand the broader social, political, and economic context in which this activism is occurring, we cannot yet predict why certain localities enter the fray while others do not. In chapter 4, political scientists S. Karthick Ramakrishnan and Tom Wong tackle this important question, as yet unexplored: why do some localities, but not others, consider, pass, or fail to pass immigration ordinances? While most analyses (indeed, many in this volume) place demographic change at the center of explanation, Ramakrishnan and Wong's national-scale quantitative analysis offers a compelling finding: that local political partisanship (the proportion of Republicans and Democrats in a given county), not demographic change, is the best predictor for local-level immigration policy activism. In building this analysis, they include both anti-immigrant ordinances, specifically IIRAs such as the local ordinance passed in Hazleton, Pennsylvania, and pro-immigrant measures, including limited cooperation and sanctuary ordinances.

Section 2: From Devolution to the Grassroots

The chapters in section 2 explore the full range of state and local immigration policy activism. First are those policies arising from the 1996 laws and the devolution of immigration enforcement authority. Second are the policies arising from the grassroots, such as the Hazleton IIRA. And third are those local ordinances that are not specifically focused on immigration or immigrants but disproportionately affect immigrants (Varsanyi 2008b and this volume).

In chapter 5, political scientist and immigration policy researcher Michele Waslin provides us with in-depth historical and contemporary coverage of the devolution of immigration policing powers from the federal government to state and local governments, and the growing involvement of state and local law enforcement agencies in civil immigration enforcement. Where Rodríguez and her coauthors present us with a careful legal analysis of 287(g) agreements, Waslin addresses a different facet of this phenomenon, exploring the impacts of local civil immigration enforcement on both the police and immigrant communities. In addition to providing a comprehensive overview of the issue, she concludes her chapter with brief case studies of 287(g) agreements in action: in Prince William County, Virginia, and Maricopa County, Arizona.

Though the devolution of immigration enforcement has generated a fair share of controversy, grassroots immigration policies have been at the center of legal and political firestorms given the long-standing plenary power of the federal government and questions as to the propriety of state- and local-level immigration enforcement. In chapter 6, political scientists Marc Rosenblum and Leo Gorman examine one of the most controversial of these local policies: the development of state-level employer sanction and worksite enforcement laws. The passage of the Immigration Reform and Control Act of 1986 (IRCA) created the first system of employer sanctions in the United States, designed to penalize employers who knowingly hired undocumented immigrants. However, a tiny loophole in the bill, stating that sub-federal governments had control over the business licenses of their employers, has led to a wave of states and cities trying to use this mechanism to enforce employer sanctions at the state and local level. In their chapter, Rosenblum and Gorman provide an overview of state-level migration laws, then examine the politics and implementation of state worksite enforcement laws in Arizona, Mississippi, and Illinois, with particular focus on laws requiring employers to use the federal government's evolving employer verification database, E-Verify. They conclude by weighing the pros and cons of state immigration enforcement.

Localities have also developed ordinances that are not, at face value, about policing immigrants, but which *indirectly* impact the lives of (undocumented) immigrants in their jurisdictions, a strategy that I, as a geographer and migration scholar, call "immigration policing through the back door" or "immigration policing by proxy." In chapter 7, I provide an overview of these grassroots policies, focusing specifically on land use and public space ordinances designed to regulate and manage day labor markets and day laborers, who by the nature of their work are highly visible and have become the focus of anti-immigrant efforts throughout the United States. I conclude my chapter with a brief look at the strategies developed and employed by three city governments in the Phoenix metro area to appease community tensions and manage their growing day labor markets.

Section 3: Tracing the Evolution of Local Policy Activism

The chapters in section 3 open a window onto the evolution of immigration politics in four "new destination" locales: Prince William County, Virginia; Phoenix, Arizona; Hazleton, Pennsylvania; and Charlotte, North Carolina.[15] Though the media frequently paint a simple "us versus them" portrait of local immigration policy activism, the authors in this section take pains to emphasize the varying roles of different actors in these debates. They stress the centrality of rapid demographic change in the evolution of local immigration policy activism and note that certain local actors, particularly the

---

15. North Carolina and Pennsylvania are the states in which the largest number of anti-immigrant local ordinances were passed in 2005 and 2006 (Nguyen n.d.).

business and government elite, benefit greatly from economic development and population growth, whereas other local actors are more readily threatened by rapid demographic change and stress the local costs—real and perceived—of immigration.

One of the most prominent recent cases of local anti-immigration policy activism can be found in Hazleton, Pennsylvania, where in the summer of 2006 the city government passed one of the first IIRAs designed to sanction local employers and landlords for hiring and renting to undocumented immigrants. Sociologists Ben Fleury-Steiner and Jamie Longazel do not explore the ordinance itself. Rather, the authors trace the political and economic reasons for which Latino immigrants have moved to Hazleton in increasing numbers over the past decades. Specifically, they follow the economic development strategies pursued by the city's community development organization, CAN DO, which has been more recently supported by pro-business state laws such as the Keystone Opportunity Zone Initiative. As Fleury-Steiner and Longazel recount, this economic development strategy has ultimately attracted large firms, such as Cargill Meat Solutions, with reputations for hiring low-wage and frequently undocumented labor. In their explanation, rapidly shifting demography may still be at the root of IIRAs, but these authors weave a careful political economic analysis that takes one step further back and explores the root causes of this demographic change.

In chapter 9, Owen Furuseth and Heather Smith, both geographers, also track the evolution of immigration policy activism, this time in Charlotte, North Carolina, and its surrounding Mecklenburg County. They search out the origins of large-scale Latino migration to Charlotte back to the early 1980s and divide the ensuing years into four phases: early Latino immigration (early 1980s–early 1990s); early immigration maturity (mid-1990s–2000); mature and sustained immigration (post 2001); and the phase that brings us to the present day: Charlotte at an immigrant crossroads. As evidenced by their periodization, they draw direct connections between shifting demography and growing political tensions over immigrant settlement and integration. Furuseth and Smith also highlight an important dynamic in the emergence of local immigration policy: the frequently contradictory pathways taken by central cities and their surrounding counties and towns, as evidenced in these authors' discussion of the divergent strategies pursued in Charlotte and surrounding Mecklenburg County.

The chapter by demographers Jill Wilson, Audrey Singer, and Brooke DeRenzis focuses on another locus of the "new destination" dynamic:

suburbs. Not only are immigrants increasingly settling outside of traditional immigration-receiving regions in the United States, they are also settling
outside of central cities in suburban and exurban developments, where jobs
may be plentiful and costs lower (Singer, Hardwick, and Brettell 2008). As
with Hazleton, Pennsylvania, Prince William County, Virginia (a suburb of
Washington, DC) has received considerable media attention for developing
one of the most anti-immigrant, enforcement-oriented local strategies in the
country. Wilson, Singer, and DeRenzis provide a careful analysis of rapid
population growth, demographic shifts, and economic growth in the region,
and make connections between these abrupt changes, involvement of local,
regional, and national grassroots politics, and the evolution of anti-immigrant activism in the community.

As discussed by all the authors in this section, economic development
policies play a central role in demographic change and population growth,
which, in turn, have played a central role in the emergence of local immigration policy activism. However, how do immigration politics influence
the "global city" aspirations of a local business and government elite? As
political scientist and lawyer Doris Marie Provine discusses in her chapter,
economic growth–oriented strategies in Phoenix and Vancouver have confronted markedly different political contexts. In Phoenix, local, state, and
national politics are actively anti-immigrant, whereas the local, provincial,
and federal governments of Vancouver, British Columbia, and Canada have
long favored and promoted immigration and immigrant integration. Thus,
undocumented immigration is relatively tolerated in Vancouver, while
Phoenix city boosters face the challenges of one of the most anti-immigrant
climates in the United States.

Section Four: Exploring Tensions at the Local Scale

Lastly, the chapters collected in section 4 offer fine-grained discursive and
qualitative analyses of the politics surrounding the passage of anti-immigrant
measures at the local level. As with the chapters in the preceding section,
those in this closing section grapple with politics in several high-profile cases.
Analysis of these cases is crucial for three reasons: they have received the
majority of popular media coverage; they have been at the forefront of policy
activism and have been emulated by localities across the nation; and in several instances they are the named defendants in legal cases currently making
their way through the courts. Thus an understanding of these cases sheds
valuable light on the broader phenomenon.

In chapter 12, political scientist Michael Danielson analyzes the passage of the Vista, California, day labor ordinance, and argues that the introduction, passage, and legal struggles surrounding the ordinance have resulted from the convergence of local demographic change and political pressures from both local and national actors. As with all of the chapters in this section, Danielson is careful to explore the wide range of views represented in debates over the ordinance and notes, provocatively, that day laborers—most directly affected by the ordinance—were least present in these debates, given their political marginalization.

In chapter 13, sociologists Jill Esbenshade, Benjamin Wright, Paul Cortopassi, Arthur Reed, and Jerry Flores provide us with a close reading and discursive analysis of the transcripts from the City Council meetings at which four of the most scrutinized and controversial local immigration policies have been passed: in Hazleton, Pennsylvania; Farmers Branch, Texas; Escondido, California; and Prince William County, Virginia. They find that supporters of the local ordinances frequently voiced their concerns over the local economic costs of immigration and made ready connections between deteriorating quality of life and immigration. Above all, however, Esbenshade and her coauthors find that a "law-and-order" argument stressing the illegality of immigrants was most pervasive in these debates.

These findings are echoed in chapter 14, in which anthropologist Hinda Seif analyzes a unique data source: letters written to a California state legislator in response to debates over whether California should issue driver's licenses to undocumented residents. As with the chapter by Esbenshade and coauthors, Seif finds that the arguments voiced against the proposal have less to do with the substance of the proposal itself and more to do with racist discourse, perceived threats to U.S. sovereignty, and a growing perception that the government is tolerating lawlessness. Seif also explores a jurisdictional tension not addressed elsewhere in the volume: specifically, the tensions arising between a pro-immigrant locality and legislator, and others in the state (though not necessarily in his district) opposed to an immigrant-friendly agenda.

STATE AND LOCAL IMMIGRATION POLICY: THE END, OR JUST THE BEGINNING?

As the chapters in this volume make abundantly clear, the outcome of this era of state and local immigration policy activism is decidedly unclear. The emergence of these policies has been marked by a variety of tensions—legal, political, demographic, economic, and cultural—highlighting not only the growing involvement of cities, counties, and states in immigration policy formation and enforcement, but also raising important questions as to whether sub-federal governments *should* be involved in this policy realm. Has this recent explosion of state and local immigration policy activism been a temporary diversion from business as usual—plenary power—or is the current proliferation of policies a challenge to the federal government's century-long plenary powers and a hint as to future reconfigurations of jurisdictional responsibilities? And what are the impacts of state and local immigration policy activism on communities across the United States, immigrant and otherwise?

At one level, as evidenced by a number of the chapters in this volume, there is still a great deal of legal ambiguity surrounding these policies. For example, in the district court cases deciding the initial fates of the IIRA passed in Hazleton, Pennsylvania, and a similar, high-profile ordinance passed in Valley Park, Missouri, the judges came to opposite conclusions. The business licensing portion of the Hazleton ordinance, designed to penalize employers who knowingly hire undocumented workers, was overturned, whereas a similar section of the Valley Park IIRA was upheld (see *Lozano v. City of Hazleton*, 2007 and *Gray v. City of Valley Park*, 2008, respectively). It remains to be seen what the outcome will be if and when these cases reach the Supreme Court. Even the devolution of immigration policing powers—authorized by federal statute and thus seemingly less susceptible to legal challenge—has been subject to considerable scrutiny, with some legal scholars arguing that local and state police have inherent authority to enforce federal immigration law (Hethmon 2004) and others arguing exactly the opposite, raising concerns that local immigration enforcement has the potential to encourage racial profiling and challenge carefully nurtured relationships between local police and their immigrant communities (Pham 2004; Wishnie 2004).

Beyond legal debates, the emergence of state and local immigration enforcement also creates a patchwork of immigration-related policies across the nation-state. What is the impact of this enforcement patchwork on local communities? On immigrants? With "new destination" settlement in full swing, some communities are voicing concerns over the costs and challenges—real and perceived—of immigration. However, as voiced by opponents of California's Prop. 187 in the mid-1990s and opponents of enforcement-oriented policies today, local immigration enforcement will likely have two outcomes—to make undocumented residents and their families (which often include citizen children) increasingly marginalized and vulnerable, and possibly to drive them into neighboring and more welcoming jurisdictions—neither of which necessarily "solves" the "illegal immigration problem" as it is frequently framed by supporters of IIRAs and 287(g) agreements. This patchwork effect is even more problematic in places such as Maricopa County, Arizona, in which city and county law enforcement hold contradictory policies yet have overlapping jurisdictional authority. The Phoenix Police Department has voiced concerns and opposition to local immigration enforcement, at the same time as Sheriff Joe Arpaio has terrorized local immigrant communities by training the most officers in the United States under a 287(g) MOU and made explicit attempts to arrest as many unauthorized residents as possible with his agency's newfound devolved policing authority (Gabrielson 2008; see also Waslin, this volume).

At yet another level, the era of state and local immigration policy activism brings to the fore questions about federalism, an emerging "immigration federalism" (Spiro 1997; Skerry 1995), and the rescaling of the nation-state. As Morton Grodzins (1966, 32) stated in the mid-1960s, "It is difficult to find any governmental activity which does not involve all three of the so-called levels of the federal system." True enough. As noted above, even throughout the long century of plenary power, there has been ad hoc and informal cooperation between local, state, and federal authorities in the realm of immigration enforcement (McDonald 1999). But as Hannah Arendt wrote in the mid-twentieth century, "Sovereignty is nowhere more absolute than in matters of emigration, naturalization, nationality, and expulsion" (2004, 278). For over a century, nation-states have been defined in part by their "monopolization of the legitimate 'means of movement'" (Torpey 2000), not only vis-à-vis one another but, crucially as well, vis-à-vis other scales of political organization: cities, subnational states, and supranational organizations. How will this era of state and local immigration policy activism rework long-held assumptions about federalism and the relationships between cities, states, and the federal government? And taking our inquiry beyond debates over federalism, what might this era of local immigration policy activism tell us about the rescaling and restructuring of state power in an era of neoliberal globalization (Peck 2001; Brenner 2004; Harvey 2005; Varsanyi 2008a)?

Finally, what will happen with these policies should Congress eventually pass comprehensive immigration legislation, including legalization of the undocumented residents in the United States? Perhaps this is overly pessimistic, but it is unlikely that comprehensive immigration reform will completely and permanently solve the problems and challenges of undocumented immigration, for immigrants themselves and for their communities. Although comprehensive immigration reform certainly holds great potential to improve the lives of millions, as illustrated by Rosenblum and Gorman's case study of E-Verify in this volume, the challenges of immigration enforcement will not be easily solved, particularly as the demand for low-wage, exploitable labor persists in the United States.

It seems that the involvement of cities, counties, and states in the creation and enforcement of immigration and immigrant policy faces an uncharted future. The chapters in this volume illuminate the significant challenges and opportunities of such a future, highlight the range of issues at stake, and chart a research agenda that will more deeply explore the impacts of these policies on immigrant communities, as well as the ethical and justice implications of the growing and continued involvement of cities, counties, and states in the formation and implementation of immigration policy.

WORKS CITED

Aleinikoff, T. Alexander. 2002. *Semblances of Sovereignty: The Constitution, the State, and American Citizenship.* Cambridge, MA: Harvard University Press.

Alexander, M. 2007. *Cities and Labour Immigration: Comparing Policy Responses in Amsterdam, Paris, Rome, and Tel Aviv.* Burlington, UK: Ashgate.

Andreas, Peter. 2000. *Border Games: Policing the U.S.-Mexico Divide.* Ithaca, NY: Cornell University Press.

Antiterrorism and Effective Death Penalty Act (AEDPA), P.L. 104-132 (1996).

Arendt, Hannah. 2004 [1951]. *The Origins of Totalitarianism.* San Diego, CA: Harcourt, Brace, Jovanovich.

Balderrama, F. E., and R. Rodriguez. 1995. *Decade of Betrayal: Mexican Repatriation in the 1930s.* Albuquerque, NM: University of New Mexico Press.

Body-Gendrot, Sophie, and Martin A. Schain. 1992. "National and Local Politics and the Development of Immigration Policy in the United States and France: A Comparative Analysis." In *Immigrants in Two Democracies: French and American Experiences,* ed. David L. Horowitz and Gerard Noiriel. New York: New York University Press.

Brenner, Neil. 2004. *New State Spaces: Urban Governance and the Rescaling of Statehood.* Oxford, UK: Oxford University Press.

Brownell, Peter. 2005. "The Declining Enforcement of Employer Sanctions," *Migration Information Source.* Washington, DC: Migration Policy Institute.

Cabell v. Chavez-Salido, 454 U.S. 432, 102 S.Ct. 735 (1982).

Calavita, Kitty. 1992. *Inside the State: The Bracero Program, Immigration, and the I.N.S.* New York: Routledge.

Chae Chan Ping v. United States, 130 U.S. 581, 9 S.Ct. 623 (1889).

Clinton, B. 1993. State of the Union Address. http://www.cspan.org/executive/transcript.asp?cat=current_event&code=bush_admin&year=1993.

Cole, David. 2003. *Enemy Aliens: Double Standards and Constitutional Freedoms in the War on Terrorism.* New York: New Press.

Coleman, Mathew. 2007. "Immigration Geopolitics beyond the Mexico-US Border," *Antipode* 39, no. 1: 54–76.

———. 2008. "Between Public Policy and Foreign Policy: U.S. Immigration Law Reform and the Undocumented Migrant," *Urban Geography* 29, no. 1: 4–28.

Cornelius, Wayne A. 1998. "The Structural Embeddedness of Demand for Mexican Immigrant Labor: New Evidence from California." In *Crossings: Mexican Immigration in Interdisciplinary Perspective,* ed. Marcelo M. Suárez-Orozco. Cambridge, MA: Harvard University Press.

———. 2005. "Controlling 'Unwanted' Immigration: Lessons from the United States, 1993–2004," *Journal of Ethnic and Migration Studies* 31, no. 4: 775–94.

Cornelius, Wayne A., Takeyuki Tsuda, Philip Martin, and James Hollifield, eds. 2004. *Controlling Immigration: A Global Perspective.* 2d ed. Stanford, CA: Stanford University Press.

De Canas v. Bica, 424 U.S. 351 (1976).

DeSipio, Louis. 1996. *Counting on the Latino Vote: Latinos as a New Electorate.* Charlottesville, VA: University of Virginia Press.

Dunn, Timothy J. 1996. *The Militarization of the U.S.-Mexico Border, 1978–1992: Low-Intensity Conflict Doctrine Comes Home.* Austin, TX: University of Texas Press.

Ellis, Mark. 2006. "Unsettling Immigrant Geographies: US Immigration and the Politics of Scale," *Tidschrift voor Economische en Sociale Geografie* 97, no. 1: 49–58.

Filindra, Alexandra, and Daniel J. Tichenor. 2008. "Beyond Myths of Federal Exclusivity: Regulating Immigration and Noncitizens in the States." Paper prepared for the American Political Science Association meeting, Boston.

Foner, Nancy. 2002. *From Ellis Island to JFK: New York's Two Great Waves of Immigration.* New Haven, CT: Yale University Press.

Gabrielson, Ryan. 2008. "Reasonable Doubt" series of articles, *East Valley Tribune.*

Gans, Herbert J. 1962. *Urban Villagers: Group and Class in the Life of Italian-Americans.* New York: Free Press.

García, Angela S. 2007. "Internalizing Immigration Policy within the Nation-State: The Local Initiative of Aguaviva, Spain." Working Paper No. 151. San Diego, CA: Center for Comparative Immigration Studies, University of California, San Diego.

Gray v. City of Valley Park, Mo. (2008) Slip Copy, 2008 WL 294294 (E.D.Mo.).

Grodzins, Morton. 1966. *The American System*. New York: Rand McNally.

Harvard Law Review. 2005. "The Constitutionality of Immigration Federalism," *Developments in the Law: Jobs and Borders*, vol. 118: 2247–69.

Harvey, David. 2005. *A Brief History of Neoliberalism*. Oxford, UK: Oxford University Press.

Hayduk, Ronald. 2006. *Democracy for All: Restoring Immigrant Voting Rights in the United States*. New York: Routledge.

Hethmon, Michael. 2004. "The Chimera and the Cop: Local Enforcement of Federal Immigration Law," *University of the District of Columbia Law Review* 8: 83–140.

Hines v. Davidowitz, 312 U.S. 52 (1941).

Hollifield, James F. 2008. "The Politics of International Migration: How Can We 'Bring the State Back In'?" In *Migration Theory: Talking across Disciplines*, ed. Caroline B. Brettell and James F. Hollifield. New York: Routledge.

Illegal Immigration Reform and Immigrant Responsibility Act (IIRIRA), P.L. 104-208 (1996).

Immigration and Customs Enforcement. 2009. "Delegation of Immigration Authority Section 287(g) Immigration and Nationality Act." http://www.ice.gov/pi/news/factsheets/section287_g.htm#signed-moa.

Johnson, Kevin R. 1995. "An Essay on Immigration Politics, Popular Democracy, and California's Proposition 187: The Political Relevance and Legal Irrelevance of Race," *Washington Law Review* 70: 629–73.

Jones-Correa, Michael. 1998. *Between Two Nations: The Political Predicament of Latinos in New York City*. Ithaca, NY: Cornell University Press.

Kasinitz, Philip, John H. Mollenkopf, and Mary C. Waters, eds. 2006. *Becoming New Yorkers: Ethnographies of the New Second Generation*. New York: Russell Sage Foundation.

Kasinitz, Philip, John H. Mollenkopf, Mary C. Waters, and Jennifer Holdaway, eds. 2008. *Inheriting the City: The Children of Immigrants Come of Age*. Boston, MA: Harvard University Press.

Kemp, Adriana, and Rebeca Raijman. 2004. "'Tel Aviv Is Not Foreign to You': Urban Incorporation Policy on Labor Migrants in Israel," *International Migration Review* 38, no. 1.

Lahav, Gallya. 1998. "Immigration and the State: The Devolution and Priva-
tisation of Immigration Control in the EU," *Journal of Ethnic and Migration Studies* 24, no. 4: 675–94.

League of United Latin American Citizens (LULAC) v. Wilson, 908 F.Supp. 755 (1995).

Light, Ivan. 2006. *Deflecting Immigration: Networks, Markets, and Regulation in Los Angeles*. New York: Russell Sage Foundation.

Lozano v. City of Hazleton (2007) 496 F.Supp.2d 477.

Massey, Douglas S., ed. 2008. *New Faces in New Places: The Changing Geography of American Immigration*. New York: Russell Sage Foundation.

Massey, Douglas S., Jorge Durand, and Nolan J. Malone. 2002. *Beyond Smoke and Mirrors: Mexican Immigration in an Era of Economic Integration*. New York: Russell Sage Foundation.

Mathews v. Diaz, 426 U.S. 67, 96 S.Ct. 1883 (1976).

McDonald, William F. 1999. *The Changing Boundaries of Law Enforcement: State and Local Law Enforcement, Illegal Immigration, and Transnational Crime Control*. Washington, DC: National Institute of Justice.

Meyer, Josh, and Anna Gorman. 2009. "Homeland Security Shifts Focus to Employers," *Los Angeles Times*, March 31.

Motomura, Hiroshi. 1999. "Federalism, International Human Rights, and Immigration Exceptionalism," *University of Colorado Law Review* 70: 1361–94.

———. 2008. "Immigration Outside the Law," *Columbia Law Review* 108: 2037–97.

Nelson, Lise K., and Nancy A. Hiemstra. 2008. "Latino Immigrants and the Renegotiation of Place and Belonging in Small Town America," *Social and Cultural Geography* 9, no. 3: 319–42.

Neuman, Gerald L. 1996. *Strangers to the Constitution: Immigrants, Borders, and Fundamental Law*. Princeton, NJ: Princeton University Press.

Nevins, Joseph. 2002. *Operation Gatekeeper: The Rise of the "Illegal Alien" and the Remaking of the U.S.-Mexico Boundary*. New York: Routledge.

———. 2007. "Dying for a Cup of Coffee? Migrant Deaths in the US-Mexico Border Region in a Neoliberal Age," *Geopolitics* 12, no. 2: 228–47.

———. 2008. *Dying to Live: A Story of U.S. Immigration in an Age of Global Apartheid*. San Francisco, CA: Open Media/City Lights.

Newton, Lina, and Brian E. Adams. 2009. "State Immigration Policies: Innovation, Cooperation or Conflict?" *Publius: The Journal of Federalism* 39: 408–31.

Ngai, Mai. 2004. *Impossible Subjects: Illegal Aliens and the Making of Modern America*. Princeton, NJ: Princeton University Press.

Nguyen, Mai Thi. n.d. "Anti-Immigrant Ordinances in North Carolina: Consequences on Local Communities and Governance." Manuscript. Chapel Hill, NC: Department of City and Regional Planning, University of North Carolina, Chapel Hill.

Olivas, Michael A. 2007. "Immigration-Related State and Local Ordinances: Preemption, Prejudice, and the Proper Role for Enforcement," *University of Chicago Legal Forum* 2007: 27–56.

Papademetriou, Demetrios G., and Aaron Terrazas. 2009. "Immigrants and the Current Economic Crisis: Research Evidence, Policy Challenges, and Implications." Washington, DC: Migration Policy Institute. http://www.migrationpolicy.org/pubs/lmi_recessionJan09.pdf.

Park, Robert E., and Ernest W. Burgess. 1925. *The City: Suggestions for Investigation of Human Behavior in the Urban Environment*. Chicago, IL: University of Chicago Press.

Passel, Jeffrey S. 2006. "The Size and Characteristics of the Unauthorized Migrant Population in the U.S.: Estimates Based on the March 2005 Current Population Survey." http://pewhispanic.org/files/reports/61.pdf.

Passel, Jeffrey S., and D'Vera Cohn. 2008. "Trends in Unauthorized Immigration: Undocumented Inflow Now Trails Legal Inflow." Washington, DC: Pew Hispanic Center. http://pewhispanic.org/files/reports/94.pdf.

Peck, Jamie. 2001. "Neoliberalizing States: Thin Policies/Hard Outcomes," *Progress in Human Geography* 25, no. 3: 445–55.

Penninx, Rinus, Karen Kraal, Marco Martiniello, and Steven Vertovec, eds. 2004. *Citizenship in European Cities: Immigrants, Local Politics and Integration Policies*. Aldershot, UK: Ashgate.

Personal Responsibility and Work Opportunity Reconciliation Act (PRWORA), P.L. 104-193 (1996).

Pham, Huyen. 2004. "The Inherent Flaws in the Inherent Authority Position: Why Inviting Local Enforcement of Immigration Laws Violates the Constitution," *Florida State University Law Review* 31: 965–1003.

Plyler v. Doe, 457 US 202 (1982).

Portes, Alejandro, and Min Zhou. 1993. "The New Second Generation: Segmented Assimilation and Its Variants," *Annals of the American Academy of Political and Social Science* 530: 74–96.

Progressive States Network. 2008. "The Anti-Immigrant Movement That Failed: Positive Integration Policies by State Governments Still Far Outweigh Punitive Policies Aimed at New Immigrants." http://www.progressivestates.org/content/903.

Ridgley, Jennifer. 2008. "Cities of Refuge: Immigration Enforcement, Police, and the Insurgent Genealogies of Citizenship in U.S. Sanctuary Cities," *Urban Geography* 29, no. 1: 53–77.

Rodríguez, Cristina M. 2008. "The Significance of the Local in Immigration Regulation," *Michigan Law Review* 106: 567–642.

Rogers, Alisdair, and Jean Tillie, eds. 2001. *Multicultural Policies and Modes of Citizenship in European Cities*. Aldershot, UK: Ashgate.

Romero, Victor C. 2002. "Migration Regulation Goes Local: The Role of States in U.S. Immigration Policy. Devolution and Discrimination," *New York University Annual Survey of American Law* 58: 377–86.

Schuck, Peter H. 2007. "Taking Immigration Federalism Seriously," *University of Chicago Legal Forum* 2007: 57–92.

Singer, Audrey, Susan W. Hardwick, and Caroline B. Brettell. 2008. *Twenty-First-Century Gateways: Immigrant Incorporation in Suburban America*. Washington, DC: Brookings Institution Press.

Skerry, Peter. 1995. "Many Borders to Cross: Is Immigration the Exclusive Responsibility of the Federal Government?" *Publius* 25, no. 3: 71–85.

Smith, Heather A., and Owen J. Furuseth, eds. 2006. *Latinos in the New South: Transformations of Place*. Aldershot, UK: Ashgate.

Spiro, Peter. 1994. "The States and Immigration in an Era of Demi-Sovereignties," *Virginia Journal of International Law* 35: 121–78.

———. 1997. "Learning to Live with Immigration Federalism," *Connecticut Law Review* 29: 1627–46.

———. 2001. "Federalism and Immigration: Models and Trends," *International Social Science Journal* 53, no. 167: 67–73.

Sugarman v. Dougall, 413 U.S. 634, 93 S.Ct. 2842 (1973).

Thacher, David. 2005. "The Local Role in Homeland Security," *Law and Society Review* 39: 635–73.

Tichenor, Daniel J. 2002. *Dividing Lines: The Politics of Immigration Control in America*. Princeton, NJ: Princeton University Press.

Torpey, John. 2000. *The Invention of the Passport: Surveillance, Citizenship and the State*. Cambridge, UK: Cambridge University Press.

Tsuda, Takeyuki, ed. 2006. *Local Citizenship in Recent Countries of Immigration: Japan in Comparative Perspective*. New York: Lexington.

Varsanyi, Monica W. 2005. "The Paradox of Contemporary Immigrant Political Mobilization: Organized Labor, Undocumented Migrants, and Electoral Participation in Los Angeles," *Antipode* 37, no. 4: 775–95.

———. 2007. "Documenting Undocumented Migrants: The *Matrículas Consulares* as Neoliberal Local Membership," *Geopolitics* 12, no. 2: 299–319.

———. 2008a. "Rescaling the 'Alien', Rescaling Personhood: Neoliberalism, Immigration and the State," *Annals of the Association of American Geographers* 98, no. 4: 877–96.

———. 2008b. "Immigration Policing through the Backdoor: City Ordinances, the 'Right to the City' and the Exclusion of Undocumented Day Laborers," *Urban Geography* 29, no. 1: 29–52.

Wells, Miriam. 2004. "The Grassroots Reconfiguration of U.S. Immigration Policy," *International Migration Review* 38, no. 4: 1308–47.

Wishnie, Michael. 2001. "Laboratories of Bigotry? Devolution of the Immigration Power, Equal Protection, and Federalism," *New York University Law Review* 76: 493–569.

———. 2004. "Civil Liberties in a New America: State and Local Police Enforcement of Immigration Laws," *University of Pennsylvania Journal of Constitutional Law* 6: 1084–115.

Zolberg, Aristide. 2006. *A Nation by Design: Immigration Policy in the Fashioning of America*. Cambridge, MA: Harvard University Press.

Zúñiga, Víctor, and Rubén Hernández-León, eds. 2005. *New Destinations: Mexican Immigration in the United States*. New York: Russell Sage Foundation.

SECTION ONE

National Overview

2   Legal Limits on Immigration Federalism

CRISTINA M. RODRÍGUEZ, MUZAFFAR CHISHTI, AND
KIMBERLY NORTMAN

For over a century, courts and commentators have regarded the power to regulate immigration as exclusively federal. Throughout U.S. history, however, states and localities have played some role in the regulation of immigration. Before the Supreme Court clearly articulated the plenary scope of the federal immigration power in the late nineteenth century, states imposed duties on migrants' entrance into their jurisdictions and used their inspection laws to control immigrant movement, largely without constraint (Neuman 1996, 23; Legomsky 1987, 189–90). In the twentieth century, states occasionally adopted measures restricting immigrant access to welfare benefits and public employment, and cracked down on employers who hired unauthorized workers. Courts evaluating these measures came to mixed conclusions on their legality. Despite holding that many of them exceeded the bounds of state authority, the Supreme Court also made clear that not all state and local immigration-related measures are illegal.

In recent years, sub-federal activity with respect to immigration has been pervasive, loudly contested, and widely reported. Congress's inability to pass comprehensive immigration reform in 2006 and 2007, coupled with the scale of migration (legal and illegal) into the United States since the 1990s, has helped fuel the proliferation of state and local measures covering a wide swath of territory. In 2007 alone, the fifty states considered over a thousand different measures regulating immigrants, and 167 of these measures became law (Laglagaron et al. 2008).

The laws that states and localities have debated in the last decade have included numerous measures intended to help immigrants integrate into their communities through the extension of services and legal protections to authorized and unauthorized immigrants alike. In 2007, for example, state legislatures enacted sixty laws designed to expand the rights and benefits given to immigrants and to combat their exploitation (Laglagaron et al. 2008). Much of the breathless media coverage of state and local efforts to combat unauthorized immigration fails to capture the extent to which state and local governments are also pursuing innovative solutions to help integrate immigrants (see Mitnik and Halpern-Finnerty, this volume).

That said, the recent escalation of sub-federal attempts to deter unlawful immigration by cracking down on employers and expanding police enforcement efforts raises a variety of legal concerns and therefore demands special scrutiny. Many supporters of these measures cite the federal government's failure to do its job as justification for state and local involvement in an area traditionally considered a federal domain. Commentators also have attributed the rapid spread of this form of regulation to the conservative media's ability to tap into the frustration felt in local communities with immigration patterns perceived to be out of control.

Whatever the causal explanation, it is important to put this renewed interest in immigration enforcement in its proper legal context. In this chapter, we provide a framework for assessing the legality of state and local efforts to sanction employers who hire unauthorized immigrants and enlist state and local police in the enforcement of immigration law—two of the most popular and controversial forms of sub-federal immigration enforcement.

We focus our analysis on the preemption question, or whether certain state and local laws violate the Constitution's Supremacy Clause by interfering or conflicting with federal law. In the larger scheme of things, it is also important for advocates, policy makers, and scholars to develop an understanding of how current state and local activity violates or threatens to undermine the individual rights of citizens and noncitizens alike. Some of the immigration measures passed of late create a climate hostile to bedrock constitutional protections, including the due process and equal protection guarantees of the Fourteenth Amendment and the free speech and association rights of the First Amendment. But given that the principle of exclusive federal responsibility over immigration is entrenched in law, the lines that separate federal and state authority must be articulated with as much precision as possible.

THE PREEMPTION FRAMEWORK

The Supreme Court repeatedly has declared: "the power to regulate immigration is unquestionably exclusively a federal power" (*De Canas v. Bica*, 1976,

354). Though scholars are divided on whether justification exists for this sweeping a conception of federal authority (Rodríguez 2008), conventional wisdom holds that state and local authority in this area is narrowly circumscribed and that states cannot constitutionally regulate immigration. What constitutes the regulation of immigration is, of course, the question posed by the state and local laws we consider in this chapter. The Supreme Court has said that the regulation of immigration is "essentially a determination of who should or should not be admitted into the country, and the conditions under which a legal entrant may remain" (*De Canas v. Bica*, 1976, 355). This definition provides only the most general of guidance, however, not only because most any regulation could be defined as imposing a condition on residence, but also, more importantly, because it explicitly addresses only legal entrants and not unauthorized immigrants.

The parameters of state and local authority in relation to immigration are most clearly set out in the Supreme Court's decision in *De Canas v. Bica*, in which the Court upheld a California legislative scheme that imposed sanctions on employers who hired unlawful immigrants. In deciding the case, the Court noted that regulating immigration is the exclusive responsibility of the federal government (354). But the Court also made clear that not every state or local measure related to immigrants is per se preempted by this constitutional federal power, whether latent or exercised (355). The Court observed: "the fact that aliens are the subject of a state statute does not render it a regulation of immigration" (11, n. 16). The Court concluded that a court may find that the federal government has superseded completely the state's authority to regulate only when Congress has clearly manifested the intent to do so (357). In upholding the California scheme regulating employers, the Court clearly contemplated that some state and local regulation related to immigration and harmonious with federal law is permissible.

De Canas was decided before Congress enacted the Immigration Reform and Control Act of 1986 (IRCA) and the federal scheme of employer sanctions, and the case's outcome clearly would be different today. Congress passed IRCA after several years of debate, creating the sanctions regime and legalizing a substantial segment of the unauthorized population then in the United States. During the debates over how to design the sanctions regime, some members of Congress feared placing too heavy a burden on employers; others worried about document fraud and the risk that the regime would lead to the adoption of a national identity card; still others expressed concern that employers inevitably would discriminate against Latino, Asian, and other would-be employees who appeared or sounded foreign (Aleinikoff, Martin, and Motomura 2003, 1130–33). In other words, IRCA instituted a comprehensive regulatory regime that carefully balanced a range of interests, thus shifting the terrain on which *De Canas* was decided.

Even in light of the dramatic changes of IRCA, it is important to recognize that the Court in *De Canas* came to its conclusion in the face of comprehensive congressional immigration regulation in existence at the time. In other words, *De Canas* still suggests that state and local laws are not automatically prohibited simply by virtue of having an impact on immigrants. As was the case in *De Canas*, the legal validity of current state and local measures rises and falls on whether the measures are inconsistent with existing federal statutory law and therefore in violation of the Supremacy Clause of the Constitution. The relevant inquiry is threefold. Is there (1) express preemption, (2) field preemption, or (3) conflict preemption?

Express preemption analysis is relatively straightforward and requires a clear statement from Congress of its intent to preempt a particular sort of state law, though the scope of express preemption provisions can be difficult to define. Because Congress cannot be expected to anticipate every state action that might interfere with its regulatory objectives, state and local law also can be preempted by implication. Implied preemption breaks down into whether a state statute is field preempted or conflict preempted.

Field preemption requires an inquiry into whether the federal government has occupied the field such that there is no room for the exercise of state authority. The Supreme Court defined field preemption most comprehensively in *Hines v. Davidowitz* (1941), noting that where the government has enacted a "complete scheme of regulation," states cannot "conflict or interfere with, curtail or complement, the federal law, or enforce additional or auxiliary regulations" (52). Where Congress has occupied the field, even state regulations that purport to supplement the federal scheme are not permissible.

In *De Canas*, while echoing the observation that even state regulations in harmony with federal law might be preempted, the Court made clear that to establish a claim of field preemption, it is not sufficient to point to the complex immigration schemes Congress has adopted to preempt all state and local regulation related to immigration. The definition of the field cannot be as broad as "immigration law" or "immigration enforcement." It must be shown that Congress intended to oust state regulatory authority that intersects with the field Congress has occupied (357), the boundaries of which must be defined with a certain level of specificity. As the Court has observed, every act of Congress occupies some field, "but we must know the boundaries of that field before we can say that it has precluded a state from the exercise of any power reserved to it by the Constitution" (360, n. 8).

Most immigration preemption cases decided by the Supreme Court ultimately have been conflict preemption cases. States and localities tend not to contravene express preemption provisions because of their clarity, and field preemption has become increasingly rare as a general matter, probably because of its malleability and capaciousness. In the immigration context, as in all other contexts, most cases turn on whether a state law creates an obstacle to the effectuation of the federal regulatory scheme. In these instances, a finding of conflict depends on the particular facts of the case and the statutes at issue. As the Court observed in *De Canas*, state laws should be preempted only to the extent necessary to "protect the achievement of the aims of the federal law" in view of the fact that the "proper approach is to reconcile the operation" of the federal and state schemes (238, n. 5). Conflict analysis clearly requires courts to make judgments regarding the effects of state and local schemes that have not yet been implemented. The analysis therefore can be both complicated and speculative, particularly when the federal government is not a party to the case and has not taken a position on whether conflict exists.

THE LEGALITY OF STATE AND LOCAL LAWS TARGETING EMPLOYERS

The state and local measures intended to prevent employers from hiring unauthorized workers that have been passed to date have three key features in common, though they naturally differ in institutional design, and the application of preemption principles to them will depend on these details. First, the ordinances passed by localities such as Hazleton, Pennsylvania, declare it unlawful to "knowingly recruit, hire for employment, or continue to employ . . . any person who is an unlawful worker." Similarly, Arizona, Colorado, Georgia, and Oklahoma have passed laws that prohibit employers and/or contractors who provide services to the state from knowingly or intentionally employing an unauthorized alien. These prohibitions mirror language in sec. 274A of IRCA, which establishes that "it is unlawful for a person or other entity to hire, or to recruit or refer for a fee, for employment in the United States an alien knowing the alien" is not authorized to be employed (*IRCA*, 1986, sec. 1372A).

Second, the local ordinances generally require city agencies to enroll in the federal government's E-Verify program (formerly known as Basic Pilot), a database that enables employers to verify whether an individual is authorized to work in the United States but that has been criticized as error prone. The ordinances also make receipt of any city contracts or grants worth $10,000 or more contingent on the contract recipient enrolling in E-Verify. Similarly, the laws passed by Colorado, Georgia, and Oklahoma require state contractors and subcontractors to enroll in E-Verify as a condition of receiving state contracts. Arizona's HB 2779 goes a step further and requires all employers in the state to verify employee eligibility through E-Verify. By contrast, federal law makes the enrollment by employers in E-Verify voluntary.

Some of the state and local employment measures also attach consequences to the knowing violation of the prohibition on hiring unlawful workers. The Legal Arizona Workers Act (HB 2779), for example, requires the attorney general or the county attorneys of Arizona to investigate complaints from individuals that an employer is knowingly or intentionally employing an unauthorized alien. State agents are required to verify an individual's work authorization through consultation with the federal government. Employers found to have committed a first violation may have their business licenses suspended, and employers found to have committed a second violation may have their licenses permanently revoked. For more on Arizona's employer sanctions law, see Rosenblum and Gorman, this volume.

Applying Preemption Principles

Analysis of the state and local laws must begin with the text of IRCA to determine whether Congress has preempted the measures expressly. Congress has provided that "the provisions of this section preempt any State or local law imposing civil or criminal sanctions (other than through licensing and similar laws) upon those who employ, recruit or refer for a fee for employment, unauthorized aliens" (IRCA, 1986, sec. 1324a(h)(2)).

The state and local laws that declare it unlawful to hire anyone unauthorized to work under federal law simply restate federal law and are not inconsistent with IRCA's express preemption clause. Of the measures that impose consequences on employers for failure to comply with the law, including fines, loss of public contracts, and vulnerability to suit by discharged citizen workers, only those regulations that amount to "sanctions" are expressly preempted.

Black's Law Dictionary defines "sanction" as "a penalty or other mechanism of enforcement used to provide incentives for obedience with the law or with rules and regulations" (Nolan and Nolan-Haley 1990). This definition clearly encompasses civil and criminal fines, as well as imprisonment. Some states, including Oklahoma and Tennessee, have considered adopting laws that would fine employers directly for hiring unauthorized workers. In 2007, West Virginia went so far as to enact an employer sanctions provision that mandates a $5,000 fine for a second violation of the statute's prohibition on the hiring of an unlawful worker. These measures, as fines or penalties, are clearly and expressly preempted by federal law. Indeed, at the time that Congress passed IRCA, the twelve states that had employer sanctions laws on their books all imposed civil or criminal fines on employers who hired unauthorized workers, underscoring that Congress had such penalties in mind when it enacted IRCA's express preemption clause.

The suspension or revocation of a business permit also could be categorized as a sanction or mechanism of enforcement designed to induce conformity with the law. But IRCA contains an exception to its general rule of preemption, or a savings clause, which provides that state and local governments can use "licensing and similar laws" to impose sanctions on employers. Congress thus clearly contemplated leaving state and local governments with some authority to regulate employers who hire unauthorized aliens. Hazleton, the state of Arizona, and the other governments that have followed their lead appear to be the first to rely on this twenty-year-old licensing provision in IRCA, and so its meaning, until now, has not been explored. Courts today find themselves faced with the question: does the authority to impose a licensing or similar sanction on an employer include the authority to suspend or revoke a business license or permit if an employer knowingly hires an unauthorized alien?

From the face of IRCA, it is difficult to determine precisely how Congress thought states should be permitted to use their licensing power. The legislative history of the statute provides virtually no guidance on this question. As noted above, at the time Congress passed IRCA, at least twelve states had laws on the books imposing fines on employers who hired unlawful workers, but none of these laws included licensing-related sanctions, and the origins of IRCA's licensing exception have proven difficult to uncover. As a result, courts determining whether a state or local licensing regulation falls within the exception likely will have to resort to a common-sense interpretation of "licensing and similar laws." To date, the federal courts have come to different conclusions on the meaning of the licensing provision in IRCA in cases decided in Pennsylvania and Arizona in 2007 and 2008—*Lozano v. City of Hazleton* and *Chicanos por la Causa v. Napolitano*, respectively. This disagreement could prompt eventual Supreme Court or congressional intervention to clarify the meaning of the statute.

One possible interpretation of "licensing and similar laws" is that they constitute laws that impose conditions on applicants seeking permission to engage in particular occupations or trades. In the legislative history of the preemption provision, Congress noted that "the Committee does not intend to preempt licensing or 'fitness to do business laws,' such as state farm labor contractor laws or forestry laws, which specifically require such licensee or contractor to refrain from hiring, recruiting or referring undocumented aliens" (U.S. House 1986, 5633). Because the licensing sanctions at issue today differ in kind from the specific examples Congress lists in the legislative history, there is some evidence that Congress did not contemplate the types of licensing sanctions now being adopted. But the list of examples in the legislative history does not purport to be exhaustive, and the Ninth Circuit Court of Appeals has found that no support exists for such a narrow definition of licensing laws, concluding instead that "licensing" should be interpreted according to its general meaning.

The question then becomes: who determines that an employer has knowingly violated the law? Can a state or local government determine that the employer has violated the statute by knowingly hiring an unauthorized immigrant and then subsequently impose a licensing-related sanction? The legislative history of the express preemption clause declares that the provision is "not intended to preempt . . . state or local processes concerning . . . a license to any person who has been found to have violated the sanctions provisions" of IRCA (U.S. House 1986, 5662). The question both the statute and its history raise is what it means "to have been found" to have violated the sanctions provisions. Must a state's use of its power be preceded by a determination by the federal government that an employer has violated the provisions?

On the face of the statute, no mention is made of the need for a federal determination of liability before a state can use its licensing authority. The federal statute simply authorizes state and local governments to impose licensing-related sanctions on employers who have hired unauthorized aliens. The state laws now on the books define "unauthorized alien" with reference to federal eligibility standards, creating no new standards of their own, though early versions of the Hazleton ordinance in particular did not clearly adopt federal definitions. A state or locality that imposes a licensing sanction upon finding that an employer has hired workers ineligible for employment as a matter of federal law appears to be acting within the express terms of the statute.

But can state and local officials accurately determine that an employer has violated federal law? Again, neither IRCA itself nor its legislative history provides a direct answer to this question. At first glance, given that IRCA permits an employer to base his or her hiring decisions on either consultation with E-Verify or a simple document check, it is intuitive that a state or local government may similarly determine that a worker is unauthorized.

However, an E-Verify finding of ineligibility is not the final word on whether the employer has violated IRCA. Under federal law and practice, employees can contest a finding of non-confirmation. Employers also have a right to contest allegations that they have violated the statute, and only after a statutorily specified hearing before an administrative law judge can penalties be imposed on an employer for knowingly violating the statute (*IRCA*, 1986. sec. 1324a(e)(3)). Many of the state and local laws that impose licensing sanctions establish procedures for employers to challenge the charges against them. But the existence of a parallel state procedure for determining liability could result in targeting employers who have not been determined definitively by a federal tribunal to have hired unauthorized aliens, arguably creating confusion and inefficiencies in the system.

The Ninth Circuit has rejected this analysis, finding instead that because Arizona HB 2779 was premised on the enforcement of federal standards, it passed muster. The court also refused to strike down the statute as a whole because of the speculative possibility that state and federal tribunals might come to different conclusions regarding whether a particular employer hired an individual unauthorized to work. The extent of state authority to regulate employers may thus depend on how the law works in practice, and individual employers may be required to litigate the preemption question on a case-by-case basis should the law ever be enforced by state officials.

Implied Preemption

Even if the penalties state and local governments have legislated are not expressly preempted, the laws may be impliedly preempted, either because they regulate in a field occupied by the federal government or because they conflict with federal law.

A field preemption challenge against the state and local employment provisions would be based on the observation that Congress, when it passed IRCA, enacted a comprehensive scheme to regulate employer hiring, thus occupying the field of employment-related immigration enforcement and leaving no room for the states to supplement the scheme. Though IRCA is indeed comprehensive, a field preemption claim would be difficult to defend because IRCA's express preemption clause clearly contemplates some enforcement role for state and local governments. That role may be limited, but the existence of the licensing exception indicates that Congress did not intend the total ouster of state and local authority in the context of immigration-related employment regulation.

The inquiry must therefore proceed to conflict preemption. The state and local regulations here at issue share a common goal with IRCA: to prevent employers from hiring individuals ineligible under federal law to work in the United States. As noted above, though the original ordinance passed by Hazleton did not clearly conform to federal standards regarding work eligibility, each of the state and local measures now on the books carefully defines employment eligibility with reference to federal law. Indeed, the requirement that agencies, contractors, and employers participate in the federal E-Verify program is intended to ensure that the licensing penalties apply only to employers who have hired workers who are not eligible to work as defined by the federal government.

The pursuit of a common goal and the adoption of common standards do not mean, however, that the state and local laws at issue do not conflict with federal law. If states and localities adopt implementation mechanisms that conflict with federal law, their measures are preempted by operation of the Supremacy Clause. The questions become whether and in what sense this sort of conflict arises.

The argument that the measures as a whole impede the federal government's enforcement of its laws has merit. To be sure, the mere fact that the state and local licensing schemes contain different features from the federal law that pursues the same objective—preventing the hiring of unlawful workers—should not be the decisive factor in favor of preemption. A finding of conflict preemption requires more than that the state and federal laws address the same subject matter and have different features. It must be established that the state law presents an obstacle to the enforcement or implementation of federal law, a flexible standard that requires judges to make somewhat speculative judgments. And it ultimately is not difficult to define a state law that regulates in the same territory as federal law as an obstacle to the full enforcement of federal law, particularly in an area such as immigration, where the federal regulatory scheme is tremendously complex. Whether a court strikes down a particular state or local measure on conflict preemption grounds will depend on the degree of conflict that the court expects to see. To understand the nature of the obstacle preemption inquiry, it is helpful to consider instances in which state and local licensing laws diverge from IRCA.

Preemption and E-Verify. There is a reasonable case to be made that state and local laws requiring employers and contractors to participate in E-Verify are preempted, though the Ninth Circuit has rejected this challenge. Whether the decision, at the state and local level, to mandate E-Verify conflicts with federal law depends in part on why the federal government has made participation in E-Verify voluntary. If its purpose was to promote experimentation with different means of verifying workers' status without provoking the employer backlash that likely would result from making participation mandatory, then whether to participate in E-Verify could be characterized as a federally protected choice made available to advance effective enforcement of IRCA, a choice a state government cannot take away without conflicting with federal law (*Geier v. American Honda Motor Company*, 2000, 866).

This sort of conflict claim would be strongest as applied to the Arizona law, which requires all employers to participate in E-Verify, thus removing the choice whether to participate from all employers in the state. The requirement that contractors enroll before receiving grants from the state or a city in the state poses a slightly more difficult question. These requirements may be taking a choice contemplated by the federal government away from entities seeking contracts, but state and local governments are taking this action in the process of doling out grants and other monetary benefits different in kind from the license to do business.

But, as the Ninth Circuit has pointed out, Congress could have prevented states from requiring that employers participate in the program explicitly, and Congress chose not to do so. More important, the federal government seeks broad-based participation in E-Verify. The state requirement that all employers participate in E-Verify thus arguably furthers the federal scheme.

Preemption and enforcement priorities. The strongest conflict preemption argument against the state laws that impose licensing or similar sanctions on employers is that the enforcement priorities such laws set interfere with or upset the federal government's effectuation of its own priorities. With IRCA,

Congress struck a balance between penalizing employers who hire unauthorized workers and not burdening employers unduly while protecting the rights of workers from overbroad enforcement (Aleinikoff, Martin, and Motomura 2003, 1325–28). The federal government's use of its discretion to prosecute some employers and not others reflects its efforts to effectuate this balance. If state and local governments are permitted to use their licensing authority against employers whom the federal government has not decided to prosecute, those governments arguably upset the enforcement balance the federal government has struck, particularly if the penalties the state governments apply to employers far exceed those prescribed by federal law.

It may be that the federal government would welcome states and localities supplementing their immigration enforcement capacities. Even if the federal government has decided to under-enforce IRCA, as some critics charge, state and local regulations that penalize employers who knowingly hire workers ineligible for employment under federal law appear to be fully consistent with federal law on its face. But by intervening in an area in which the federal government has calibrated its regulatory priorities carefully, the state and local governments that have adopted employer sanctions schemes are arguably creating obstacles to the implementation and effective enforcement of federal law.

THE ENFORCEMENT OF FEDERAL IMMIGRATION LAW BY STATE AND LOCAL POLICE

Though the federal government is chiefly responsible for enforcing its immigration laws, state and local governments increasingly are taking positions on whether their police forces and corrections officers should participate in immigration enforcement. Some state and local governments have entered or are seeking to enter cooperative agreements with the federal government that would enable their law enforcement officials to enforce federal immigration law directly. A number of jurisdictions also have passed laws requiring police to inquire into the immigration status of individuals arrested or detained for serious crimes. At the same time, several associations of chiefs of police have warned that becoming involved in immigration enforcement compromises law enforcement generally. Some jurisdictions have eschewed cooperation and passed measures that would restrain the authority of public officials, including police, to inquire into immigration status. Each of these positions contains the potential for conflict either with the Constitution or with federal statutes.

Direct Enforcement

An initial question that must be addressed in the law enforcement context is whether state and local police possess inherent constitutional authority to make arrests for violations of federal immigration law. Courts have not spoken at length or with much clarity on this issue. In 1983 the Ninth Circuit concluded that Congress had not occupied the field of *criminal* immigration enforcement but that the *civil* provisions of federal immigration law consti- tuted a pervasive regulatory scheme that field preempted state and local civil arrest authority (*Gonzales v. City of Peoria*, 1983, 474–75) (*United States v. Salinas-Calderon*, 1984, 1301, n. 3). In 1996 Congress enacted major immigra- tion reforms, including a provision that authorizes state and local govern- ments to participate in the enforcement of immigration law under federal supervision. Since those reforms, the Ninth and Third Circuits have declared the scope of state and local authority uncertain (*Mena v. City of Simi Valley*, 2003, 1265, n. 15) (*Carrasca v. Pomeroy*, 2002, 827).

In 2002 the Office of Legal Counsel (OLC) of the Department of Justice issued an opinion concluding that state and local police have inherent au- thority to enforce both the criminal and civil immigration laws and therefore need not wait for delegated authority from the federal government to par- ticipate in enforcement (Department of Justice 2002). OLC based this conclu- sion on the states' status as "sovereign entities," the assumption that state police have authority to make arrests for general federal criminal violations, and the conclusion that it would be irrational for the federal government to deprive itself of assistance from the states. In coming to this conclusion, OLC contradicted at least two previous memos concluding that no inherent authority existed (Department of Justice 1996, 1989). Claims of inherent au- thority, like the 2002 OLC memo, remain controversial today.

This constitutional confusion aside, most direct enforcement-related con- troversies can be resolved on statutory grounds. Whether the Constitution confers inherent authority on state and local police to make immigra- tion-related arrests, Congress almost certainly has impliedly preempted state and local authority to make both criminal and civil arrests. The federal government clearly has contemplated and narrowly defined the terms under which state and local police can participate in enforcement.

In 1996 Congress added sec. 287(g) to the Immigration and Nationality Act, authorizing states and localities to enter into agreements with the fed- eral government that would give local and state officials authority to arrest and detect individuals for immigration violations and to investigate immigration cases (*Illegal Immigration Reform and Immigrant Responsibility Act*, 2000, sec. 1376(g)). The states and localities that enter into 287(g) agreements may designate officers to receive training and supervision by Immigration and Customs Enforcement (ICE). The Department of Homeland Security has approved at least sixty-six agreements, the vast majority of which have been initiated in the last few years. By enacting sec. 287(g), Congress sought to provide an avenue for the federal government to enlist state and local resources to assist in immigration enforcement while superintending state and local involvement in immigration policing. In other words, the existence of sec. 287(g) strongly suggests that state and local authority to enforce immigration law must be preceded by federal authorization and accompanied by federal supervision.

Though most immigration law is civil in nature, the immigration code contains criminal provisions as well. As a general matter, state and local police have the authority to enforce federal criminal laws. But strong statutory evidence exists to support the conclusion that Congress intended to circumscribe criminal enforcement authority in the immigration context. Congress explicitly has authorized state and local police to arrest violators of two criminal immigration provisions: the prohibition on the smuggling, transporting, or harboring of illegal immigrants, and the provision establishing criminal penalties for illegal reentry following removal. The specific grants of authority to state and local police in these provisions suggest that Congress understood all other forms of criminal immigration enforcement to be off-limits to nonfederal law enforcement (Wishnie 2004).

Given these various statutory provisions, state and local measures that purport to authorize police to enforce both civil and criminal federal immigration law without federal authorization or supervision are likely unconstitutional. Any attempts at immigration enforcement that are not ancillary to regular law enforcement (as discussed below), or otherwise expressly authorized by federal law, have been preempted based on Congress's determination that the federal government should supervise state participation in this area. Not surprisingly, no state or locality appears to have passed a measure declaring its independent authority to enforce federal immigration law.

Importantly, though Congress has provided a channel for state and local governments to participate in immigration enforcement, federal law does not require participation. Indeed, any such mandate likely would constitute commandeering of state executive officials, which the Supreme Court declared to be a violation of the principles of federalism embodied in the Tenth Amendment in *United States v. Printz* (1997).

Some state and local governments have eschewed cooperation altogether by prohibiting the disclosure of immigration status information. Whether state and local governments can take this step remains a source of debate. In 1996 Congress addressed the noncooperation phenomenon by adopting two provisions that prohibited state and local governments from preventing their employees from voluntarily conveying information regarding an individual's immigration status to federal authorities (*Welfare Reform Act*, 2000, sec. 1644) (*Illegal Immigration Reform and Immigration Responsibility Act*, 2000, sec. 1373(b)). In the last year, numerous states have contemplated adopting similar laws to restrain their localities from prohibiting disclosure of immigration status information.

In the mid-1990s, the City of New York challenged the congressional provisions, arguing that the measures interfered with the city's authority to direct the operations of its own officials (*City of New York v. United States*, 1999). The Second Circuit Court of Appeals ultimately rejected New York City's challenge to federal law but suggested that, were the city to adopt a general confidentiality policy (the policy Mayor Michael Bloomberg eventually adopted), the city might be able to substantiate its claim that federal preemption amounts to an unconstitutional intrusion on the city's power to regulate its officials. This sort of claim would be unavailable to a locality seeking to challenge a state law prohibiting noncooperation, because localities are creatures of their states and are protected by federalism doctrines only in their relationship to the federal government.

Enforcement Ancillary to Routine Policing

The most common of the law enforcement provisions adopted by states and localities directly require law enforcement officers to question individuals arrested and detained for driving-under-the-influence offenses, felonies, and/ or particularly serious crimes. According to measures enacted by jurisdictions such as Georgia, Oklahoma, and Prince William County, Virginia, if an arrestee is determined upon questioning (in some cases conducted only if police have probable cause to believe the individual is unlawfully present) to be a foreign national, police are directed to consult the Department of Homeland Security to determine if the individual is lawfully present in the United States. If not, police are instructed to report the individual to ICE.

Under Colorado's recently passed law and under an executive order recently issued by the attorney general of New Jersey, if police have probable cause to believe an individual arrested on other grounds is present unlawfully, the law directs police to report the arrestee to ICE.

Most of the states and localities that have adopted these particular enforcement measures also have directed law enforcement officials to enter into 287(g) agreements, but a formal 287(g) is not a prerequisite for an ancillary enforcement statute, for reasons discussed below. Though both sorts of measures are intended to involve state and local police in the apprehension of unauthorized immigrants, the powers given by the ancillary enforcement statutes are different in kind from the 287(g) agreements. Whereas the 287(g) agreements authorize state and local police to enforce federal immigration law generally, the questioning statutes merely direct officials to attempt to elicit immigration status information from individuals arrested or detained for non-immigration reasons.

Despite the risk that these ancillary enforcement measures will compromise trust between the police and immigrant communities, these laws are not susceptible to legal challenge on their face and are reflective of standard practice. Legal challenges to these measures likely will have to proceed on an as-applied basis, in response to particular instances of police violating the civil or constitutional rights of arrestees. Though state and local police have virtually no authority to stop, arrest, or detain an individual solely for immigration-related reasons, they may inquire into an individual's immigration status if the inquiry is ancillary to the performance of ordinary law enforcement duties. If the inquiry is conducted while a suspect is in custody, which is the case with most if not all of the laws that have passed, the questioning cannot extend the duration of the detention beyond what is necessary for criminal law enforcement purposes, a specification that most states and localities have written into their measures. As with any police questioning, individuals have the right to refuse to answer police questions, and those in custody have the right to request an attorney.

If, during an otherwise lawful investigatory stop or detention, state or local police uncover information regarding a removal order against or the unauthorized status of the person in their custody, the police may (and routinely do) inform ICE. In general, state and local police cannot detain an individual for civil immigration purposes longer than the time appropriate or necessary for the original criminal arrest, traffic stop, or other non-immigration law enforcement purpose (*Farm Labor Organizing Committee v. Ohio State Highway*

Patrol, 1997). Federal authorities may place a detainer on a suspect, asking state officials to keep the suspect in custody pending a determination of his or her status. Whether ICE may authorize state and local police to detain an individual for immigration purposes beyond the time necessary for the original law enforcement purpose that brought the individual into state or local custody remains unresolved. Such detention could be unlawful on the ground that it utilizes a civil, administrative justification to prolong detention precipitated by criminal law enforcement (*Abel v. United States*, 1960, 230).

The Risk of State and Local Immigration Enforcement

The limited possibilities for legal challenge aside, immigrant advocates and law enforcement officials alike have articulated strong policy arguments in opposition to 287(g) agreements, as well as to overzealous immigration-related questioning during routine policing. The arguments are familiar and compelling. The International Association of Chiefs of Police has emphasized that effective law enforcement depends on building trust in immigrant communities, where immigrants are often suspicious of police as the result of their experiences with corrupt and violent law enforcement in their home countries (International Association 2007, 13). The absence of trust leads to underreporting of crimes, particularly domestic violence, sexual assault, and gang-related activity. As the Immigration Committee of the Major Cities Chiefs (MCC) has cautioned, immigration enforcement by local police could lead immigrants to avoid contact with police for fear that they or their family members might be deported (MCC 2006, 5–6).

The MCC also has emphasized that police are ill equipped to deal with the complexity of immigration law. In a world of limited resources, immigration enforcement is likely to be too great a fiscal burden to justify extensive state and local involvement (MCC 2006, 6–7). In addition, the potential for racial profiling and violating the civil rights of Latinos and other minority groups is high and pernicious when state and local police become involved in immigration enforcement, particularly when immigration enforcement becomes a part of the routine and quotidian activity of law enforcement officials.

Notably, the New Jersey executive order calling for police to question suspects in custody about their immigration status also explicitly restricts law enforcement from inquiring into or investigating the immigration status of any victim, witness, or person requesting assistance from the police (Department of Law and Public Safety 2007, 4). The order recognizes that "the overriding mission of law enforcement [is to] enforce the state's criminal laws and to protect the community that they serve," which "requires the cooperation of, and positive relationships with, all members of the community." According to the attorney general of New Jersey, "public safety suffers if individuals believe that they cannot come forward to report a crime or cooperate with law enforcement" (Department of Law and Public Safety 2007, 1). Whether legal or not, then, state and local participation in immigration enforcement raises serious policy concerns that should give public officials pause. For a more detailed discussion of this issue, see Waslin, this volume.

CONCLUSION

Though the regulation of immigration has long been considered an exclusive federal responsibility, state and local governments in this decade have been asserting their regulatory authority to address the consequences of large-scale immigration. Much of this state activity raises no legal concerns and serves as the United States' de facto integration policy (Rodríguez 2008, 581–609), but laws designed to deter unauthorized immigration have raised legal controversy for testing the limits of state authority. Whether legal challenges to these measures ultimately succeed, the costs of implementing, enforcing, and defending some of these laws in court could pressure states and localities to rescind or reformulate some of their recent legislation. Policy dangers, such as the risk of racial profiling by employers and police, also may force states to reconsider these laws. But whether states and localities reverse course, they have made it clear that immigration is having a significant impact on state and local budgets and communities and that Congress should recognize the states as partners in the management of immigration and integration.

WORKS CITED

Abel v. United States, 362 U.S. 217 (1960).

Aleinikoff, T. Alexander, David Martin, and Hiroshi Motomura, eds. 2003. *Immigration and Citizenship Law*. St. Paul, MN: Thomson West.

Carrasca v. Pomeroy, 313 F.3d 828 (3rd Cir. 2002).

Chicanos por la Causa v. Napolitano, 544 F.3d 975 (9th Cir. 2008).

City of New York v. United States, 971 F. Supp. 789 (S.D.N.Y. 1997), *aff'd*, 179 F.3d 29 (2nd Cir. 1999).

De Canas v. Bica, 424 U.S. 351 (1976).

Department of Justice. Office of Legal Counsel. 1989. *Handling of INS Warrants of Deportation in Relation to NCIC Wanted Persons File*. Memorandum to Federal Bureau of Investigation, by Douglas W. Kmiec. http://www.aclu.org/immigrants/gen/29970lgl19900101.html.

———. 1996. *Assistance by State and Local Police in Apprehending Illegal Immigrants*. Memorandum to U.S. Attorney for Southern District of California, by Teresa Wynn Rosenborough. http://www.usdoj.gov/olc/immstopo1a.htm.

———. 2002. *Non-Preemption of the Authority of State and Local Law Enforcement Officials to Arrest Aliens for Immigration Violations*. Memorandum to Attorney General John Ashcroft, by Jay S. Bybee. http://www.aclu.org/FilesPDFs/ACF27DA.pdf.

Department of Law and Public Safety. Office of the Attorney General of the State of New Jersey. 2007. *Attorney General Law Enforcement Directive 2007-3*. Trenton, NJ. http://www.nj.gov/oag/newsreleases07/ag-le-directive-2007-3.pdf.

Farm Labor Organizing Committee v. Ohio State Highway Patrol, 991 S. Supp. 895 (N.D. Ohio 1997).

Geier v. American Honda Motor Co., 529 U.S. 861 (2000).

Gonzalez v. City of Peoria, 722 F.2d 468 (9th Cir. 1983).

Hines v. Davidowitz, 312 U.S. 52 (1941).

Illegal Immigration Reform and Immigrant Responsibility Act. 2000. *U.S. Code*. Vol. 8, sec. 1376(g).

Immigration Reform and Control Act. 2000. *U.S. Code*. Vol. 8, sec. 1200.

International Association of Chiefs of Police. 2007. *Police Chiefs' Guide to Immigration Issues* (July). http://www.theiacp.org/documents/pdfs/Publications/PoliceChiefsGuidetoImmigration.pdf.

Laglagaron, Laureen, Cristina Rodríguez, Alexa Silver, and Sirithon Thanasombat. 2008. *Regulating Immigration at the State and Local Level*. Washington, DC: Migration Policy Institute.

Legomsky, Stephen. 1987. *Immigration and the Judiciary: Law and Politics in Britain and America*. New York: Oxford University Press.

Lozano v. City of Hazleton, 996 F. Supp.2d 477 (M.D. Pa. 2007).

MCC (Major Cities Chiefs) Immigration Committee. 2006. *Recommendations for Enforcement of Immigration Laws by Local Police Agencies*. http://www.houstontx.gov/police/pdfs/mcc_position.pdf.

Mena v. City of Simi Valley, 332 F.3d 1255 (9th Cir. 2003).

Neuman, Gerald. 1996. *Strangers to the Constitution: Immigrants, Borders and Fundamental Laws*. Princeton, NJ: Princeton University Press.

Nolan, Joseph R., and Jacqueline M. Nolan-Haley. 1990. *Black's Law Dictionary*. St. Paul, MN: West.

Rodríguez, Cristina M. 2008. "The Significance of the Local in Immigration Regulation," *Michigan Law Review* 106: 567–642.

United States v. Printz, 521 U.S. 898 (1997).

United States v. Salinas-Calderon, 728 F.2d 1298 (10th Cir. 1984).

U.S. House of Representatives. 1986. *Immigration Control and Legalization Amendments Act of 1986*. 99th Cong. 2nd sess. H. Rept. 682(I).

Welfare Reform Act. 2000. *U.S. Code*. Vol. 8, sec. 1644.

Wishnie, Michael J. 2004. "State and Local Police Enforcement of Immigration Law," *University of Pennsylvania Journal of Constitutional Law* 6: 1084–1114.

3   Immigration and Local Governments: Inclusionary Local Policies in the Era of State Rescaling

PABLO A. MITNIK AND JESSICA HALPERN-FINNERTY

The acceleration of migration flows into rich countries is a central feature of the post-Fordist era. In Western Europe and the United States this has generated a new sociodemographic reality characterized by a high share of foreign-born in the population, in particular in traditional immigration cities; by the emergence of new settlement destinations; and by the rapid growth of the proportion of unauthorized immigrants (Mitnik, Halpern-Finnerty, and Vidal 2008, 2–5; Penninx et al. 2004a). Simultaneously, the state has been rescaled. National state functions have been shifted both upward, to supranational or international bodies, and downward, to subnational governments and local quasi-public institutions (Brenner 2004; Jessop 2002a, 2004; Moulaert, Swyngedouw, and Wilson 1988; Swyngedouw 1997). Most crucially, cities and regions have been charged with the task of promoting economic growth, innovation, and international competitiveness (Jessop 2002b; Peck and Tickell 2002), thus becoming the nodes of "glocalization" strategies (Brenner 2003).

The downward shift of functions and powers has involved areas of government beyond the economic sphere, including immigration policy. Over the last three decades, European Union member states have increased their reliance on local governments for the monitoring and implementation of immigration policy (Lahav 1998). Likewise, in the United States there has been a devolution of some immigration powers to subnational governments (Varsanyi 2008a) and increasing attempts by the federal government to push state- and local-level agencies into participating in the policing of unauthorized immigrants. More importantly, both in Europe and in the United States, immigrants have concentrated geographically in some cities and regions, prompting many local governments to use their increased autonomy and authority to develop policies directed specifically at immigrants or immigrants' issues.

In any local jurisdiction, these immigrant-specific policies contribute to the constitution of what we may call a *local mode of integration*, in analogy to the notion of "national mode of integration" (Heckmann 1998; Heckmann and Schnapper 2003). However, these policies are not the only local policies that do so. Following Thomas Hammar's understanding of national immigration policy (1985), Friedrich Heckmann and Dominique Schnapper have stressed that both special (that is, immigrant-specific) and general policies help determine the nature of a mode of integration.[1] Along the same lines, Michael Alexander has argued that in studying local policies toward immigrants, researchers need to pay attention to all policies that are "initiated or largely determined by the local authority, and have significant impacts on the local migrant population, either through specific (migrant-targeted) or general (population- or area-based) measures" (2004, 59). Here we adopt a similar position. We focus on both immigrant-specific local policies and local policies that are not immigrant-specific but that centrally affect immigrants' welfare, rights, and opportunities, and thus contribute to the constitution of differentiated local modes of integration.

In Western Europe, researchers have shown that specific and general local policies affecting immigrants in a variety of domains—policing, employment, political participation, housing, education, culture, and so forth—have varied greatly across cities, from very exclusionary to very inclusionary (Alexander 2003, 2007; Penninx et al. 2004b). In contrast, in the United States the bulk of the research in this area has been concerned with local policies that are immigrant-specific and mostly exclusionary, although some inclusionary immigrant-specific policies—almost all in the juridical and political domains—have also received attention (Almonte 2006–2007; Cuison Villazor 2008; Ellis 2006; Esbenshade 2007; Harwood and Myers 2002; Hayduk 2004; Hopkins 2008; Lewis and Ramakrishnan 2007; Ridgley 2008; Varsanyi 2005, 2007, 2008b; Wells 2004; see also Provine and Seif, both in this volume).

In this chapter, we seek to change this state of affairs by documenting the existence, all over the country, of both immigrant-specific and non-immigrant-

---

1. Indirect or general policies refer to "policies and measures resulting from general socio-structural principles of societal integration," while direct or special policies refer to "intentionally and consciously devised policies and measures for the integration of immigrants" (Heckmann 1998, 2).

specific inclusionary local policies in a variety of domains. We show that in many counties, cities, and other smaller jurisdictions, elected officials have implemented policies that help immigrants to get settled in their new communities, improve their wages and working conditions, reduce their risk of being taken advantage of by unscrupulous employers, give them access to health care and other social services, promote their social integration, and contribute to an overall climate of trust, respect, and welcome. Many of these policies are not immigrant-specific.

The chapter is organized as follows. In the following section we examine local governments' efforts to prevent the involvement of their personnel with the enforcement of civil immigration law. We then discuss a variety of inclusive local immigration policies aimed at regulating employment and self-employment. Next we focus on local policies that boost immigrants' access to health care, and we follow this with a brief look at a few additional institutional innovations or policies that local governments have implemented to support the social and political integration of immigrants.

THE ENFORCEMENT OF IMMIGRATION LAW

Under the widely predominant interpretation of current federal law, agencies at the state and local levels lack statutory or constitutional authority to enforce immigration law's civil provisions, with the exception of those agencies that have entered into a formal agreement with the Department of Homeland Security (DHS) to do so (Seghetti, Viña, and Ester 2005; Smith, Sugimori, and Yasui 2003–2004, 626–28; see also Rodríguez, Chishti, and Nortman, this volume). In addition, state and local agencies and officials are not legally required to collaborate with Homeland Security's Immigration and Customs Enforcement (ICE) in finding or arresting unauthorized immigrants, or even to report to ICE information about a person's unauthorized presence in the country, unless that person has committed a crime. Nevertheless, city, county, and other local agencies and officials often play an important de facto role in the enforcement of the civil provisions of immigration law. This can lead to community mistrust, racial profiling, and civil rights violations (Smith, Sugimori, and Yasui 2003–2004, 624; Waslin 2003 and this volume). It also jeopardizes the achievement of these agencies' primary goals, in particular, public safety (see, among others, King 2006; Waslin 2003).

For these and other reasons (see Mitnik, Halpern-Finnerty, and Vidal 2008, 7–8), many local governments have attempted to curtail any involvement of their personnel with the enforcement of civil immigration law. Sixty-eight counties, cities, and other smaller local governments are known to currently limit cooperation explicitly, by which we mean that they have implemented an ordinance, resolution, executive order, or some other juridical instrument to this effect. Sixty-five of these sixty-eight local governments prohibit the participation of the police and other government officials in, and the use of government resources for, the enforcement of civil immigration law; twenty-six prohibit the collection of information on immigration status or instruct officials not to collect such information; and fifteen ban information sharing, either directly or by embedding this prohibition in a broad privacy or confidentiality provision. Many local governments employ two or more of these strategies simultaneously.[2] Based on the available information, the total number of foreign-born people living in at least one jurisdiction that limits cooperation is approximately 8.5 million, that is, about 27 percent of the total number of foreign-born living in the country.[3]

The strategies observed today are the result of the co-evolution of the actions of the federal and local governments over the last three decades. Los Angeles was the first city to officially withdraw cooperation when, in 1979, the police chief issued the now-famous Special Order 40. This order, which remains in force, establishes that "officers shall not initiate police action with the objective of discovering the alien status of a person" and "shall not arrest nor book persons for" illegal entry. The chief of police of the District of Columbia followed suit in 1984 by issuing an emphatic General Order indicating that the Metropolitan Police Department "is not in the business of inquiring about the residency status of the people we serve and is not in the business of enforcing civil immigration laws" (underlined in the original).[4] In the same year, a memo from the mayor to the heads of all departments and agencies prohibited making inquires about immigration status unless "federal or District regulations and judicial decisions require that inquiries be made to determine eligibility for benefits."[5]

2. The National Immigration Law Center compiles a list of local governments with limited-cooperation policies (http://www.nilc.org/immlawpolicy/LocalLaw/index.htm). Taking the local governments in this list as of April 2008 as our point of departure, we analyzed the ordinances, executive orders, police directives, and so forth, used to limit cooperation, and produced a table indicating for each local government the legal instrument utilized, year of implementation, and the strategy employed. This table is available on request.
3. Estimated using the 2000 Census of Population and Housing.
4. District of Columbia's Police Department General Order 201.26 (1984).
5. District of Columbia's Mayor's Memorandum 84-41 (1984).

The city of Takoma Park, Maryland, in 1985, and the cities of Chicago, San Francisco, and New York, in 1989, went further and passed ordinances or issued executive orders prohibiting city employees from gathering, keeping, or sharing with ICE's precursor, the Immigration and Naturalization Service (INS), information on the immigration status of their residents, and establishing that neither city personnel and facilities, nor any other city resources, would be employed in the enforcement of civil immigration law (cf. Rodríguez 2008, 600–605).

City bans on sharing information with the federal government were outlawed in 1996 by the Illegal Immigration Reform and Immigrant Responsibility Act (IIRIRA).[6] Many local governments responded by forbidding agencies and officials from *collecting* information about immigration status, unless required by law.[7] This is legal. In effect, IIRIRA establishes that local governments cannot prohibit agencies or officials from exchanging information about people's citizenship or immigration status with the federal government, but it does not require them to collect such information and says nothing about prohibiting its collection. Four cities and one county prohibit not only the collection of information about immigration status but also the disclosure of any information on that matter that local government agencies or officials may possess. To protect themselves from legal challenges, these local governments have embedded their prohibitions in broad privacy or confidentiality provisions banning the disclosure of information about a broad range of issues, including immigration status.[8] In what seems to violate IIRIRA's ban, ten cities prohibit information sharing outright, without embedding this prohibition in a broader confidentiality provision.

IIRIRA and federal legislation proposed in the last few years aim not only at making it more difficult for local governments to impede cooperation with the federal government but also at fully involving the former in the enforcement of civil immigration law. IIRIRA made it possible for any subnational government to sign a "memorandum of understanding" (MOU) with the DHS by which officials or employees of that government get authorized to carry out the function of an immigration officer "in relation to the investigation, apprehension or detention of aliens in the United States," at their government's

---

6. The Welfare Reform Act, passed the same year, also includes a provision to the same effect.

7. Access to some federally funded social programs mandates the collection of this information.

8. We have counted the county/city of San Francisco as a city.

expense. If a state or local agency signs such an agreement, ICE trains and certifies state and local officers as qualified to perform this enforcement function (Carafano and Keith 2006). Recently proposed legislation—for example, the Clear Law Enforcement for Criminal Alien Removal Act (H.R. 3137) and the Homeland Security Enhancement Act (S. 1362)—attempts to use carrots and sticks to induce the participation of local governments in immigration law enforcement allowed by IIRIRA, and to implement measures to increase the capacity of state and local police to arrest foreigners who violate immigration law (for details, see Mitnik, Halpern-Finnerty, and Vidal 2008, 12–13).

In general, *local* governments have not reacted positively to these ideas. Since 1996, law enforcement agencies in only two towns, eleven cities, and thirty-nine counties have signed MOUs with DHS.[9] Moreover, many cities have passed resolutions and have actively lobbied against the more recently proposed legislation. Lastly, dozens of police agencies and several police associations have voiced their opposition to the proposed federal legislation.[10]

IMMIGRANTS AND WORK: THE LOCAL REGULATION OF EMPLOYMENT AND SELF-EMPLOYMENT

Immigrants fill many jobs in the United States: nearly one of every seven people in the civilian labor force in 2005 was an immigrant. Immigrants' share in the low-wage workforce is even higher. In 2002 there were 8.6 million low-wage immigrant workers—one out of every five U.S. low-wage workers—and almost half of all immigrant workers were low-wage (Capps et al. 2003). Undocumented immigrants, most of whom are from Mexico and other Latin American countries, constituted an estimated 4.9 percent of the labor force in 2005 (Passel 2006).

Immigrants not only have a very high probability of holding low-wage jobs, but they also are very likely to be the subjects of a range of employment and labor law violations and to hold dangerous jobs (Bernhardt, McGrath, and DeFilippis 2007; Smith, Sugimori, and Yasui 2003–2004). In 2002, two million immigrants were paid less than the minimum wage (Capps et al. 2003). In addition, immigrants are overrepresented among the self-employed: they have been more likely than natives to be self-employed in every census from 1880 to 1990 (Beeler and Murray 2007). Immigrants' low wages and their concomitant

9. http://www.ice.gov/partners/287g/Section287_g.htm.
10. For police agencies and police associations opposed to the local enforcement of civil immigration law, see the list compiled by the National Immigration Forum, at http://www.immigrationforum.org/DesktopDefault.aspx?tabid=567.

reduced access to health care (see next section) are very detrimental to their families' welfare. In 2001, 12 percent of working immigrant families were poor, and fully 42 percent were low-income. Moreover, children of immigrants were far more likely than children with U.S.-born parents to be poor and to have inadequate food, housing, and health care (Capps et al. 2005).

Because immigrants, especially undocumented immigrants, are so likely to be low-wage and highly vulnerable workers, they benefit greatly from the implementation of higher wage floors and other employment standards, and from policies aimed at curbing violations of employment and labor rights. These policies are not directed specifically at immigrants, but they benefit them disproportionately. Moreover, when enacted at the local level, these and other related policies are often motivated, at least in part, by concerns regarding immigrant workers, and are supported by coalitions that include immigrant and ethnic organizations in addition to unions and workers' rights advocates.

We briefly discuss below six ways in which local governments have regulated labor markets.

Mandating Employment Standards

Local governments do not have inherent sovereign powers (Dalmat 2005, 101). Whatever powers they have are delegated by the states they are in. As state constitutions and statutes frequently specify these powers in a very imprecise way, the authority of local governments to mandate employment standards—wage floors in particular—has been an important object of political struggles. As a result, several citywide minimum wage laws passed since 2002 were later overturned in court or banned by new state statutes. Nevertheless, today five cities have citywide minimum wage laws in force: Albuquerque ($7.15/hour); Baltimore ($6.55/hour); the District of Columbia ($7.55/hour); San Francisco ($9.36/hour); and Santa Fe, New Mexico ($10.50/hour). All but Baltimore's law mandate wage floors higher than their federal and state counterparts.

Studies of the economic effects of minimum wages in San Francisco and Santa Fe—both cities with sizable immigrant populations—indicate that these cities' wage laws have achieved their purpose of substantially boosting wages at the bottom of the labor market, with negligible negative effects (Dube, Naidu, and Reich 2005, 2006; Reich, Dube, and Vickery 2006; Potter 2006; Reynis and Potter 2006; Reynis, Segal, and Bleecker 2005; Dube et al. 2006).[11] In the case of San Francisco, a study of the restaurant industry—which

---

11. San Francisco and Santa Fe are the only cities for which studies of actual effects exist.

employs a large proportion of immigrants—showed that the introduction of a citywide minimum wage greatly reduced the share of poverty-wage workers while having no effect on employment growth or store closures (Dube, Naidu, and Reich 2005, 2006; Reich, Dube, and Vickery 2006).

Citywide minimum wage laws frequently do more than just raise earnings. For instance, Baltimore's law expands coverage to workers left out in federal and state legislation, while both Baltimore's and San Francisco's include stronger enforcement mechanisms and harsher penalties than their federal and state counterparts for noncompliant employers (Mitnik 2007, 3–5). Some of the enforcement mechanisms in San Francisco's law are particularly effective in helping immigrants exercise their rights by, for example, granting the right to initiate civil action against noncompliant employers not only to affected individual workers and the city but also to any other person or entity acting on behalf of the public, including unions, community-based organizations, and immigrant worker centers.

In some cases, economic and political considerations have made it more desirable for local governments to mandate minimum wages in particular industries, types of establishments, or geographic areas rather than jurisdiction-wide (Mitnik 2007, 5). Three California cities (Berkeley, Emeryville, and Los Angeles) have passed and successfully upheld in court this type of "targeted" minimum wage law. In 2000 Berkeley established that large employers in the city's Marina Zone had to pay a minimum wage equal to the city's "living wage." In 2005, Emeryville passed legislation regulating compensation for all employees in hotels with more than fifty guest rooms and, indirectly, regulating work conditions for room cleaners. Lastly, Los Angeles passed an ordinance in 2007, which was upheld by the California Supreme Court in 2008, regulating minimum compensation and other aspects of employment conditions for hotel employees in a corridor situated immediately adjacent to Los Angeles International Airport. In all three cities, a sizable proportion of benefited workers are immigrants.

Cities have also used their legislative powers to regulate aspects of employment relations other than minimum wages. Some of these are of great concern for immigrant workers. For instance, Baltimore and the District of Columbia mandate that employers pay overtime at 1.5 times the employee's usual wage, and specify that employers must pay due wages to an employee who resigns, retires, or is fired. These are not secondary additions to these cities' minimum wage provisions: noncompliance with the overtime provision and the lack of wage payment, especially after termination, are much more common violations in Baltimore than the payment of sub-minimum wages.[12] The District of Columbia also requires employers to provide seating for those working in stores, shops, offices, or factories; to pay extra for split shifts; and to pay for the purchase and cleaning of mandatory uniforms and protective clothing. San Francisco, for its part, requires that all businesses provide paid sick leave to their employees and allow employees to use their paid sick leave to care for their family members. Kansas City, Missouri, has made it a crime to steal a person's wage. Finally, New York City has a comprehensive antidiscrimination employment law that protects immigrants from discrimination based on national origin or citizenship status (Mitnik 2007, 7–9).

Mandating Hourly-Pay Standards for Independent Contractors

In order to reduce payroll costs, low-wage employers often misclassify their employees as "independent contractors." These misclassified workers are not covered by most employment and labor laws, and they pay more taxes than they would pay as employees. Historically common in agriculture and day labor jobs, misclassification is now present in most sectors of the economy, but in particular "in the low-wage immigrant dominated sectors of home health care, construction, delivery services, and janitorial" (National Employment Law Project 2005). Misclassification not only affects misclassified workers. To compete, firms that do not misclassify their workers may be forced into a race to the bottom, which often means cutting wages and benefits.

San Francisco has passed an ordinance aimed at alleviating the negative effects of misclassification on workers. It mandates that any person, firm, proprietorship, partnership, or corporation that in any month obtains twenty or more hours of personal services, from the same or from different persons, has to pay an hourly contractual rate at least equal to the city's minimum wage. This effectively extends the city's minimum wage law to many independent contractors, regardless of whether they have been rightly or wrongly classified. It may also reduce employers' incentives to misclassify their workers.

Regulating the Activities of Domestic Employee Placement Agencies

Housecleaners and other domestic or household employees, a large proportion of whom are foreign born, are often subject to exploitative working conditions, including violations of their most basic workers' rights (Domestic

---

12. Sheldon Shugarman, executive director of Baltimore's Wage Commission, personal communication, April 5, 2007.

Workers United and DataCenter 2006). Intermediary placement agencies frequently contribute, by commission or omission, to the generation of those exploitative working conditions. In 2003 New York City passed an ordinance aimed at ameliorating the problem. It mandates that employment agencies provide to each applicant and prospective employer a written statement indicating the employee's rights and the employer's obligations under state and federal law.[13] It also requires that employment agencies provide each applicant with a detailed written statement of the job conditions for the recommended positions, and that agencies keep these statements on file for three years following placement, along with a written confirmation by employers that they have read and understood the statement of rights and obligations. Together, these measures reduce employers' and agencies' incentives to mislead employees with false promises or representations, and empower employees by making them aware of their rights and by generating evidence they can use against their employers or the placing agencies in the case of wrongdoing.

Using Proprietary Interests to Induce Changes in Employers' Behaviors

So far we have focused on cities' regulatory powers in a narrow sense, that is, their power to make the law in some domains. However, because cities are also "financial entities and market participants with expenses, assets, and incomes, as well as rights and responsibilities to their investors [that is, the citizenry]" (Wells 2002, 124), cities can also act as proprietors. When a city acts in this capacity it may commit itself, for instance, to only contracting with, giving financial aid to, and renting property to firms that pay a "living wage," that is, a minimum wage specified by the city. The same principle also applies—with more limitations, given potentially preemptive federal statutes—to conditions other than wages.

Living wage ordinances have been passed and implemented in more than one hundred cities, and many other cities are discussing similar legislation.[14] In 2005, the minimum wages required by already implemented living wage ordinances, which are frequently indexed to inflation, averaged more than $9 per hour (Fairris and Reich 2005). There are many disadvantaged

---

13. The statement, prepared by the city and distributed in both English and Spanish, describes laws regarding minimum wage, overtime and hours of work, record keeping, Social Security payments, unemployment insurance coverage, disability insurance coverage, and workers' compensation.

14. The Association of Community Organizations for Reform Now (ACORN) keeps a list of local governments that have passed living wage ordinances and a list of living wage campaigns under way. See http://www.livingwagecampaign.org.

immigrants working for city service contractors that tend to pay poverty wages (for example, in services like facility and building maintenance, janitorial, landscaping, laundry, pest control, tree trimming, and security). Likewise, sometimes cities have proprietary interests in businesses such as hotels and restaurants, which hire a large number of immigrants at similarly low wages. Hence, although living wage ordinances generally cover a relatively small fraction of workers within a city, they are likely to cover a much higher proportion of immigrants.

Living wage ordinances often address employment issues other than wages, while a few cities have passed separate legislation conditioning financial support for economic development projects on employment standards other than wages as well. Most living wage ordinances require a higher minimum wage if employers do not provide health care benefits, while a few cities require all covered firms to provide health care benefits (more on this in the next section). Several cities require the provision of vacations or sick leave. Others allow retirement and childcare benefits to count as part of the minimum compensation they demand. A few require that the jobs created with the help of public money be full-time or almost full-time (for more details, see Mitnik 2007, 13).

Cities have also used their proprietary interests to support workers' right to organize (see Mitnik 2007, 12–16). Because unions tend to improve wages and other forms of compensation the most at the bottom of the labor market (Mishel, Bernstein, and Allegretto 2007, 181–89) and to substantially reduce employment and labor law violations (Bernhardt, McGrath, and DeFilippis 2007), immigrants benefit greatly from cities' support of workers' right to organize.

Supporting Worker Centers for Day Laborers

Many immigrants seek employment on the day labor market, often congregating daily at informal hiring sites. In 2004, close to 120,000 workers were either looking for day labor jobs or working as day laborers in the United States on any given day (Valenzuela et al. 2006, 4). The day labor workforce is overwhelmingly Latino and immigrant, mostly undocumented. Day laborers are mainly employed by homeowners, renters, or contractors. Their annual earnings are unlikely to exceed $15,000, and they are very often victims of employer abuse, wage theft, and workplace injuries. Lastly, rapid growth of day labor markets and the public health and safety concerns associated with their operation in open-air hiring sites have generated tensions in many cities (Valenzuela et al. 2006; see also Valenzuela 2003).

In some cities, the creation of (day laborer) worker centers has been an effective response to the challenges of day labor markets (España 2002; Fine 2006; Valenzuela et al. 2006). Worker centers are community-based organizations that serve low-wage workers—in most cases, immigrants. Those working with day laborers provide a formal location for day labor markets—thus alleviating community tensions—and basic amenities for workers and employers. They also constitute a basic form of regulation of an otherwise exploitative labor market. Indeed, they "monitor the actions of employers, increase the transparency of the hiring process and provide an institutional foundation for holding employers accountable for workplace abuses." In addition, "they organize and normalize the hiring of day laborers, monitor worker quality and provide opportunities for worker incorporation into the mainstream economy" (Valenzuela et al. 2006, 23). Several local governments have sponsored and provided funds to help set up or finance the operation of day labor worker centers. Of the sixty-three day labor worker centers identified in the 2006 National Day Labor Survey, ten were run by city government agencies, and many of the others (run by community or faith-based organizations) received some form of support from municipal governments (Valenzuela et al. 2006, 7).

IMMIGRANTS' ACCESS TO HEALTH CARE

Over half of noncitizens lack health care coverage, compared to 15 percent of native-born citizens (Kaiser Commission 2004). There are several reasons for this disparity. First, immigrants are far less likely to have employer-based insurance; this is primarily the result of most immigrants being employed in low-wage jobs that do not offer health insurance. Second, many immigrants are ineligible for public programs like Medicaid or its state counterparts, and some are eligible but lack knowledge about how to access those programs or fear that applying for public assistance will affect their visa or citizenship procedures or cause them to be targeted by ICE. Only Emergency Medicaid, which covers the cost of emergency medical treatment, is offered to all immigrants who meet an income requirement, regardless of their immigration status. In 2004, twenty-five states offered some form of expanded coverage to immigrants ineligible for Medicaid and the State Children's Health Insurance Program (SCHIP), but in most cases this expansion was targeted at very specific subpopulations (Kaiser Commission 2004, 2).

Local governments often bear the burden of this deficit in health care coverage, both financially and in terms of public health. Residents without insurance are less likely to have access to health care and to seek preventative care, leading to more serious health problems and a greater number of emergency room visits, as well as to the potential spread of communicable diseases (Mohanty 2006, 4). Local governments' power to effect change in this arena, however, is limited by the Employer Retirement Income Security Act of 1974 (ERISA), which prevents state and local regulation of employer benefits plans. The preemption clause of ERISA continues to be open to interpretation regarding how it applies to state and local regulation of businesses' provision of health insurance. In general, ERISA asserts that state and local governments are not allowed to mandate that private employers offer or pay for health insurance or to directly regulate private employer–sponsored health plans, but the debate about whether laws that indirectly affect or relate to these plans are preempted has not been resolved.

We discuss here a few policies that local governments have implemented, sponsored, or funded, and that aim at (1) maximizing the enrollment of people already eligible for health insurance, or (2) expanding access to health insurance and health care to those not eligible for existing programs. The policies we discuss have substantially benefited immigrants, and some of them were indeed motivated, at least in part, by the goal of improving immigrants' access to health care.

Maximizing the Enrollment of People Already Eligible for Health Care Programs

Two successful examples of (quasi-public) local policies aimed at maximizing the number of eligible people enrolled are Citrus Valley, California's Get Enrollment Moving (GEM) plan and the Indigent Care Collaboration (ICC) in central Texas. GEM was implemented in 2001 by the health care provider Citrus Valley Health Partners, with partial funding from the Los Angeles County Department of Health Services. It combats under-enrollment by addressing both lack of knowledge about health insurance options and fears about the consequences of enrolling in public programs. The foundation of GEM is hundreds of volunteer health educators, the *promotoras de salud*. Recruited from the communities targeted by the plan, the *promotoras* go door-to-door to talk with people about their health care options and to encourage enrollment by providing information about health care and identifying those eligible for some type of coverage. GEM follows up on these efforts by providing application assistance with multilingual staff members at the central office. Since it began, GEM has been able to enroll nearly thirty thousand people in federal or California state public health programs. GEM reports that nearly 35 percent of those enrolled live in a family with at least one adult unauthorized immigrant (Petsod, Wang, and McGarvey 2006, 115).

ICC is an alliance of health care safety net providers that came together in Travis County, Texas, in 1997 and expanded to Williams and Hayes counties in 2000. Its goals are expanding access, improving quality, and increasing affordability of health care for the low-income and uninsured residents of central Texas.[15] The coalition includes hospitals, health care networks, clinics, city and county health departments, nonprofit organizations, individual providers, and others. ICC uses a computation software called Medicaider which can quickly screen for an individual's eligibility for Medicaid, SCHIP, Supplemental Security Income, other federal and state programs for the low-income uninsured, local public programs, and charity care services. This allows ICC to direct each patient to the program for which he or she is eligible and that entails the most efficient use of local, state, and federal resources. As a result, ICC has been able to vastly improve access to health care in Austin and the surrounding region without significantly expanding care programs themselves. A large proportion of those benefited by the program are immigrants.

Expanding Access to Health Insurance and Health Care

We discuss here three approaches that local governments have used to expand access to health insurance and health care: San Francisco's unique health care program, which offers medical services to its uninsured residents; the use by local governments of their proprietary interests to induce firms to offer health insurance to their employees; and the provision of subsidized health care through public hospitals and clinics.

The approach of the city/county of San Francisco is by far the most ambitious and the one that should benefit immigrants the most. It aims at offering universal coverage with the Healthy San Francisco (HSF) program, which began on a pilot basis in July 2007 and today has a total enrollment of twenty-eight thousand (the program is being phased in over time). HSF offers primary care, hospitalization services, specialty care, and prescription drugs for uninsured residents of San Francisco regardless of employment,

---

15. See http://www.icc-centex.org/abouticc.cfm.

immigration status, or medical condition. Individuals can enroll in the program (directly or through their employer) for a sliding monthly fee, heavily subsidized for small and medium-sized businesses and for low-income individuals (the fee is zero for people from very low income households).

Part of the program is financed with public money, and the remainder is covered through the fees that enrolled individuals (or their employers) pay and with the money collected from those large and medium-sized employers that do not meet an "employer spending requirement" established by the ordinance that created HSF. HSF attempts to avoid conflicting with ERISA in two ways. First, the coverage provided by HSF is not portable outside of San Francisco and therefore is not technically health insurance. Second, the ordinance does not directly regulate employer spending on health insurance, instead offering multiple health spending options (one of which is HSF). Still, the employer spending requirement has been actively resisted by San Francisco's employers, in particular the Golden Gate Restaurant Association.

As discussed in the previous section, cities and other local governments acting as proprietors can pass a living wage ordinance that commits them to do business only with firms that pay a living wage. The same principle is valid for health care benefits. To avoid potential conflicts with ERISA, cities typically avoid requiring health care benefits in their living wage legislation. They demand, instead, a higher living wage if those benefits are not offered (Reynolds and Kern 2003, 40). A few cities, however, require covered firms to provide health care benefits (Mitnik 2007, 18).

A third and straightforward way for local governments to address the problem of the uninsured is to directly provide health care through public hospitals and clinics, partially or fully subsidizing provision. For instance, the New York City public health system, the Health and Hospitals Corporation (HHC), operates the HHC Options program, which offers subsidized health care for low- and moderate-income individuals utilizing the public system (Commission on the Public's Health System 2005; Ku and Papademetriou 2007). HHC ensures immigrants' right to access health care, regardless of immigration status, by keeping information on this status confidential and making this policy widely known. In an open letter to immigrant New Yorkers released in twelve languages as part of a 2006 public awareness campaign, HHC President Alan Aviles and New York City Commissioner of Immigrant Affairs Guillermo Linares stated that information about immigration status was not going to be shared with anyone, including immigration and law enforcement officials.

OTHER INCLUSIONARY INSTITUTIONAL INNOVATIONS AND POLICIES

In this section we briefly refer to four institutional innovations or policies that local governments have implemented to support the social and political integration of immigrants: establishing a multipurpose agency aimed at serving the needs of immigrant residents; accepting *matrículas consulares* as valid forms of identification and promoting their acceptance by third parties; offering municipal identification cards; and allowing noncitizen residents to vote in local elections.

New York City has had, for some time now, a multipurpose agency charged with the exclusive task of dealing with immigrant issues.[16] The New York Mayor's Office of Immigrant Affairs (MOIA) declares as its goal the promotion of the full and active participation of immigrant New Yorkers in the civic, economic, and cultural life of the city.[17] Founded in 1984 as the Office of Immigrant Affairs within the Department of City Planning, MOIA has been a separate agency since 1990. It works with three groups: immigrants, community-based organizations serving immigrants, and New York City agencies and officials. It helps immigrants identify city services they can receive and community-based organizations able to address their needs. It also helps immigrants get information regarding citizenship and change of legal status applications and procedures, and it offers them information regarding employment, housing, public schools, small business services, and the city's privacy policies. MOIA works with nearly three hundred community-based organizations (Pecorella and Stonecash 2006, 14) to find city agencies that can assist them with resources or to which they can refer immigrants, and it arranges meetings with appropriate city officials to address community-specific concerns. Finally, MOIA educates city agencies about best practices for reaching immigrant communities, identifies community-based organizations serving specific immigrant communities for these agencies to contact, teams with city agencies to provide bulletins and advisories in multiple languages and to assist them in accessing translation services, and offers expertise to the mayor regarding issues important for immigrants. In addition, MOIA has an important symbolic value, highlighting the city's stance regarding immigration and immigrants' rights.

---

16. New York City is the only local government that has established an agency of this type. In 2004 Los Angeles took some steps toward creating an office of immigrant affairs (Mayor Hahn's 2004 Executive Directive IC-2), but the project did not move forward.

17. See http://www.nyc.gov/html/imm/html/about/about.shtml.

Matrículas consulares are identity cards that the Mexican government issues to Mexicans living abroad who request them. Although these consular IDs have existed for almost 140 years, cities and counties only recently started to accept them as a valid form of identification after many states tightened their documentation requirements for issuing driver's licenses following the events of September 11, 2001. These local governments have also urged banks and other financial institutions to accept the *matrículas consulares* as a valid identification with which to open accounts, with the goal of reducing undocumented immigrants' need to carry and store cash and thus also reducing their chances of being targets of crime. By the end of 2005, *matrículas consulares* were accepted as valid identification by 1,204 police agencies, 393 cities, and 168 counties (Varsanyi 2007, 306).

New Haven, Connecticut, has followed a different strategy. In June 2007, New Haven became the first city to offer a multipurpose municipal identification card to all its residents, regardless of age or immigration status. Although this institutional innovation is not immigrant-specific, its central motivation was to help illegal immigrants (Medina 2007). Recognized as official documentation within city limits, New Haven's ID allows immigrants easy access to all city services and provides them with legal documentation for use at hospitals, banks, public libraries, and stores. In addition, the ID is meant to improve public safety in two ways. First, immigrants can use it to open bank accounts. Second, the ID is expected to make immigrants who lack other proof of identification more likely to report crimes they may suffer or witness.

Finally, some cities have enfranchised or, more precisely, re-enfranchised immigrants. Over a 150-year period starting in 1776, noncitizens were allowed to vote in local, state, and, in some cases, federal elections in twenty-two states and federal territories. However, state by state, noncitizens lost their right to vote in the first quarter of the twentieth century (Raskin 1992–1993). In more recent times, however, Takoma Park and five other, smaller jurisdictions in Maryland have restored noncitizens' right to vote, while cities in several other states are considering similar legislation (Hayduk 2004). In addition, Chicago has allowed noncitizens to vote in local school board elections since 1988, as did New York between 1970 and 2003 (when school boards were dissolved), and there are campaigns under way to permit immigrants to participate in these elections in several other cities as well (Kini 2005; Varsanyi 2005; Yang 2006).

CONCLUDING REMARKS

Place matters greatly for the large number of immigrants, both authorized and unauthorized, living in the United States today. In part this is a result of the rescaling of the state and the concomitant intensification of geographical variation in immigrant-specific local policies and in "universal local policies" that centrally affect the welfare, rights, and opportunities of immigrants. We have examined here inclusionary policies that are likely to be associated with significant differences in local modes of integration across the country. We have shown that many counties, cities, and other smaller jurisdictions have implemented policies that boost unauthorized immigrants' chances of remaining in the country, as well as other policies that grant important social, economic, and political rights to immigrants, improve their life chances, and promote their integration in various ways. The variety and potentially substantial effects on immigrants of the inclusionary local immigration policies we have discussed suggest that conducting systematic research on local modes of integration in the United States would be warranted. The theoretical, methodological, and policy payoffs of that research are likely to be large.

WORKS CITED

Alexander, Michael. 2003. "Local Policies towards Migrants as an Expression of Host-Stranger Relations," *Journal of Ethnic and Migration Studies* 29, no. 3: 411–30.

———. 2004. "Comparing Local Policies toward Migrants." In *Citizenship in European Cities,* ed. Rinus Penninx, Karen Kraal, Marco Martinielo, and Steven Vertovec. Aldershot, UK: Ashgate.

———. 2007. *Cities and Labour Immigration.* Aldershot, UK: Ashgate.

Almonte, Michael J. 2006–2007. "State and Local Law Enforcement Response to Undocumented Immigrants," *Brooklyn Law Review* 72: 655–88.

Beeler, Amy, and Julie Murray. 2007. "Improving Immigrant Workers' Economic Prospects." In *Securing the Future,* ed. Michael Fix. Washington, DC: Migration Policy Institute.

Bernhardt, Annette, Siobhán McGrath, and James DeFilippis. 2007. *Unregulated Work in the Global City.* New York: Brennan Center for Justice.

Brenner, Neil. 2003. "'Glocalization' as a State Spatial Strategy." In *Remaking the Global Economy,* ed. Jamie Peck and Henry Yeung. London: Sage.

———. 2004. *New State Spaces.* Oxford: Oxford University Press.

Capps, Randolph, Michael Fix, Everett Henderson, and Jane Reardon-Anderson. 2005. "A Profile of Low-Income Working Immigrant Families." Washington, DC: Urban Institute.

Capps, Randolph, Michael Fix, Jeffrey Passel, Jason Ost, and Dan Perez-Lopez. 2003. "A Profile of the Low-Wage Immigrant Workforce." Washington, DC: Urban Institute.

Carafano, James J., and Laura Keith. 2006. "The Solution for Immigration Enforcement at the State and Local Level." Web memo. Washington, DC: Heritage Foundation.

Commission on the Public's Health System. 2005. *HHC Options*. New York: New York City Health and Hospitals Corporation.

Cuison Villazor, Rose. 2008. "What Is a Sanctuary?" *Southern Methodist University Law Review* 61, no. 133: 133–56.

Dalmat, Darin. 2005. "Bringing Economic Justice Closer to Home," *Columbia Journal of Law and Social Problems* 39: 93–147.

Domestic Workers United and DataCenter. 2006. "Home Is Where the Work Is." New York: Domestic Workers United and DataCenter.

Dube, Arindrajit, Ethan Kaplan, Michael Reich, and Felix Su. 2006. "Do Businesses Flee Citywide Minimum Wages?" Berkeley, CA: Institute for Research on Labor and Employment, University of California, Berkeley.

Dube, Arindrajit, Suresh Naidu, and Michael Reich. 2005. "Can a Citywide Minimum Wage Be an Effective Policy Tool?" Berkeley, CA: Institute for Research on Labor and Employment, University of California, Berkeley.

———. 2006. "The Economic Impacts of a Citywide Minimum Wage." Berkeley, CA: Institute for Research on Labor and Employment, University of California, Berkeley.

Ellis, Mark. 2006. "Unsettling Immigrant Geographies," *Tijdschrift voor Economische en Sociale Geografie* 97, no. 1: 49–58.

Esbenshade, Jill. 2007. "Division and Dislocation." Washington, DC: Immigration Policy Center, American Immigration Law Foundation.

España, Mauricio. 2002. "Day-Laborers, Friend or Foe," *Fordham Urban Law Journal* 30: 1979–2005.

Fairris, David, and Michael Reich. 2005. "The Impacts of Living Wage Policies," *Industrial Relations* 44, no. 1: 1–11.

Fine, Janice. 2006. *Worker Centers*. Ithaca, NY: Economic Policy Institute and Cornell University Press.

Hammar, Tomas. 1985. *European Immigration Policy*. London: Cambridge University Press.

Harwood, Stacy, and Dowell Myers. 2002. "The Dynamics of Immigration and Local Governance in Santa Ana," *Policy Studies Journal* 30, no. 1: 70–91.

Hayduk, Ronald. 2004. "Democracy for All," *New Political Science* 26, no. 4: 499–523.

Heckmann, Friedrich. 1998. "National Modes of Immigrant Integration." EFMS Paper No. 24. Bamberg, Germany: Europäisches Forum für Migrationsstudien.

Heckmann, Friedrich, and Dominique Schnapper. 2003. "Introduction." In *The Integration of Immigrants in European Societies*, ed. F. Heckmann and D. Schnapper. Stuttgart: Lucius and Lucius.

Hopkins, Daniel J. 2008. "Threatening Changes: Explaining Where and When Immigrants Provoke Local Opposition." Manuscript.

Illegal Immigration Reform and Immigrant Responsibility Act (IIRIRA), P.L. 104-208 (1996).

Jessop, Bob. 2002a. *The Future of the Capitalist State*. Cambridge: Polity Press.

———. 2002b. "Liberalism, Neoliberalism, and Urban Governance," *Antipode* 34, no. 3: 452–72.

———. 2004. "Hollowing Out the 'Nation State' and Multi-Level Governance." In *A Handbook of Comparative Social Policy*, ed. P. Kennett. Cheltenham, UK: Edward Elgar.

Kaiser Commission. 2004. "Key Facts: Health Coverage for Immigrants." Washington, DC: Henry J. Kaiser Family Foundation.

King, Martha, ed. 2006. *Justice and Safety in America's Immigrant Communities*. Princeton, NJ: Policy Research Institute for the Region and Woodrow Wilson School of Public and International Affairs, Princeton University.

Kini, Tara. 2005. "Voting Rights in Local School Board Elections," *California Law Review* 93: 271–322.

Ku, Leighton, and Demetrios Papademetriou. 2007. "Access to Health Care and Health Insurance." In *Securing the Future*, ed. Michael Fix. Washington, DC: Migration Policy Institute.

Lahav, Gallya. 1998. "Immigration and the State," *Journal of Ethnic and Migration Studies* 24, no. 4: 675–94.

Lewis, Paul G., and S. Karthick Ramakrishnan. 2007. "Police Practices in Immigrant-Destination Cities," *Urban Affairs Review* 42, no. 6.

Medina, Jennifer. 2007. "New Haven Approves Program to Issue Illegal Immigrants IDs," *New York Times*, June 5.

Mishel, Lawrence, Jared Bernstein, and Sylvia Allegretto. 2007. *The State of Working America, 2006/2007*. Ithaca, NY: Cornell University Press.

Mitnik, Pablo. 2007. "Cities and Jobs." Madison, WI: Center on Wisconsin Strategy, University of Wisconsin, Madison. Updated April 2008.

Mitnik, Pablo, Jessica Halpern-Finnerty, and Matt Vidal. 2008. "Cities and Immigration." Madison, WI: Center on Wisconsin Strategy, University of Wisconsin, Madison.

Mohanty, Sarita. 2006. "Unequal Access," *Immigration Policy in Focus* 5, no. 5.

Moulaert, Frank, Erik Swyngedouw, and Patricia Wilson. 1988. "Spatial Responses to Fordist and Post-Fordist Accumulation and Regulation," *Papers of the Regional Science Association* 64: 11–23.

National Employment Law Project. 2005. "1099'd." New York: National Employment Law Project.

Passel, Jeffrey. 2006. "The Size and Characteristics of the Unauthorized Migrant Population in the U.S." Washington, DC: Pew Hispanic Center.

Peck, Jamie, and Adam Tickell. 2002. "Neoliberalizing Space," *Antipode* 34, no. 3: 380–404.

Pecorella, Robert, and Jeffrey Stonecash. 2006. *Governing New York State*. Albany, NY: SUNY Press.

Penninx, Rinus, Karen Kraal, Marco Martinielo, and Steven Vertovec. 2004a. "Introduction." In *Citizenship in European Cities*, ed. R. Penninx, K. Kraal, M. Martinielo, and S. Vertovec. Aldershot, UK: Ashgate.

———, eds. 2004b. *Citizenship in European Cities*. Aldershot, UK: Ashgate.

Petsod, Daranee, Ted Wang, and Craig McGarvey. 2006. "Investing in Our Communities: Strategies for Immigrant Integration." Sebastopol, CA: Grantmakers Concerned with Immigrants and Refugees.

Potter, Nicholas. 2006. "Measuring the Employment Impacts of the Living Wage Ordinance in Santa Fe, New Mexico." Albuquerque, NM: Bureau of Business and Economic Research, University of New Mexico.

Raskin, James B. 1992–1993. "Legal Aliens, Local Citizens," *University of Pennsylvania Law Review* 141: 1391–1470.

Reich, Michael, Arindrajit Dube, and Gina Vickery. 2006. "The Economics of Citywide Minimum Wages." Berkeley, CA: Institute for Research on Labor and Employment, University of California, Berkeley.

Reynis, Lee, and Nicholas Potter. 2006. "Supplemental Analysis of the Impacts of the $8.50 Minimum Wage on Santa Fe Business, Workers and the Economy." Albuquerque, NM: Bureau of Business and Economic Research, University of New Mexico.

Reynis, Lee, Myra Segal, and Molly Bleecker. 2005. "Preliminary Analysis of the Impacts of the $8.50 Minimum Wage on Santa Fe Business, Workers, and the

Santa Fe Economy." Albuquerque, NM: Bureau of Business and Economic Research, University of New Mexico.

Reynolds, David, and Jen Kern. 2003. *Living Wage Campaigns,* January 2003 ed. Washington, DC: Association of Community Organizations for Reform Now (ACORN).

Ridgley, Jennifer. 2008. "Cities of Refuge," *Urban Geography* 29, no. 1: 53–77.

Rodríguez, Cristina. 2008. "The Significance of the Local in Immigration Regulation." Public Law and Legal Theory Research Paper Series Working Paper No. 08-22. New York: New York University School of Law.

Seghetti, Lisa, Stephen Viña, and Karma Ester. 2005. "Enforcing Immigration Law." CRS Report for Congress. Washington, DC: Congressional Research Service, Library of Congress.

Smith, Rebecca, Amy Sugimori, and Luna Yasui. 2003–2004. "Low Pay, High Risk," *New York University Review of Law and Social Change* 28: 597–654.

Swyngedouw, Erik. 1997. "Neither Global Nor Local." In *Spaces of Globalization,* ed. K. Cox. New York: Guilford Press.

Valenzuela, Abel, Jr. 2003. "Day Labor Work," *Annual Review of Sociology* 29: 307–33.

Valenzuela, Abel, Jr., Nik Theodore, Edwin Meléndez, and Ana Luz González. 2006. "On the Corner." Los Angeles, CA: Center for the Study of Urban Poverty, University of California, Los Angeles.

Varsanyi, Monica. 2005. "The Rise and Fall (and Rise?) of Non-Citizen Voting," *Space and Polity* 9, no. 2: 113–34.

———. 2007. "Documenting Undocumented Migrants," *Geopolitics* 12, no. 2: 299–319.

———. 2008a. "Rescaling the 'Alien,' Rescaling Personhood," *Annals of the Association of American Geographers* 98, no. 4: 877–96.

———. 2008b. "Immigration Policing through the Backdoor," *Urban Geography* 29, no. 1: 29–52.

Waslin, Michele. 2003. "Immigration Enforcement by Local Police." Issue Brief No. 9. Washington, DC: National Council of La Raza.

Wells, Miriam J. 2002. "When Urban Policy Becomes Labor Policy," *Theory and Society* 31: 115–46.

———. 2004. "The Grassroots Reconfiguration of U.S. Immigration Policy," *International Migration Review* 38, no. 4: 1308–47.

Yang, B. Y. F. 2006. "Fighting for an Equal Voice," *Asian American Law Journal* 13: 57–89.

4 Partisanship, Not Spanish: Explaining Municipal Ordinances Affecting Undocumented Immigrants

S. Karthick Ramakrishnan and Tom (Tak) Wong

Though there is widespread recognition that localities are playing a more significant role in regulating the lives of low-skilled immigrant residents, there is little systematic understanding of why some localities may adopt restrictionist policies while others may adopt more permissive policies or do nothing at all. Part of the difficulty in understanding why these ordinances are being proposed in some places but not in others is the fact that many of the localities considering restrictionist ordinances are small municipalities that rarely get coverage in state newspapers and wire stories, let alone in national outlets such as the *New York Times* and *Washington Post* or more regional newspapers like the *Chicago Tribune*. Thus, as suggested by a number of chapters in this volume, the dominant understanding of the factors compelling local action on immigration is shaped by heavy coverage of such places as Hazleton, Pennsylvania, Carpentersville, Illinois, San Bernardino, California, and Farmers Branch, Texas, with likely explanations centering around the size and growth of Latino populations and attendant challenges such as overcrowded schools and housing, growth of Spanish-language communities, erosion of wages among native-born workers, and perhaps xenophobia or racial prejudice among native-born populations (Scolforo 2006; Kotlowitz 2007).

We thank the ACLU, Migration Policy Institute, and Fair Immigration Reform Movement for sharing their data on local ordinances; participants in the 2007 Omaha Cumbre, Politics of Race, Immigration, and Ethnicity Consortium, and Warren Institute Roundtable at UC-Berkeley for their comments; and the Chief Justice Earl Warren Institute on Race, Ethnicity and Diversity for financial support.

Although these demographic explanations are clearly relevant in the ways that policy analysts, local officials, community advocates, and journalists make sense of these ordinances, it is important to expand the analysis to the larger universe of over twenty thousand municipalities in the United States to gain a better understanding of whether demographic pressures are indeed of the utmost salience in explaining the recent rash of immigration-related ordinances. Also, it is important to consider other factors that have heretofore been marginal in explanations of local ordinance activity related to immigration, including the partisanship and ideology of local voters and the political empowerment or fallout from the spring 2006 immigration rallies. Finally, it is important to examine the proposal and passage not only of restrictionist ordinances (Esbenshade 2007; Hopkins 2010) but also of various "pro-immigrant" ordinances at the local level, including so-called sanctuary laws.

In this chapter we show that partisanship and politicization are crucial in explaining why some localities have considered or passed restrictionist ordinances while a few others have considered "pro-immigrant" ordinances and—just as importantly—why most communities have done nothing at all on the issue. Political factors remain significant even after controlling for factors related to the competing explanation of "local demographic pressures," including the growth of Latino populations, the prevalence of recently arrived immigrants, overcrowded housing, and rising poverty rates at the local level. Thus, as a number of the case studies in this volume suggest, while demographic pressures at the local level may be a common feature to many localities that have considered restrictionist ordinances, political factors are important in shaping how such pressures find policy expression at the local level.

EMERGING QUESTIONS ON LOCAL GOVERNMENT POLICIES

There is a long tradition in political science of studies on the role of immigrants and racial minorities in local governance. Early pluralists such as Robert Dahl (1961) pointed to an assimilationist trend in immigrant political incorporation based on the mobilization of potential electorates. Others such as Steven Erie (1988) and Gerald Gamm (1989) demonstrated the problem of incorporation of immigrants into local party structures, while those in the tradition of minority political incorporation (Browning, Marshall, and Tabb 1984) pointed to the need for minority groups to forge electoral coalitions with white liberals and Democrats. Contemporary studies of immigrants and local political structures (Jones-Correa 1998; Ramakrishnan and Lewis 2005; Rogers 2006; Wong 2006; Ramakrishnan and Bloemraad 2008) suggest that the pluralist vision is largely inapplicable to contemporary immigrants and that significant barriers to entry remain among both political and civic institutions.

Although these newer studies shed some light on the continued relevance of earlier models of political incorporation, the current state of knowledge on local politics is inadequate to understand the entry of local governments into questions that have heretofore been the purview of the federal government (Varsanyi 2008). Indeed, in recent years, news stories and reports by organizations such as the Migration Policy Institute and the Puerto Rican Legal Defense and Education Fund point to a rise in the consideration and use of local ordinances targeting immigrants, especially undocumented immigrants. Examples of restrictionist ordinances include attempts to compel landlords to verify the legal immigrant status of tenants, denying business licenses or city contracts to those who hire illegal immigrants, using local police to facilitate deportations in conjunction with Immigration and Customs Enforcement (ICE), and establishing English as a city's official language. On the other hand, there also has been a steady increase in the number of cities passing measures explicitly designed to shield undocumented immigrants, including "sanctuary" ordinances that limit cooperation with ICE to matters of national security, establishing or funding day labor centers that protect the rights of workers regardless of their legal status, and even providing city-issued identification cards for residents, even those who are in the United States illegally.

There is a small but growing number of studies that examine local government policies toward immigrants (Jones-Correa 2004; Ramakrishnan and Lewis 2005; Varsanyi 2008; Esbenshade 2007). While these studies have helped to lay some important theoretical groundwork on new types of policies that specifically target immigrants or undocumented immigrants, this chapter presents one of the first national studies of local government policies toward immigrants, especially as they relate to restrictive and permissive policies toward unauthorized or undocumented immigrants.

The chapter examines variation in municipal government policies related to low-skilled immigrant labor in localities across the United States. It builds on prior research conducted in California, which indicates that city policies toward immigrants vary according to local population size and the partisanship of local jurisdictions, and that these effects hold true even after controlling for demographic factors such as the proportion of the population that is foreign born or recently arrived in the United States (Ramakrishnan and Lewis 2005). While California is important to the study of local government policies, it is also important to compare policies across states, each with its own history of immigration and varying rules and institutional arrangements on matters such as partisan local elections, ballot initiatives, and local government autonomy.

Our research questions revolve around the extent to which city governments consider and pass restrictionist or permissive policies regarding issues such as day labor markets, housing, unlicensed businesses, and cooperation with federal immigration authorities.[1] In addition to answering the "what" and "where" questions of the passage of such ordinances, we also seek to answer the question of why these policies are considered in some places but not in others and, once they are considered, why they pass in some localities but fail in others. Answering these "why" questions entails the collection of various kinds of contextual data (on demographic changes, local economies, and local political opportunity structures) and using such data in a multivariate regression context to assess the relative significance of each in relation to local efforts to legislate on immigration-related issues.

ASSESSING COMPETING EXPLANATIONS

The simplest explanation for the consideration and passage of restrictionist ordinances across the United States centers on the demographic changes associated with recent migration and the socioeconomic dislocations resulting from such migrations. However, localities with restrictionist policies are but a small fraction of the thousands of communities in the United States that are transforming due to recent international migration. Thus, while demographic changes and labor market outcomes may be necessary factors, they are unlikely to be sufficient ones.

Past research on local government policies toward immigrant integration indicates that the ideological and partisan leanings of governing institutions and the electorate play an important role. For instance, in a 2003 survey of more than three hundred California cities, Ramakrishnan and Lewis found that municipal governments with Republican-leaning electorates and

---

1. The restrictive ordinances in our sample include measures whereby local governments use their official capacities to enforce federal immigration laws or to address perceived negative societal consequences of illegal immigration. Illegal Immigration Relief Act (IIRA) ordinances and variants of them constitute the majority of these restrictive measures. IIRAs commonly refer to the fiscal and governance challenges arising from the presence of illegal immigrants. The pro-immigrant ordinances in our sample include resolutions and mandates that express opposition to immigration raids and restrictionist national legislation, those barring the use of public funds to enforce immigration laws, and those with explicit "sanctuary" policies whereby local officials do not inquire about legal status and do not notify immigration authorities about the status of individuals unless they are convicted of serious crimes.

conservative city councils were less likely to provide translation of city hall documents and interpretation services in public meetings. We believe that partisanship may play an even stronger role today than in 2003, given that immigration reemerged as a salient and sharply partisan issue in 2005 when the U.S. Congress considered a measure (H.R. 4437) to make illegal immigration a federal felony. Thus we hypothesize that Republican-majority areas are more likely to sponsor restrictionist ordinances, either because residents in these regions are more likely to clamor for measures to repel undocumented immigrants from their cities or because such regions afford policy entrepreneurs with the opportunities to seek political office or pass particular policies by framing undocumented immigration as one of the most significant problems for local governance.

In some ways, the proportion of Republicans in a region can be seen as a proxy for political ideology and issue preferences on immigration at the local level: not only are registered Republicans more likely than registered Democrats to describe themselves as ideologically conservative (National Election Studies 2004), but they are also more likely to take conservative positions on the issue of illegal immigration in particular (Ramakrishnan et al. 2007). At the same time, evidence from Arizona and elsewhere suggests that the proportion of Republicans in a region also indicates the extent to which candidates can challenge incumbents in Republican primaries or expand the base of Republican voters in the general election (Lelyveld 2006; Roarty 2008).

In the process of testing the importance of local partisanship, we also analyze the relative merit of other factors that may arguably be related to the proposal of restrictionist ordinances:

- *The Latino share of the citizen population* is a measure of the potential electoral strength of Latinos to push for liberal measures and to counteract conservative measures on immigration. We expect the Latino share of the citizenry to be positively related to the proposal of "pro-immigrant" ordinances and negatively related to the proposal of restrictionist ordinances.

- By contrast, *the growth of recent immigrants to the United States* would be associated with less electoral strength for immigrants and also with greater challenges to local manifestations of rapid demographic change such as:

    High proportions of households that are linguistically isolated. One of the most prominent concerns about recent migration to new destinations, especially of Latino immigrants, is the fear of linguistic balkanization and the visibility of Spanish in public spaces (Huntington 2004).

Wage competition with blacks and whites. We expect the effects of wage competition due to low-skilled migration and group conflict over resources to be felt most strongly among those whites and blacks living below the poverty line (Borjas 2006). Indeed, for assessments of the explanatory power of group conflict over resources, it is the difference in poverty rates among blacks, whites, and Latinos that may be most important (Gay 2006).

Overcrowded housing. Past research on the politics of immigration at the local level has shown that issues of overcrowding are more common in immigrant destination cities. However, these problems are rarely addressed by municipal governments (Ramakrishnan and Lewis 2005), so we may fail to see a positive association between overcrowded housing and city ordinances related to immigrant tenants.

- *The existence of immigrant protests in the area.* There was some concern among political analysts that the immigrant protests of spring 2006 would spark a backlash among nativists. The proposal of ordinances in many localities in the summer of 2006 reinforced the plausibility of this assertion. Here we can test whether such protests did indeed spark a restrictionist backlash or whether there was no such effect.

- *Places with industries that are heavily dependent on immigrant labor,* such as agriculture, mining, and construction, may be less likely to pass restrictionist ordinances because of the importance of low-skilled migrants to the local economy.

- Finally, the *state-level policy climate* toward immigrants may itself bear a significant relationship to ordinance activity at the local level. For instance, a municipality may be more likely to consider a restrictionist ordinance in states where recent policies have been pro-immigrant. Similarly, those seeking to pass such policies may be less likely to do so in places where there have been restrictionist measures passed at the statewide level. On the other hand, having restrictionist legislation may bear a positive relationship to similar measures at the local level, with either serving as a precursor or model for the other.

Given the number of potentially competing explanations, we cannot rely on a few case studies to explicate the relative importance of each. Thus we have created a database of local ordinances and enriched it with contextual data at the state and local level. First we obtained lists of municipalities that have proposed restrictive ordinances and regulations from various sources, including the ACLU, the Puerto Rican Legal Defense and Education Fund, the Fair Immigration Reform Movement, the National Immigration Law Center, and the Migration Policy Institute. We also derived lists of jurisdictions that have proposed "sanctuary" or "limited cooperation" ordinances from these sources. We then validated these lists by making phone calls to jurisdictions noted as considering or passing ordinances, as well as by monitoring news stories on local ordinances. We merged information on the proposal and passage of ordinances with census data on various demographic factors.[2] Finally, we came up with a measure of state-level legislative activity on immigrant integration based on reports from the National Conference of State Legislatures from 2005, 2006, and 2007, and included any measures that bear a significant relationship to illegal immigration.

In order to capture the partisan and/or ideological dimension of local politics, we use the 2000 vote share of Bush versus Gore (an open-seat presidential election) at the county level. Thus we can talk of municipalities in "Republican areas" and "Democratic areas." Using this right-left measure presents two challenges: First, while it would be ideal to also include measures of party registration, such data are not readily available across states (and, indeed, are not public information in several states). Nevertheless, given the relatively high correlation between Democrat-Republican party identification and presidential vote choice, the latter can serve as an adequate measure of partisanship at the local level. The second challenge is that we are using information on "proportion Republican" at the county level but information on ordinances at the municipality level. The error associated with this measure is related to a municipality's share of the county population. We ran an alternative, weighted least squares model based on the municipality's share of the total county population. This correction for heteroskedasticity does not invalidate our findings regarding the significance of partisanship at the local level.

FINDINGS

Based on our compilation of data from various sources, by July 2007 ninety-eight municipalities had proposed restrictionist ordinances and seventy-eight had proposed pro-immigrant ordinances, including measures limiting cooperation with federal authorities on deportations (table 4.1). On the restrictionist side, approximately 55 percent of proposals had passed, about 15 percent

---

2. The census data are primarily from 2000. More recent data are not available for the majority of places where restrictionist ordinances have been proposed or in the universe of census places more generally.

had been voted down or tabled, and more than a quarter were still pending. On the "pro" side, the vast majority of proposals had passed, with only one pending and three classified as failed or tabled.

Table 4.1 Proposal and Passage of Immigration-Related Ordinances at the Municipal Level as of July 2007

Ordinance	Status	Number	As Share of Total
Pro	Pending	1	
	Passed	74	
	Failed/tabled	3	
	Subtotal	*78*	0.3%
Restrictionist	Pending	29	
	Passed	55	
	Failed/tabled	14	
	Subtotal	*98*	0.4%
No action		25,448	99.3%
	Total	25,622	

These findings are significant for several reasons. First, it is important to note that restrictionist proposals outnumber pro-immigrant proposals. Further, the total number of proposals jumped from very few to nearly two hundred in the course of two years. Still, the overwhelming majority of cities (99.3 percent) have not taken any formal steps—"pro" or "con"—on the immigration issue. Another important finding is that a far greater proportion of pro-immigrant proposals have passed. This may indicate a greater selectivity among cities considering "pro" ordinances, choosing to propose only when there is a good chance of passage. It is also possible that restrictionist ordinances gain more opposition once they are proposed, although the presence of national advocacy groups that monitor, advocate, and file lawsuits on either side of the local ordinances debate suggests that differences in the selectivity of choosing ordinances (between backers on the pro-immigrant and restrictive sides, respectively) may be the likelier explanation.[3]

---

3. These include the ACLU, Fair Immigration Reform Movement, Mexican American Legal Defense and Education Fund, Puerto Rican Legal Defense and Education Fund, and Southern Poverty Law Center (among others) on the pro side, and the Immigration Reform Law Institute, Federation for American Immigration Reform, and Minuteman Project (among others) on the restrictionist side.

What Characterizes Ordinance Cities?

One of the conventional wisdoms about the recent spate of restrictionist ordinances is that they are being proposed in places that are experiencing new and rapid growth in immigration, especially by recent arrivals to the United States. Other potential explanations include resentment in places with high wage competition for low-skill jobs, lack of linguistic assimilation among recent immigrants, and potential backlash from nativists over the immigrant marches of spring 2006. In table 4.2 we provide comparisons for each of these factors to see whether reality is in line with the conventional wisdom. The data are presented for cities based on their proposal activity (whether restrictionist, "pro," or none), although similar relationships hold when applied to the ultimate passage of such policies.

Table 4.2 Characteristics of Cities Based on *Proposal* of Local Ordinances, 2000

Characteristic	Restrictionist	No Proposal	"Pro"
Percent with Republican majority in county***	71	67	25
Any pro-immigration protest (% likelihood)***	5	1	61
Latino share of population***	10.5	8.1	24.5
Latino share of citizens***	7.7	7.0	20.9
Growth in Latino population (%), 1990–2000	261	183	62.9
Percent of immigrants arrived since 1995***	25	19	29
Percent of Spanish linguistic-isolated households***	2.2	1.6	6.4
Percent employed in agriculture	1.1	2.6	1.0
Percent of households overcrowded***	1.9	1.7	6.7
Black poverty rate***	24.0	15.0	24.9
White poverty rate	9.7	10.3	11.1
Latino poverty rate***	20.4	16.9	24.0
Population***	58,779	8,621	907,671

*** significant at the 1% level

Comparing characteristics across these three types of cities reveals complicated relationships that are not apparent in examinations of restrictionist cities alone (Esbenshade 2007; Hopkins 2010). Thus, for instance, factors such as overcrowded housing and language isolation are slightly higher in restrictionist cities than in cities that have taken no action. However, these differences are not statistically significant, and the differences are indeed highest for cities that have proposed immigrant-friendly ordinances. Thus, for factors such as Spanish prevalence and overcrowded housing, we find non-significant differences on the restrictionist end when compared to cities that have taken no action, but statistically significant and counterintuitive relationships on the "pro-immigrant" end. Similar findings hold true for the Latino share of the population and the Latino share of the citizen population. Finally, we find very strong support for our hypotheses regarding partisanship and group political power. Restrictionist and pro-immigrant cities are distinguished most by their partisan composition, with pro-immigrant cities much more Democrat than the U.S. average. Pro-immigrant ordinances are also most likely in those cities where Latinos account for a large share of the citizen population.

There is also evidence suggesting a nativist backlash to the immigrant rallies and protests, given that cities with restrictionist proposals were more likely than "no action" cities to have had immigrant rallies in spring 2006. However, we cannot rule out the possibility that nativist reactions to the presence of immigrants preceded the protests. Also, pro-immigrant cities are by far the most likely to have experienced immigrant protests in 2006, suggesting that the factor may represent different political dynamics when considering the pathway toward restrictionist or pro-immigrant proposals. The same can be said for the role played by the recency of the immigrant population: restrictionist proposals are more likely in places where the immigrant population is composed heavily of recent immigrants (25 percent of immigrants are recent arrivals, compared to 19 percent in cities that took no action). However, the same also holds for pro-immigrant cities (29 versus 19 percent), so the recency of immigration cannot be deemed to be determinative of restrictionist activity. Thus, while the recency of migration may pose challenges to local governance in terms of overcrowded housing, linguistic isolation, and the like, it is actually associated with pro-immigrant proposals in large, Democratic cities and with restrictionist proposals in smaller, Republican cities.

Finally, we find that pro-immigrant and restrictionist activity is not evenly distributed across municipalities in all fifty states. The number of pro-immigrant proposals is highest in California (sixteen), followed by

Massachusetts and Oregon (five each), Alaska (four), and Illinois, Michigan, New Jersey, Ohio, and Pennsylvania (three each). On the restrictionist side, Pennsylvania had by far the highest number (twenty-five), followed by California (seven), Virginia (six), and Alaska and Texas (five each).

Multivariate Results

While comparisons of city characteristics may provide a "reality check" on assumptions regarding restrictionist and pro-immigrant ordinances, they tell only part of the story. In order to arrive at systematic answers about the conditions under which cities may consider and pass restrictionist and pro-immigrant ordinances, it is important to run statistical analyses that can show the contribution of each factor while controlling for all other factors. At the same time, it is important to be attuned to issues of multicollinearity. Since some of these factors are highly correlated (see appendix table), we ran alternative model specifications instead of putting every factor in the same regression model. We report our findings from these alternative specifications where relevant in the text.

Given the potential for varying dynamics related to the same variable in predicting a shift from "no policy" to restrictionist policies versus a shift from "no policy" to permissive policies, we run two separate logit models, where the dependent variable takes on a value of −1 if restrictionist, 0 if no policy, and 1 if pro-immigrant.[4] Finally, we also analyze the results separately with proposals as the dependent variable and with policy passage as the dependent variable.

As the regression results in table 4.3 indicate, the dynamics that explain the proposal of restrictive policies are indeed different from those that explain pro-immigrant proposals. Thus, for instance, the effects of immigrant-related protests, the recency of immigration, and being outside the U.S. South are significant in predicting liberal proposals but not restrictionist ones. On the other hand, the relative deprivation of blacks and whites relative to Latinos is significant in predicting restrictionist proposals but not liberal ones. The only factors that are significant for both Model I and Model II are city size and partisan composition.

---

4. If we conceive of policies along a continuum from restrictionist to status quo to explicitly pro-immigrant, it would be appropriate to use an ordered logit model. However, based on the way that policy processes have unfolded at the local level, it is more accurate to model policy making as starting in a neutral state, from which cities can go "pro" or "con." Thus we need two separate models to estimate deviations from the neutral status-quo state. Another limitation of using an ordered logit model is that we may be forcing one model to fit two different types of policy pathways.

Table 4.3 Multivariate Model Estimations of Ordinance Proposal

	Model I	Model II
	Logit (1 = Restrictive)	Logit (1 = "Pro")
Republican majority in county	**0.647** **(0.264)****	**−0.8** **(0.337)****
Any protest	−0.641 (0.660)	**2.054** **(0.398)*****
Hispanic share of citizens	−0.004 (0.014)	0.017 (0.012)
Growth in Hispanic population, 1990–2000	0.0001 (0.000)	−0.002 (0.002)
Agriculture jobs (share)	−0.037 (0.061)	−0.02 (0.045)
Percent of immigrants who are recent arrivals	0.0002 (0.007)	**0.038** **(0.013)*****
Overcrowded households (% of total)	−0.022 (0.056)	0.032 (0.032)
Black relative deprivation (poverty)	**0.011** **(0.005)****	0.007 (0.013)
White relative deprivation (poverty)	**−0.016** **(0.008)***	−0.013 (0.019)
Population (ln), 2000	**0.727** **(0.092)*****	**1.109** **(0.141)*****
Anti-immigrant organizations	0.336 (0.246)	−0.322 (0.225)
State policy climate	0.017 (0.034)	0.055 (0.045)
Southern state	−0.19 (0.266)	**−1.92** **(0.541)*****
Constant	**−12.193** **(0.890)*****	**−17.433** **(1.615)*****
Observations	18,016	18,007
Pseudo-R^2	0.12	0.55

* significant at 10%; ** significant at 5%; *** significant at 1%, based on two-sided t tests

Significance (*p*) values in brackets

A similar divergence in explanations can be found with respect to models that predict the *passage* of restrictionist and liberal ordinances related to unauthorized immigrants (table 4.4). As before, protest activity is positively associated with the passage of liberal ordinances, as is being outside the U.S. South. Also, the only factors that are significant on both the pro and restrictionist sides are population size and party composition. There are two factors on the restrictionist side, however, that bear special mention: a higher proportion of agricultural jobs in the locale reduces the likelihood of passage of restrictionist ordinances, while the growth in the Latino population (but not the immigrant population) increases the likelihood of restrictionist policies being enacted.

Table 4.4 Multivariate Model Estimations of Ordinance Passage

	Model I	Model II
	Logit (1 = Restrictive)	Logit (1 = "Pro")
Republican majority in county	**0.829** **(0.357)****	**−0.854** **(0.345)****
Any protest	−1.299 (0.996)	**2.141** **(0.408)*****
Hispanic share of citizens	−0.01 (0.020)	0.016 (0.012)
Growth in Hispanic population, 1990–2000	**0.0002** **(0.0000)***	−0.001 (0.002)
Agriculture jobs (share)	**−0.403** **(0.202)****	−0.021 (0.045)
Percent of immigrants who are recent arrivals	−0.003 (0.010)	**0.038** **(0.013)*****
Overcrowded households (% of total)	0.04 (0.057)	0.036 (0.032)
Black relative deprivation (poverty)	−0.003 (0.010)	0.008 (0.013)
White relative deprivation (poverty)	−0.011 (0.012)	−0.012 (0.020)
Population (ln), 2000	**0.75** **(0.123)*****	**1.064** **(0.143)*****
Anti-immigrant organizations	0.407 (0.282)	−0.289 (0.223)
State policy climate	0.031 (0.046)	0.053 (0.046)
Southern state	−0.069 (0.358)	**−1.823** **(0.540)*****
Constant	**−12.851** **(1.207)*****	**−17.052** **(1.631)*****
Observations	18,019	18,041
Pseudo-R²	0.15	0.55

* significant at 10%; ** significant at 5%; *** significant at 1%, based on two-sided t tests

Significance (*p*) values in brackets

Given the difficulties in interpreting logit coefficients for substantive effects, we summarize the substantive effects of the statistically significant factors in the analyses in table 4.5.[5] We see that city size is by far the most significant predictor of proposals and passage, with large cities nearly five times as likely as small cities to propose restrictive ordinances. Pro-immigrant ordinances are also eleven times more likely to be proposed in large cities than in small cities. Similar relationships also hold for proposal passage, suggesting that the relationship between city size and ordinance activity is a complicated one, increasing the likelihood of restrictionist proposals but also that of pro-immigrant proposals. This is in line with the bivariate findings in table 4.2, where restrictionist ordinances typically happen in medium-sized cities and "pro" ordinances appear in very large cities.

Table 4.5 Simulated Changes in the Likelihood of Ordinance Proposal and Passage

	Proposal		Passage	
	Restrictive	*Pro*	*Restrictive*	*Pro*
Republican majority in county	1.87	0.46	2.17	0.42
Any protest	—	1 (8.4)[a]	—	1 (9.7)[a]
Agriculture jobs (share)	—	—	0.36	—
Percent of immigrants who are recent arrivals	—	2.76	—	2.73
Growth in Hispanic population, 1990–2000	—	—	1.03	—
Overcrowded households (% of total)	—	—	—	—
Black relative deprivation (poverty)	1.20	—	—	—
White relative deprivation (poverty)	0.71	—	—	—
Population (ln), 2000	4.84	10.38	4.89	9.39
Southern state		0.17		0.19

Note: Standardized effects on statistically significant variables are changes in probability of the outcome when the variable is moved from the 25th to 75th percentile and all other variables are kept at their means.

[a] Figures in ( ) represent changes in probability of the outcome when the variable value changes from 0 to 1

5. We use CLARIFY (Tomz, Wittenberg, and King 2000) to simulate the effects on the dependent variable of changes in each individual variable while holding other variables at their means.

The next strongest set of effects is associated with political factors. Cities in Republican areas are about twice as likely as those in Democratic areas to propose and pass restrictionist legislation and about half as likely to propose or pass pro-immigrant measures. Also, the presence of protests does not support the hypothesis of nativist backlash leading to restrictionist legislation. Indeed, pro-immigrant ordinances are eight times more likely in protest areas than in areas without protests. This lends support to the hypothesis that the spring 2006 protests were related more to immigrant empowerment and system responsiveness than to restrictionist policy backlash.

What is also important to note from tables 4.3 through 4.5 is the number of factors that are weakly related to the consideration and proposal of immigrant-related ordinances. Below, we return to our initial set of hypotheses to examine how they fare in our models.

- *Party composition.* This factor has the strongest and most consistent effects after city size. Cities in Republican areas are nearly twice as likely to propose restrictionist ordinances and more than twice as likely to pass such ordinances compared to Democratic areas. Similarly, cities in Democratic areas are about twice as likely as those in majority-Republican areas to consider and pass pro-immigrant ordinances.

- *Growth of the Latino population.* This oft-cited factor for the rise in restrictionist ordinance activity has very weak effects, with slightly higher chances of restrictionist policies passing in cities with the highest percentage growth of Latino populations.

- *Latino share of the citizen population.* This factor does not bear any significant relationship to the proposal and passage of ordinances, either pro or con. This further reinforces findings from other studies of local immigrant incorporation that immigrant electoral power may be less important in predicting local government policies toward immigrants today than in the past.

- *Recency of migration.* Having an immigrant population that is composed primarily of recent arrivals is not associated with restrictionist ordinances. Indeed, it is associated with a greater likelihood of pro-immigrant legislation. Other factors related to recent arrivals, such as the proportion of households that are Spanish-speaking and the proportion of households that are overcrowded, also bear no relationship to the proposal or passage of restrictionist ordinances.

- *Wage competition.* Higher levels of disadvantage to blacks relative to Latinos are associated with a slightly higher likelihood of proposals of restrictionist legislation. These results are in line with Claudine Gay's (2006) findings in Los Angeles neighborhoods, where economic competition between blacks and Latinos erodes African-American support for policies favorable to Latinos. A similar dynamic *cannot* be found for poor whites, where the relationship is indeed slightly positive where poverty rates among whites exceed poverty rates among Latinos. Another way to interpret this finding is that restrictionist legislation is happening in places where whites are better off than Latinos, on average, and blacks are worse off than Latinos. Finally, neither advantage nor disadvantage bears a significant relationship to policy passage.

- *Immigrant protests.* The 2006 protests are strongly associated with the proposal and passage of pro-immigrant legislation. However, their average effect is close to nil because, even though protests occurred in scores of municipalities across the United States in 2006, that number is still small compared to the twenty-five thousand or so cities in the country. Still, those cities that had protests were eight times more likely to have pro-immigrant legislation.

- *Local economic interests.* The prevalence of industrial sectors that are heavily dependent on immigrant workers was generally not significant, with one important exception: the likelihood of restrictionist policies being passed is much lower in places where agriculture accounts for a sizable number of jobs. It is important to note, however, that the effects are evident in the stage of ordinance passage and not ordinance proposal. This suggests that policy entrepreneurs in agricultural areas may have overreached by pushing for restrictionist policies only to find an organized opposition from local businesses to such plans.

- *State-level policy climate toward immigrants.* This factor bears no significant relationship to ordinance activity at the local level, on either the restrictive or permissive side.

Diagnostics and Corrections to Multivariate Models

There are a few potential issues with our multivariate models that merit examination. First, as we have already noted, county political data can be seen as a valid measure of political context (a city in a Republican county, for instance), but they may also be subject to heteroskedasticity if the variable is supposed to accurately capture party composition in the city itself. We ran weighted least squares models separately (weighting by the city's proportion of the county population and gaps in household income) and found that the effects of party composition remain significant. We also ran the logit models on a much smaller sample of cities because of potential biases and inflated standard errors in using the full sample for the analysis of rare events (King and Zeng 2001). We used a normal randomization technique to select a total of about one thousand cities. The coefficients for party composition remain significant in the models on pro-immigrant legislation but drop in statistical significance (albeit with the same signs) for the restrictionist models.

CONCLUSIONS

Our analysis suggests that the *restrictionist* responses of local governments to undocumented immigration are largely unrelated to demographic pressures, whether it be the growth of recent immigrants or the proportion of Spanish-dominant households. They are also unrelated to the electoral empowerment of Latinos, given that places with large proportions of Latino residents and citizens are no more or no less likely to propose legislation, whether it be restrictionist or pro-immigrant. Instead, we find that political factors are more important, most notably partisan composition and the politicization of national immigration reform legislation at the local level through protests and rallies.

The partisan composition of the area plays an important role, second only to city size, which is by far the most important predictor of policy proposal and passage. However, because city size is positively associated with both pro and restrictionist ordinances, party composition is the only factor that displays statistically significant and theoretically consistent effects (negative on the restrictionist side and positive on the pro side). Also, it is important to note that because we control for all factors simultaneously, the finding on party registration is not simply a function of demographic change or city size (since Republican party registration tends to be greater in smaller cities).

The politicization of federal immigration reform efforts is also relevant in terms of pro-immigrant policies by localities. In reaction to punitive policies being considered at the federal level, immigrants in hundreds of localities across the United States participated in rallies to plead for fair treatment by their host society. There was some concern about a backlash from local nativist populations, in the form of either legislation or hate crimes. Our evidence does not support the localized backlash hypothesis as it relates to restrictionist ordinances. Indeed, it supports the alternative hypothesis: immigrants protesting in relatively friendly jurisdictions. Thus pro-immigrant proposals, and not restrictionist ones, are more likely in cities that had protests, although it is still possible that policy backlashes occurred elsewhere in the same region or media market. Our findings suggest, therefore, that political factors (party composition at the local level and the receptivity of local jurisdictions to Latino protests) play a more important role in shaping local ordinance activity related to immigration than do demographic factors that capture economic or cultural challenges to local governments and native-born populations.[6]

Having established, using large-N statistical analysis, that local partisan contexts matter greatly in accounting for the rise in ordinance activity related to the incorporation of undocumented immigrants, the next step is to explore *how* these factors play out in particular localities. For instance, it is difficult to ascertain from our dataset whether the dominant pathway for the relevance of partisanship is related to mobilization *from below* among conservative activists frustrated by the failure of immigration enforcement, or to mobilization *from above* by elected officials such as Lou Barletta in Hazleton, Pennsylvania, and policy entrepreneurs such as Joseph Turner in San Bernardino, California. We hope that case studies of particular municipalities across the United States, chosen with an eye to variation in outcomes and a few characteristics such as partisanship and demographic change, can help illustrate the ways in which demographic "realities" on the ground are shaped for political purposes, on both the "pro" and "con" sides of the immigration debate. Finally, we also need to obtain measures on the timing of such proposals and their geographic proximity to each other to say something about the diffusion effects of ordinances on each other. Findings about diffusion, however, are unlikely to change the fundamental results of this analysis, which are that local ordinances on immigration are related primarily to political factors such as partisan politics and immigrant protest activity and have little to do with the economic or cultural disruptions to local communities.

WORKS CITED

Borjas, George. 2006. "Immigrants In, Wages Down," *National Review*, April 25.

Browning, Rufus P., Dale R. Marshall, and David H. Tabb. 1984. *Protest Is Not Enough: The Struggle of Blacks and Hispanics for Equality in Urban Politics.* Berkeley, CA: University of California Press.

---

6. It is possible that part of the weakness related to the demographic change explanations is the fact that information on residents in small localities is only available from the decennial census. However, even if we had the most recent information on immigration in small localities, we would still find the number of cities with restrictionist proposals to be a very small portion of the number of cities experiencing large increases in the number of immigrants, alongside a large number of municipalities in regions such as rural eastern Pennsylvania with restrictionist proposals but very few immigrants.

Dahl, Robert. 1961. *Who Governs? Democracy and Power in an American City*. New Haven, CT: Yale University Press.

Erie, Steven P. 1988. *Rainbow's End: Irish-Americans and the Dilemmas of Urban Machine Politics, 1840–1985*. Berkeley, CA: University of California Press.

Esbenshade, Jill. 2007. "Division and Dislocation: Regulating Immigration through Local Housing Ordinances." Immigration Policy Center Special Report, American Immigration Law Foundation, Summer.

Gamm, Gerald H. 1989. *The Making of New Deal Democrats: Voting Behavior and Realignment in Boston, 1920–1940*. Chicago, IL: University of Chicago Press.

Gay, Claudine. 2006. "Seeing Difference: The Effect of Economic Disparity on Black Attitudes toward Latinos," *American Journal of Political Science* 50, no. 4 (October): 982–97.

Hopkins, Daniel J. 2010. "Politicized Places: Explaining Where and When Immigrants Provoke Local Opposition," *American Political Science Review* 104, no. 1.

Huntington, Samuel P. 2004. "The Hispanic Challenge," *Foreign Policy* 141: 30–45.

Jones-Correa, Michael. 1998. *Between Two Nations: The Political Predicament of Latinos in New York City*. Ithaca, NY: Cornell University Press.

———. 2004. "Racial and Ethnic Diversity and the Politics of Education in Suburbia." Paper presented at the annual meeting of the American Political Science Association, Chicago.

King, Gary, and Langche Zeng. 2001. "Logistic Regression in Rare Events Data," *Political Analysis* 9, no. 2: 137–63.

Kotlowitz, Alex. 2007. "Our Town," *New York Times Magazine*, August 5.

Lelyveld, Joseph. 2006. "The Border Dividing Arizona," *New York Times Sunday Magazine*, October 15.

Ramakrishnan, S. Karthick, and Irene Bloemraad, eds. 2008. *Civic Hopes and Political Realities: Immigrants, Community Organizations, and Political Engagement*. New York: Russell Sage Foundation.

Ramakrishnan, S. Karthick, Kevin Esterling, David Lazer, and Mike Neblo. 2007. "What Do You Mean by 'Immigrant'? Framing Effects and Attitudes towards Immigration in a Survey Experiment." Presented at the Politics of Race, Immigration, and Ethnicity Consortium, Riverside, California, February 2.

Ramakrishnan, S. Karthick, and Paul Lewis. 2005. *Immigrants and Local Governance: The View from City Hall*. San Francisco, CA: Public Policy Institute of California.

Roarty, Alex. 2008. "Kanjorski Remains Optimistic, Says Race Proceeding as Planned," *PolitickerPA.com: Inside Politics for Political Insiders*, October 20.

Rogers, Reuel Reuben. 2006. *Afro-Caribbean Immigrants and the Politics of Incorporation: Ethnicity, Exception, or Exit.* Cambridge: Cambridge University Press.

Scolforo, Mark. 2006. "Pa. Town Enforces Illegal Immigrant Rule," Associated Press, July 14.

Tomz, Michael, Jason Wittenberg, and Gary King. 2003. "CLARIFY: Software for Interpreting and Presenting Statistical Results," *Journal of Statistical Software* 8, no. 1: 1–30.

Varsanyi, Monica W. 2008. "Immigration Policing through the Backdoor: City Ordinances, the 'Right to the City,' and the Exclusion of Undocumented Day Laborers," *Urban Geography* 29, no. 1: 29–52.

Wong, Janelle S. 2006. *Democracy's Promise: Immigrants and American Civic Institutions.* Ann Arbor, MI: University of Michigan Press.

APPENDIX

Table A.1. Correlation Matrix of Independent Variables (values 0.5 and higher in bold)

	(1)	(2)	(3)	(4)	(5)	(6)	(7)	(8)	(9)	(10)	(11)	(12)	(13)	(14)
1 Percent Rep vs. Dem	1.00													
2 Any protest	-0.04	1.00												
3 Latino share of citizens	-0.09	0.06	1.00											
4 Growth of Latino population	0.06	0.00	-0.02	1.00										
5 Percent of immigrants who are recently arrived	0.02	0.06	0.00	0.17	1.00									
6 Spanish linguistically isolated	-0.07	0.07	**0.84**	0.05	0.08	1.00								
7 Percent of households crowded	-0.09	0.09	**0.63**	0.01	0.05	**0.66**	1.00							
8 Difference, black vs. Latino poverty	-0.03	0.01	-0.09	-0.05	-0.04	-0.09	-0.07	1.00						
9 Difference, white vs. Latino poverty	0.00	-0.03	-0.13	-0.09	-0.15	-0.14	-0.10	**0.62**	1.00					
10 Population (ln)	-0.20	0.24	0.09	0.01	0.23	0.08	0.13	0.08	-0.14	1.00				
11 Anti-immigrant organizations	-0.01	0.29	0.03	0.00	0.04	0.03	0.04	0.01	-0.02	0.17	1.00			
12 State-level policy measure (net + or –)	-0.12	0.02	0.07	-0.04	-0.05	0.06	0.03	0.02	0.01	0.11	-0.03	1.00		
13 Agriculture share of jobs	0.13	-0.02	0.30	0.00	-0.01	0.35	0.32	-0.10	-0.06	-0.29	-0.03	-0.03	1.00	
14 Percent of jobs in agriculture, mining, construction	0.20	-0.04	0.30	-0.01	-0.06	0.31	0.26	-0.10	-0.03	-0.37	-0.03	-0.16	**0.70**	1.00

SECTION TWO

From Devolution to the Grassroots

5 Immigration Enforcement by State and Local Police: The Impact on the Enforcers and Their Communities

Michele Waslin

Early in U.S. history, the colonies, and then the states, had primary responsibility for the enforcement of immigration law. In fact, throughout most of the nineteenth century, the regulation of immigration was left to states, localities, and even seaports (Skerry 1995). Congress did not create the first federal immigration bureaucracy until 1882, and the Bureau of Immigration was not established until the Immigration Act of 1891. Throughout the twentieth century, the federal government took responsibility for enforcement, and the courts largely maintained that the federal government possesses exclusive authority to enforce civil immigration law.

However, the twenty-first century has witnessed unprecedented involvement by state and local police agencies in immigration enforcement. Those who advocate for an increased role for state and local police argue that the federal government needs the increased capacity—or "force multipliers"—that state and local agencies provide in order to assist in the federal authorities' efforts against terrorism and unauthorized immigration. Critics, meanwhile, argue that policies that involve local police in the enforcement of federal immigration law lead to increased discrimination and racial profiling, stretch the limited resources of law enforcement, and erode—rather than promote—trust between immigrant communities and the police, thus endangering public safety.

This chapter examines the trajectory of state and local police involvement in the enforcement of federal immigration law over the last decade; highlights the cases of Maricopa County, Arizona, and Prince William County,

Virginia; and documents the impact on immigrant communities and law enforcement agencies.

LEGISLATION REGULATING STATE AND LOCAL ENFORCEMENT OF IMMIGRATION LAW

The Immigration and Nationality Act (INA), passed in 1952, did not acknowledge a role for state or local authorities in immigration enforcement. However, on several occasions in the last half-century, the federal government has addressed the matter of state and local police authority to enforce federal immigration law. For example, in a June 23, 1978, press release, the Department of Justice (DOJ) took the position that local police should refrain from detaining "any person not suspected of a crime, solely on the ground that they may be deportable aliens." In 1989 the DOJ Office of Legal Counsel (OLC) issued an opinion confirming that local police were lawfully permitted to detain and arrest immigrants only for criminal violations of the INA, and did not have the power to arrest merely on suspicion of civil immigration violations. A second OLC opinion in 1996 declared, "state police lack recognized legal authority to arrest or detain aliens solely for purposes of civil immigration proceedings, as opposed to criminal prosecution" (Department of Justice 1996).

Only in certain circumstances, and with specific procedural safeguards in place, has Congress authorized local police to arrest and detain an individual for violations of federal immigration law. For example, the Antiterrorism and Effective Death Penalty Act (AEDPA) of 1996 explicitly authorized state and local police to arrest and detain immigrants who are unlawfully present in the United States (a violation of civil immigration law) *and* have "previously been convicted of a felony in the United States." AEDPA also, for the first time, permitted the Federal Bureau of Investigation (FBI) to include records related to previously deported felons in the National Crime Information Center (NCIC) database,[1] thereby granting state and local police the authority to detain or arrest this narrow class of immigrant offenders.

Finally, Section 133 of the Illegal Immigration Reform and Immigrant Responsibility Act of 1996 (IIRIRA), also known as Section 287(g) of the INA, created a new method to engage state and local police in the enforcement of federal immigration law. Section 287(g) allows the secretary of homeland security (or the attorney general, prior to 2003)[2] to enter into agreements that

---

1. The NCIC database is a computerized index of criminal justice information operated by the FBI as a service for local law enforcement agencies.
2. Prior to 2003, immigration services and enforcement were housed in the Immigration and Naturalization Service (INS) within the Department of Justice. The INS was abolished

delegate immigration powers to local police, but only through negotiated agreements, documented in memoranda of understanding (MOUs). These MOUs are negotiated between the Department of Homeland Security (DHS) and the local authorities, and include delegation of authority to a limited number of police officers. In authorizing these MOUs, Congress specifically requires that any officer or employee of a state performing a function under the agreement should have written certification that he or she has received adequate training regarding the enforcement of relevant federal immigration laws. The statute also requires that any and all local law enforcement officials performing these functions shall be subject to the direction and supervision of the secretary of homeland security. The statute does not authorize local law enforcement officials who have no training or experience in immigration law to enforce these laws in the normal course of their duties.

THE COURTS AND IMMIGRATION LAW ENFORCEMENT

The courts have consistently ruled that the federal government has the exclusive power to regulate immigration and create immigration law.[3] However, even though legislation has provided some guidelines, questions regarding local law enforcement's authority to enforce federal immigration law continue to arise. Over time, the courts and the executive have stepped in to resolve that uncertainty by limiting state and local authority to enforcement of criminal violations of immigration law only.

One key case on the issue is *Gonzales v. City of Peoria* (1983), in which the Ninth Circuit Court of Appeals held that local police are precluded from enforcing the civil provisions of the INA. In the *League of United Latin American Citizens (LULAC) v. Wilson* (1995), the Ninth Circuit Court struck down those portions of California's Proposition 187 that required state agents to question applicants for state services about their immigration status; to obtain and examine documents relating to their immigration status; to identify "suspected illegal" immigrants and report them to state and federal authorities; and to instruct these individuals to either obtain legal status or leave the country.

---

by the Homeland Security Act of 2002, and as of March 2003, immigration functions are now housed in several agencies within the Department of Homeland Security (DHS). Throughout this chapter, "INS" is used to refer to the agency prior to March 2003, and "DHS" is referenced for matters related to the post–March 2003 period.

3. See, for example, *De Canas v. Bica* (1976), explaining that the "power to regulate immigration is unquestionably exclusively a federal power"; *Chy Lung v. Freeman* (1875), emphasizing that the power to regulate immigration "belongs to Congress, and not to the States"; *Henderson v. Mayor of New York* (1876); and *Smith v. Turner* (1849) ("The Passenger Cases").

The court characterized these provisions as a "comprehensive scheme to detect and report the presence and effect the removal of illegal aliens" and found that they were preempted by federal law.[4]

On the other hand, in *United States v. Salinas-Calderon* (1999), the Tenth Circuit found that a local law enforcement officer had general investigatory powers to inquire into "immigration violations." However, the court did not define what it meant by an "immigration violation" and did not discuss—or even appear to recognize—the difference between civil and criminal immigration offenses. In *United States v. Vasquez-Alvarez* (1999), the Tenth Circuit Court used the general reference to an "immigration violation" found in *United States v. Salinas-Calderon* to uphold a police officer's arrest of an individual for the *civil* immigration violation of unlawful presence in the country. However, the court had relied exclusively on cases that authorized police enforcement of federal *criminal* offenses, and thus there is no support for an expanded interpretation covering civil offenses. In another Tenth Circuit case, *United States v. Santana-Garcia* (2001), the defendants faced both drug possession charges and a criminal immigration offense. On appeal, the court upheld the legality of a pre-arrest detention of the defendants by a state trooper, finding, among other things, that the trooper had probable cause to arrest for an unspecified immigration "violation."

Thus there is no agreement in the courts on the role of state/local police and the enforcement of federal immigration law. Much of the case law centers on the distinction between criminal and civil violations of immigration law, and was decided prior to the recent increase in cooperation between the police and the federal government. Some recent legislative efforts have sought to criminalize and expand the range of immigration violations, and others have attempted to clarify and strengthen the role of local police in the enforcement of immigration law. There are likely to be more lawsuits and decisions in the next several years, and the changing circumstances are likely to result in very different decisions.

NEW TOOLS FOR IMMIGRATION LAW ENFORCEMENT

While federal preemption on immigration issues has been consistently upheld (see Rodríguez, Chishti, and Nortman, this volume) and local police's authority to enforce civil immigration law has been rejected in most cases, new laws and policies have blurred the lines and have resulted in a greater de facto

---

4. For further legal analysis, see Wishnie 2004; Pham 2004.

role for state and local police. In addition, the events of September 11, 2001, reignited the debate over the authority of state and local police to enforce civil immigration law. In June 2002, Attorney General John Ashcroft announced a new policy—based on a new OLC opinion, which was not released until years later as the result of a lawsuit—that declared that state and local police have the "inherent authority" to enforce civil and criminal violations of immigration law. This was a stunning departure from the 1996 OLC opinion. Without making the legal opinion public, the announcement indicated that the DOJ had reinterpreted the law and overturned decades of legal precedent.[5]

Since that time, the use of two strategies in particular—entering immigration violations into the NCIC database and 287(g) MOUs—has increased, and these tools have allowed federal immigration authorities to cooperate more closely with state and local police.

The NCIC Database

In 1974 the Immigration and Naturalization Service determined that local police do not have the authority to arrest a person subject to an administrative warrant of deportation, and thus the FBI could not enter civil immigration records into the National Crime Information Center database. The 1989 and 1996 OLC opinions again advised the FBI that administrative warrants of deportation do not indicate violations of criminal law, reflecting a policy that distinguished between criminal and civil immigration law to delineate the role of state/local and federal authority. In 1996 Congress changed the statute and, as noted above, allowed the FBI to include records related to previously deported felons in the database. This change gave state and local police the authority to detain or arrest this specific class of immigrant offenders.

Since 1996, Congress has not amended the NCIC statute to allow entry of any categories of civil immigration violation data other than that of "previously deported felon."[6] Yet in December 2001, the INS commissioner told Congress that the agency was going to enter thousands of records of "absconders"—persons with outstanding orders of deportation, exclusion, or removal—into the NCIC (Gamboa 2001). Several months later, in June

---

5. The OLC opinion was finally made public in 2005 when the U.S. Court of Appeals for the Second Circuit affirmed a prior district court ruling directing the release of the document. See *National Council of La Raza v. Department of Justice* (2005), directing release pursuant to the Freedom of Information Act.

6. A lawsuit has challenged the DOJ's ability to expand the categories of immigration violations included in NCIC. The suit is pending appeal after the judge granted the defendant's motion to dismiss. See *National Council of La Raza v. Ashcroft* (2007).

2002, at the same time as the "inherent authority" declaration, Attorney General Ashcroft announced the creation of the National Security Entry-Exit Registration System (NSEERS)[7] and indicated that those who failed to comply with NSEERS would be added to the NCIC, be subject to removal, and possibly be subject to criminal prosecution. State and local police officers, through their access to NCIC, would have the authority to arrest and detain individuals for failing to comply with the registration requirements.

Despite several more proposals to increase the range of immigration data entered into NCIC, no new categories have been added. The NCIC Immigration Violators File (IVF) currently includes three categories of immigration law violators: persons previously convicted of a felony and deported; persons allegedly subject to a final deportation order ("absconders"); and persons allegedly in violation of the NSEERS program.

In March 2003, the DOJ exempted the NCIC database from Privacy Act standards, meaning that NCIC records no longer were required to be "accurate, timely, and reliable." This was particularly troublesome given the very high error rates contained in immigration files (Gladstein et al. 2005).

Indeed, NCIC immigration files have received a large number of "hits." The most recent available data (2002–2004) from the Legal Enforcement Support Center (LESC) show a total of 20,876 immigration hits from state and local law enforcement agencies; LESC confirmed 12,128 (58 percent) of the hits and did not confirm the remaining 8,748 (Gladstein et al. 2005). LESC is staffed by operators twenty-four hours a day to verify the information contained in the NCIC. If LESC confirms that an individual has committed an immigration violation, it issues a detainer notice and requests that the police hold that individual. If LESC informs the officer that the NCIC information is erroneous, the individual is to be released (absent any other grounds for detention).

287(g) Memoranda of Understanding

Early attempts at MOUs under the 287(g) process, following the passage of IIRIRA in 1996, were not successful. After 9/11, however, MOUs appeared more desirable, and Florida and Alabama became the first states to enter into

---

7. NSEERS required all persons from certain designated countries arriving in the United States on nonimmigrant visas to register and submit fingerprints at the point of entry, followed by further registration requirements. Finally, those who registered would be required to notify the INS of their departure from the United States. The NSEERS program was modified in December 2003 and several elements were terminated. However, departure registration, registration at ports of entry, and the government's authority to use call-in registration remain in place.

MOUs, in 2002 and 2003, respectively.[8] In recent years, armed with additional funds, the DHS has prioritized the 287(g) program and has been actively
pursuing MOUs with law enforcement entities around the country. Other
cities and states have proposed legislation to compel state and local governments to enter into MOUs with DHS. Such laws have passed in Georgia,
Oklahoma, and North Carolina, and in cities including Springfield, Arkansas,
and Herndon, Virginia. As a result of DHS efforts and state and local legislation, approximately sixty-seven MOUs had been executed, and 1,075 police
and correctional officers had been trained through January 2010.[9]

The program has become so popular that DHS has had difficulty execut-
ing the large number of MOUs that have been requested, and is now evaluating requests on a case-by-case basis. In an effort to deal with the large
number of requests, in August 2007 Immigration and Customs Enforcement
(ICE) announced the creation of the ICE ACCESS program (Agreements of
Cooperation in Communities to Enhance Safety and Security).[10] The program
allows ICE and local law enforcement agencies to choose the type of support and collaboration that they feel is most relevant for the specific needs
of the community. While 287(g) is one possibility, specific programs for border communities, child exploitation, document fraud, incarcerated criminal
aliens, and others allow for collaboration with ICE.

In March 2008, DHS announced yet another initiative—the Secure
Communities Initiative—aimed at increasing the collaborative role of state and
local law enforcement in the identification, detention, and removal of criminal
aliens.[11] The initiative aims to increase coordination between DHS and state
and local police agencies to identify criminal aliens in all federal and state prisons, assess the risk level of each alien, and remove him or her. Through this
new initiative, ICE plans to have a presence in every one of the 3,100 local jails
throughout the United States and to increase the number of 287(g) MOUs.

THE IMPACT OF ENFORCEMENT ON THE COMMUNITY

While there is strong support for these policies, there is also strong opposition
to local police enforcement of immigration law from across the spectrum—advocates for victims of domestic abuse, faith-based organizations, conservatives,

---

8. For analysis of Florida and Alabama MOUs, see Nebraska Appleseed 2007.

9. http://www.ice.gov/pi/news/factsheets/section287_g.htm, January 8, 2010.

10. http://www.ice.gov/pi/news/newsreleases/articles/070821dc.htm, August 21, 2007.

11. Secure Communities Fact Sheet, http://www.ice.gov/doclib/pi/news/factsheets/
secure_communities.pdf.

immigrant rights groups, elected officials, and law enforcement officials.[12] Criticism generally falls into three categories: the increased potential for costly mistakes and discrimination, the stress on already limited police resources, and the harmful impact on community relations and community policing.

Mistakes, Profiling, Discrimination, and Litigation

Critics argue that involving local police in immigration law enforcement activities is likely to lead to mistakes, racial profiling, discrimination, and expensive litigation. Immigration law is extremely complex and subject to constant change, and documents used to prove immigration status are not uniform. Even with extensive training and experience, mistakes are very likely, and legal immigrants and U.S. citizens can be the victims of errors.[13] Past civil rights violations have resulted in costly litigation. For example, in *Castro et al. v. City of Chandler* (1997), the City of Chandler, Arizona, was forced to pay $400,000 in settlement fees after local police were found guilty of harassing and detaining Hispanic-appearing individuals who had been in their cars, walking on the street, or sitting in their homes. In *Lopez v. City of Rogers* (2003), the Mexican American Legal Defense and Education Fund (MALDEF) settled a case with the City of Rogers, Arkansas, where Latinos were allegedly improperly stopped by local police and investigated based on their ethnicity and perceived immigration status.

The immigrant community has feared that inclusion of immigration violations in the NCIC database would lead to increased errors, profiling, and discrimination, because law enforcement officers would be more likely to stop minorities, or those perceived to be immigrants, with the intention of querying NCIC for immigration violations. In fact, false positives and disparities regarding the national origin of persons getting database hits do appear to be problematic. A 2005 Migration Policy Institute report documents the use of the immigration files of the NCIC by state and local police forces from 2002 to 2004. Among their findings, 42 percent of all NCIC immigration hits in response to police queries were "false positives," in which DHS was unable to confirm that the individual was an actual immigration violator. False positive rates varied from 90 percent in Maine to 18 percent in California (Gladstein et al. 2005).

---

12. For example, see U.S./Mexico Border Counties Coalition letter to Congress, November 11, 2003; Carafano 2004; and the November 10, 2003, report by Advocates for Immigrant Victims of Domestic Violence, at http://www.immigrationforum.org/documents/TheDebate/EnforcementLocalPolice/DV_CLEAR_letter.pdf.

13. For a recent example, see Associated Press 2007.

In addition, the report found that despite the purported emphasis on national security, not a single NSEERS violator received a hit; 85 percent of all alleged immigration violators identified through the NCIC were from Latin America, and 71 percent were from Mexico (Gladstein et al. 2005). The report concluded:

> Demographic information of immigrants identified by NCIC indicates that the NCIC immigration files are not being used to further a targeted antiterrorism agenda, the principal justification offered for the DOJ's policy. Rather, the use of these records has mostly resulted in indiscriminate arrests of Mexican and other Latin American nationals. (Gladstein et al. 2005, 4)

Stretching Limited Resources

The terrorist attacks of 9/11 and consequent security concerns placed a large fiscal burden on already overburdened cities, counties, and states. New policies encouraging or requiring state and local police departments to enforce civil immigration law add to the strain on resources. Training, arrest, processing, detention, and transport all require additional officer time, supervision, and money. Time spent processing immigration violations is also potentially time away from emergency responses, criminal investigations, and other critical needs.

The federal government is not promising any additional funding to pay for the new responsibilities. Under an MOU, while ICE does cover instructors' time and training materials, the federal government does not cover officers' salaries during the training period (approximately five weeks). In addition, the federal government does not pay for technological costs associated with connecting local MOU partners to federal databases or other coordination. And this does not take into account related or collateral costs of implementation. For example, narrowly tailoring an immigration enforcement program to target unauthorized immigrants effectively while minimizing adverse effects on community policing or abuses of legally resident aliens and U.S. citizens would require public education campaigns as well as careful training and monitoring.

As a result of the potential drain on resources, some elected officials and law enforcement officers have been critical of measures requiring them to enforce immigration law. The National Association of Counties described the resources issue in the following way:

> 72 percent of counties are facing budget shortfalls. . . . In addition to enforcing civil immigration laws, states and counties would have the new and onerous reporting requirements in a field that is neither our responsibility nor our expertise. Additional responsibilities placed on our sheriffs and police departments would only exacerbate the crisis. We have already shouldered substantial costs associated with other aspects of homeland security. (Letter to Congressman F. James Sensenbrenner, September 30, 2003)

South Tucson, Arizona, Police Chief Sixto Molina succinctly stated, "We don't have the time and the personnel to be immigration agents. Murderers, rapists, robbers, thieves, and drug dealers present a much bigger threat than any illegal immigrant" (*Tucson Citizen*, October 15, 2003).

Loss of Trust in Police

The mere suggestion that local police may have the authority to enforce immigration law sends a chill through Latino and immigrant communities, resulting in decreased willingness to cooperate with law enforcement, to report crimes, or to come forward as witnesses. Fear is not limited to immigrants in violation of immigration law; millions are affected when law enforcement officers, who may be untrained in immigration law, stop and question Latinos and other Americans who "look" or "sound" like they might be foreign. As a result of potential mistakes, discrimination, and profiling, the trust and communication built between the police and large segments of the community erode.

Anecdotal evidence that immigrants are fearful of reporting crimes is mounting. A *Los Angeles Times* headline recently read, "Immigrants Deported after Calling Police." A woman in Carrollton, Georgia, was arrested in late July 2007 when she called for help after being attacked in her home (Jarvie 2007). The Georgia Security and Immigration Compliance Act, which requires law enforcement officers to investigate the citizenship status of anyone jailed for a felony or driving under the influence, had taken effect on July 1, 2007, heightening immigrants' fear of police in that state. Rich Pellegrino, director of the Cobb Cherokee Immigrant Alliance, which worked with the Police

Department's crime prevention unit persuading immigrants to report crimes, said, "We spent months building up trust, and now we've got to start all over again" (*Arizona Republic*, April 17, 2008).

MARICOPA COUNTY, ARIZONA

All of these issues are currently coming to the fore in Maricopa County, Arizona, which has the MOU with the largest number of trained officers. Due to its proximity to the border and large undocumented population, Maricopa County has experienced the economic and social costs of the broken immigration system. In this context, Sheriff Joe Arpaio of the Maricopa County Sheriff's Office (MCSO) has made national headlines for his tough stance on immigration enforcement and his zealous implementation of the MOU.

On January 19, 2007, the Maricopa County Board of Supervisors approved a 287(g) MOU with ICE. With the mandate to enforce immigration law, Sheriff Arpaio created a Human Smuggling Unit for immigration-law enforcement purposes. The emboldened MCSO expanded its reach by interpreting the smuggling provisions of a 2005 Arizona law against human trafficking (SB 1372) to charge not only smugglers but also undocumented immigrants (who can be charged with conspiring to smuggle themselves). In July 2008 the Arizona Appeals Court upheld the expanded interpretation of the law (Maricopa County Attorney's Office 2008).

The MOU and Sheriff Arpaio have come under criticism for their methods and for the impact on the Maricopa County community. An analysis of MCSO records shows that immigration-related activities have been expensive and have resulted in few key arrests, while drawing law enforcement personnel away from investigating non-immigration-related crimes. The Sheriff's Office created a $1.3 million deficit in just three months, much of it due to overtime (Gabrielson 2008a). In order to staff the immigration team, Sheriff Arpaio pulled deputies off patrol beats and used them to staff the Human Smuggling Unit. Armed with fewer deputies, response times to emergency calls increased in 2006 and 2007; records show that patrol cars arrived late two-thirds of the time on more than six thousand of the most serious calls for service (Gabrielson 2008b). Despite the time and energy spent on immigration enforcement, MCSO has had little success building cases against violent immigrant offenders or those at the top of the smuggling rings. In 2006–2007, sheriff deputies arrested 578 illegal immigrants in the course of traffic stops, and 498 of those faced a single charge: conspiracy to smuggle themselves (Gabrielson and Giblin 2008).

Community members, church leaders, local elected officials, and others have harshly criticized Sheriff Arpaio for going beyond the scope of the MOU, engaging in "vigilante-type" activities and racial profiling, and creating a "police state" and a "dehumanizing" environment for Latinos and others. MCSO has conducted large-scale operations without any evidence of criminal activity, often in Hispanic neighborhoods or sites where day laborers convene,[14] and deputies are known to target vehicles, such as large vans and SUVs, that they believe might carry undocumented immigrants. Sheriffs have also used minor traffic offenses, such as speeding or crossing the center line, as probable cause to stop a vehicle (Giblin and Gabrielson 2008a).

Critics of Arpaio's immigration enforcement tactics have been vocal and have taken action. In May 2008, Governor Janet Napolitano withdrew $600,000 from Arpaio's immigration enforcement efforts and gave the funds to the Department of Public Safety to use to clear a backlog of thousands of felony warrants, many for violent crimes (Giblin and Gabrielson 2008b). Phoenix Mayor Phil Gordon has been loudly critical of Arpaio's methods and has requested that the Department of Justice investigate his actions for civil rights violations. An ad hoc coalition of Arizona elected officials also called for an investigation into violations of the 287(g) MOU and requested "federal oversight" of the MOU's implementation.[15] In April 2008, Mayor Gordon stated that Sheriff Arpaio had created a "sanctuary county for felons" by focusing on immigration and failing to pursue felony warrants (Newton 2008). In other words, accusations of "sanctuary" have come full circle in Maricopa County.

PRINCE WILLIAM COUNTY, VIRGINIA

Over the past several years, immigration—particularly illegal immigration—has become a hot-button issue in Prince William County, Virginia, and a priority for several county supervisors who have upped the anti-immigrant rhetoric and pushed measures to crack down on undocumented immigration.

In the summer of 2007 the Prince William Board of County Supervisors passed Resolution 07-609 stating that county personnel cannot be prohibited from communicating immigration information to other federal, state, or local government entities; requiring police to inquire about the immigration status of all detained persons; and requiring the county to enter into a 287(g)

14. Ad-Hoc Coalition of Arizona Elected Officials, letter to Representative David Price, October 23, 2007, on file with author.
15. Ibid.

agreement with ICE.[16] After making several necessary changes, in October 2007 the Board passed a final resolution, and the new measures took effect on March 3, 2008.[17]

One month after the new crackdown had been put in operation, the county proudly announced that it had resulted in eighty-nine persons being questioned as to their immigration status, with forty-one of them being detained. Most of those arrested were charged with crimes unrelated to their immigration status; only two were detained on immigration-related charges (Mack 2008a). Of the eighty-nine questioned, two were able to provide proof of legal residency. The remaining eighty-seven cases were referred to ICE, though twenty-five were cited only for minor offenses and twenty-one were released without charges.

One day later, it was reported that the new 287(g) program was putting a strain on both the county jails and ICE. Since the MOU's implementation, the jail had processed approximately 13,000 suspects, 1,199 of whom were checked for immigration status issues and 632 of whom were wanted by ICE. Prince William Jail Board Chairman Patrick J. Hurd sent a letter to ICE Director Julie Myers explaining that jail workers were "at or close to their limit" and that ICE agents had been unable to retrieve suspected unauthorized immigrants within the 72-hour limit (Miroff 2008).

The burden of holding additional inmates in an already crowded jail, as well as the added transportation and processing costs, are straining the system. Though ICE compensates the jail for holding its suspects, Prince William is spending additional resources. Those immigrants charged with state or local crimes, many of whom might have been released on bond prior to the 287(g) agreement, must serve out their sentences before ICE will take them. As a result of jail overcrowding, Prince William County is shifting inmates to facilities elsewhere in Virginia, frustrating attorneys and family members. A proposal to build a state detention center where illegal immigrants could be housed until ICE is able to collect them was rejected by the state legislature.

The cost of the immigration measure in Prince William County—an estimated $6.9 million in the first year—has been a major factor in the debate since the beginning (Mack 2008b). The county and its residents are experiencing financial hardship, with the county facing revenue shortfalls of $10

16. http://www.pwcgov.org/documents/bocs/briefs/2007/0710/res07-609.pdf. The Prince William-Manassas Adult Detention Center Jail Board already had a preexisting 287(g) MOU with ICE.

17. For more on the context in which the Prince William County resolution was passed, see Wilson, Singer, and DeRenzis, this volume.

million. As is happening across the country, the current economic slump has had a serious impact in Prince William County. In late April 2008 the Board of County Supervisors reduced the budget for immigration-law enforcement, cutting out the $3.1 million that was to have been spent on video cameras to monitor enforcement activities in order to protect the county against allegations of racial profiling. In addition, the Board cut $1.2 million in related police, foster care, and protective services for the children of deported immigrants, bringing the overall costs for the program from $6.9 million to $2.6 million (Mack 2008c).

On April 15, 2008, ICE picked up sixty suspected illegal immigrants from the Prince William County detention center, long after the agreed-upon 72-hour period. ICE Special Agent Mark X. McGraw admitted, "We've gotten ahead of ourselves. We never expected that to happen as fast as it did." County officials claim that jail employees are working sixty-hour weeks and the county is spending $3 million a year on additional transportation and processing, while $220,000 a month is expended to house inmates in facilities outside the county in order to make room for the immigrants. The jail has space for 402 inmates, but it held an average of 664 inmates a day in February 2008. An additional 275 were sent elsewhere in the state, at a daily cost of $38 to $50 per inmate (Mack 2008d).

CONCLUSION

Attempts by the administration and some in Congress to recruit local police as a "force multiplier" have had mixed results and continue to raise questions, especially regarding how collaboration with local police has affected the government's priority-setting abilities. Assuming that the federal government prioritizes targeted groups such as "absconders," "terrorists," and NSEERS violators, to what extent has the involvement of local police effectively aided ICE to identify individuals from these groups? Have the persons detained and transferred to ICE been "priority" cases? Or do local police identify and refer cases that otherwise would not have been prioritized by ICE, causing ICE to shift resources toward non-priority cases? Recently ICE announced new policies that allow the agency to prioritize among the detainees in local jails and prisons and focus their resources on the "highest threats." This suggests that the available resources are not sufficient to handle the increased workload that has resulted from collaboration with local authorities, and this situation has compelled ICE to reassess its own priorities.

Recent experience has also called into question ICE's ability to comply with the increased number of MOU requests and the additional requests stemming from local participation. The Prince William County experience suggests that when local police are highly effective in their efforts to identify and detain illegal immigrants, ICE has been unable to pick them up, transport them, or deport them in a timely manner. Though the demise of comprehensive immigration reform legislation in Congress has unleashed immigration enforcement measures at the state and local level, states and localities are still ultimately dependent upon the federal government's ability to respond.

The Maricopa County experience raises additional questions regarding the limitations and oversight of MOUs. What is ICE's responsibility in terms of overseeing and supervising local police, and what penalties are levied against local police who overstep the boundaries of the MOU? As the numbers of MOUs and other collaborative efforts between ICE and local police increase, and as local officials push the limits of the collaboration, calls for additional oversight of the program will multiply, once again stretching the reach and resources of the federal government.

The impact on the community requires additional analysis, as it is too early as yet to draw many conclusions. Certainly some members of the affected communities are happy with the results of increased immigration scrutiny, and the number of immigration-related proposals and MOUs at the state and local level continues to rise. Yet it is clear that some in these communities have experienced economic and social problems related to such proposals. Stories of high costs, litigation, mistakes, loss of community trust, damaged reputation, and other negative implications are at least as prevalent as success stories. The cases of Prince William and Maricopa counties are illustrative of many of the complicated issues surrounding police collaboration with ICE. It remains to be seen whether the negative experiences of some communities will result in a decrease in MOU requests or state/local legislation requiring police to enforce immigration law.

Deputizing police to enforce federal immigration law is another in a long chain of efforts to control and decrease the illegal immigrant population in the United States. As with any other enforcement initiative, effectiveness is measured against the policy's other consequences. Measures intended to target the undocumented population in the interior of the United States undoubtedly have had a negative impact on a much wider population, and recent immigration enforcement operations have resulted in families being separated, businesses losing workers and customers, and increased complaints of discrimination and harassment. Meanwhile, billions of dollars spent enforcing immigration laws have not reduced the number of migrants crossing into the United States. In fact, the number of undocumented immigrants in the country has increased dramatically during the same period that enforcement has grown to unprecedented levels (Ewing 2008).

Recent research has shown that migrants are not deterred by the enhanced enforcement efforts in the United States. Rather, economic factors still appear to be the most important variable determining whether or not one migrates (Cornelius 2008). Thus the key question that should drive the immigration debate is: should the United States continue to expand its arsenal of immigration enforcement tools, or should it respond to the factors that generate undocumented immigration? While high numbers of detentions and deportations, worksite raids, toughened state laws, physical barriers along the border, and other highly visible operations generate headlines and make for slick campaign ads, will their lack of effectiveness, combined with negative consequences, eventually cause the U.S. public to demand real solutions from their elected officials?

WORKS CITED

Associated Press. 2007. "Native Was Threatened with Deportation; Arlington Woman Jailed for Unpaid Tickets Mistaken for Illegal Immigrant," September 1.

Carafano, James J. 2004. "No Need for the CLEAR Act: Building Capacity for Immigration Counterterrorism Investigations." Washington, DC: Heritage Foundation, April 21.

Castro et al. v. City of Chandler, No. 97-1736 (1997).

Chy Lung v. Freeman, 92 U.S. 275, 280 (1875).

Cornelius, Wayne A. 2008. "Controlling Unauthorized Immigration from Mexico: The Failure of 'Prevention through Deterrence' and the Need for Comprehensive Reform." Immigration Policy Center and Center for Comparative Immigration Studies, University of California, San Diego, June 10. http://www.immigrationpolicy.org/images/File/misc/CCISbriefing061008.pdf.

De Canas v. Bica, 424 U.S. 351, 354 (1976).

Department of Justice. 1996. "Assistance by State and Local Police in Apprehending Illegal Aliens." Memorandum opinion, February 5. http://www.justice.gov/olc/immstopla.htm.

Ewing, Walter. 2008. "Enforcement without Reform: How Current U.S. Immigration Policies Undermine National Security and the Economy." Research Report No. 38. East Lansing, MI: Julian Samora Research Institute, Michigan State University. http://www.immigrationpolicy.org/images/File/misc/JSRIenforcementWithoutReform0308.pdf.

Gabrielson, Ryan. 2008a. "Overtime Led to MCSO Budget Crisis, Records Show," *East Valley Tribune* [Arizona], July 10.

———. 2008b. "Public Safety Shortchanged throughout County," *East Valley Tribune*, July 12.

Gabrielson, Ryan, and Paul Giblin. 2008. "MCSO Evolves into an Immigration Agency," *East Valley Tribune*, July 9.

Gamboa, Susan. 2001. "Names of Missing Foreigners Ordered Deported to be Entered in Crime Database," Associated Press, December 5.

Giblin, Paul, and Ryan Gabrielson. 2008a. "Sweeps and Saturation Patrols Violate Federal Civil Rights Regulations," *East Valley Tribune*, July 11.

———. 2008b. "Why No One Is Willing to Hold Sheriff Arpaio Accountable," *East Valley Tribune*, July 13.

Gladstein, Hannah, Annie Lai, Jennifer Wagner, and Michael Wishnie. 2005. "Blurring the Lines: A Profile of State and Local Police Enforcement of Immigration Law Using the National Crime Information Center Database, 2002–2004." Prepared for the Migration Policy Institute.

Gonzales v. City of Peoria, 722 F.2d 468, 474 (9th Cir. 1983).

Henderson v. Mayor of New York, 92 U.S. 259, 273 (1876).

Jarvie, Jenny. 2007. "Immigrants Deported after Calling Police," *Los Angeles Times*, July 30.

League of United Latin American Citizens (LULAC) v. Wilson, 908 F. Supp. 769 (9th Cir. 1995).

Lopez v. City of Rogers, U.S. District Court Case No. 01-506 (2003).

Mack, Kristin. 2008a. "Crackdown in Pr. William Yields Charges," *Washington Post*, April 6.

———. 2008b. "Pr. William to Spend $6.9 Million on Crackdown," *Washington Post*, April 17.

———. 2008c. "Board Downplays Immigrant Policy Changes," *Washington Post*, May 1.

———. 2008d. "U.S. Immigration Picks Up Detainees," *Washington Post Online*, April 15.

Maricopa County Attorney's Office. 2008. "Illegal Immigration." White Paper.

Miroff, Nick. 2008. "Detainee Program Strains Va. Jail; Pr. William Cites Delays by ICE," *Washington Post Online*, April 7.

National Council of La Raza v. Ashcroft, No. 03-CV-6324 (2007).

National Council of La Raza v. Department of Justice, 411 F.3d 350 (2d Cir. 2005).

Nebraska Appleseed. 2007. *Forcing our Blues into Grey Areas: Local Police and Federal Immigration Enforcement, A Legal Guide for Advocates*. http://www.neappleseed.org/docs/local_police_and_immigration_enforcement.pdf.

Newton, Casey. 2008. "Gordon: Arpaio Has Made County a 'Sanctuary' for Felons," *Arizona Republic*, April 15.

Pham, Huyen. 2004. "The Inherent Flaws in the Inherent Authority Position: Why Inviting Local Law Enforcement of Immigration Laws Violates the Constitution," *Florida State University Law Review* 31: 965–1003.

Skerry, Peter. 1995. "Many Borders to Cross: Is Immigration the Exclusive Responsibility of the Federal Government?" *Publius* 25, no. 3 (Summer): 71–85.

Smith v. Turner, 48 U.S. (1 How.) 283 (1849).

United States v. Salinas-Calderon, 728 F.2d 1298 (10th Cir. 1984).

United States v. Vasquez-Alvarez, 176 F.3d 1294 (10th Cir. 1999).

United States v. Santana-Garcia, 561 F.2d 1160 (10th Cir. 2001).

Wishnie, Michael J. 2004. "State and Local Police Enforcement of Immigration Laws," *University of Pennsylvania Journal of Constitutional Law* 4: 1084.

6 The Public Policy Implications of State-Level Worksite Migration Enforcement: The Experiences of Arizona, Mississippi, and Illinois

MARC R. ROSENBLUM AND LEO B. GORMAN

Although they disagree on the specifics, commentators and policy makers from across the political spectrum agree that the U.S. immigration system is broken and in need of repair. Most analysts trace the roots of these problems, at least in part, to the 1986 Immigration Reform and Control Act (IRCA), which made it illegal to knowingly employ unauthorized immigrants but failed to establish reliable mechanisms for identifying eligible workers or verifying workers' status. IRCA also established difficult standards for obtaining convictions of noncompliant employers. These design flaws, along with a history of limited enthusiasm at various levels of government for worksite enforcement, have left in place a "jobs magnet" that attracts most unauthorized immigrants; and the perverse effect of IRCA has been to drive down wages in many low-skill sectors as employers treat the possibility of being fined as a business expense and compensate by cutting wages.

These problems have been on policy makers' radar almost continuously since IRCA's passage, but federal officials have failed to address them. President George W. Bush put comprehensive immigration reform—improved enforcement along with visa reforms to match migration supply and demand—on the agenda in 2001, but initial reform efforts were derailed by the attacks of September 11, 2001, and two subsequent efforts to pass comprehensive reform bills failed in the House of Representatives in 2006 and in the Senate in 2007. As other chapters in this book document, states and even localities have taken matters into their own hands, passing hundreds of laws and ordinances of their own since 2005 as their communities respond to new migration inflows, including a large and growing unauthorized population.

This chapter briefly reviews the history of state-level migration policy making and discusses the public policy implications of states acting alone in this area. We particularly focus on state-level efforts to regulate migration labor markets by enforcing migration laws at the worksite, including through E-Verify, a federal electronic eligibility verification system which allows employers to compare workers' identity data against Department of Homeland Security and Social Security Administration databases to confirm their legal status. Worksite enforcement is a policy area widely recognized as in need of reform and one in which states have often taken action ahead of Congress. Thirteen states created or augmented laws between 2006 and 2009 that required at least some employers to use the E-Verify program (Verifications Inc. 2008a).[1] Lawmakers in Illinois moved in the opposite direction: skeptical of E-Verify's error rate and discriminatory outcomes, the state temporarily prohibited employers from using the system. Though the experiences of these states are too recent and too limited to offer firm conclusions, they seem to confirm the importance of approaching immigration reform in a comprehensive way rather than through piecemeal enforcement.

The chapter begins by briefly reviewing the history of state-level migration policy making and state-federal conflict in this area. Given the uneven distribution of immigrants around the country, states have often taken the lead on migration policy making, including with respect to labor laws. The following section examines the politics and implementation of E-Verify laws in Arizona, Mississippi, and Illinois. Next we discuss the public policy implications of state-level migration policy making and draw some early conclusions about how state-level worksite enforcement has affected migrant labor markets in Arizona and Mississippi.[2] These states' experiences highlight some of the challenges of state-level policy making and the demand for the federal government to act quickly on comprehensive immigration reform.

A BRIEF HISTORY OF STATE MIGRATION LAWS

As Peter Skerry observes, immigration policy was notable during the 1980s and 1990s for the extent to which politicians from both parties and at all

---

1. The states were Arizona, Colorado, Georgia, Minnesota, Mississippi, Missouri, North Carolina, Oklahoma, South Carolina, Tennessee, and Utah.
2. A federal restraining order has blocked implementation of Illinois's anti–E-Verify law, so we are unable to evaluate its impact.

levels of government agreed that this issue should be reserved for the federal government. State and local governments saw migration as a failed policy and were happy to place the blame squarely on Washington. Congressional liberals saw migration policy through the lens of the civil rights movement and sought federal protection for migrants as a vulnerable minority group (Skerry 1995). Restrictionists in Congress also supported a federal response but in the form of tougher enforcement at the border and through the denial of welfare and other public benefits.

Yet this hardly represents a historical consensus. Indeed, while the Constitution authorizes Congress to define criteria for naturalization, it is silent on the question of admissions requirements, and states set their own rules in early U.S. history. Major ports of entry like New York and Massachusetts restricted "pauper" migration and imposed head taxes, making it difficult for labor-poor interior and southern states to recruit new workers and citizens. A series of Supreme Court decisions in the second half of the nineteenth century affirmed the federal government's plenary power to regulate admissions, limiting the scope of aliens' due process rights, clarifying the country's sovereign authority to limit inflows, and striking down state-level head taxes as an illegal infringement on Congress's authority to regulate international commerce (Skerry 1995; LeMay 2006). Yet it was only with the Court's rejection of California's anti-Chinese restrictions in 1889 in favor of federal restrictions and the establishment of a federal Bureau of Immigration in 1891 that a truly national migration system was even put in place (*Chae Chan Ping v. United States*, 1889).

States (and localities) continue to vary in their enforcement of federal immigration law. Dozens of towns and cities joined the so-called sanctuary city movement during the 1980s, for example, pledging to protect Central American refugees from deportation as a humanitarian act and to protest U.S. policies in the region (see Mitnik and Halpern-Finnerty, this volume). On a more practical level, many city and state enforcement agencies are reluctant to play an aggressive role in migration enforcement in the interest of maintaining harmonious community relations and promoting trust between police and local immigrant populations, and also to avoid the legal complexities of migration enforcement (see Waslin, this volume). But a growing number of states and localities have taken the opposite position; and since 1996 at least sixty-six state, county, and municipal law enforcement agencies have signed agreements with the Immigration and Naturalization Service/ Department of Homeland Security (INS/DHS) to obtain immigration law training for their agents and to allow local agents to help enforce federal immigration law (see Waslin, this volume).[3] At least four states require law enforcement agents to cooperate with federal agents on immigration enforcement and status verification.[4]

A second area of intergovernmental conflict has concerned immigrants' access to schools and other public benefits. One of the most historically significant benefits disputes came in 1907, when the City of San Francisco established separate schools for Japanese immigrants and denied them access to "white" public schools. The policy sparked a diplomatic crisis with Japan, an important U.S. trade partner and a rising military and economic power; and President Roosevelt personally intervened with the mayor and San Francisco School Board to reverse the policy as part of his broader effort to block formal anti-Japanese restrictions through the "Gentleman's Agreement" signed the same year.

More recently, the Supreme Court overturned a Texas law in 1982 that would have denied undocumented children access to public schools (*Plyler v. Doe*, 1982). California voters tested these limits twelve years later by passing Proposition 187, which would have denied unauthorized immigrants access to welfare and other public benefits. Prop. 187 was immediately challenged in federal district court, and Congress passed similar legislation in 1996 at the federal level. Since then, at least a dozen states have passed laws denying unauthorized immigrants access to welfare benefits, non-emergency subsidized health care, and/or tuition breaks at public universities.[5] But ten states allow unauthorized immigrants to pay in-state tuition for public universities under certain circumstances,[6] and a dozen states prohibit their health officials or other benefits officers from inquiring about individuals' legal residency status when providing services, other than when required by federal law to do so and/or have special public health campaigns targeting immigrant groups.[7]

Conflict over public services relates to a third issue: federal-state disputes over the fiscal costs and benefits of migration. Here, too, questions go back

---

3. These are known as 287(g) agreements, so called for the section of the Immigration and Nationality Act establishing this authority.

4. These states are North Carolina, Arizona, Tennessee, and Indiana (NCSL 2008).

5. These states are Arizona, California, Colorado, Florida, Idaho, Kansas, Louisiana, Missouri, North Carolina, South Carolina, Texas, and West Virginia (NCSL 2008).

6. The states include Texas, California, Utah, Washington, New York, Oklahoma, Illinois, Kansas, New Mexico, and Nebraska (Gonzales 2007).

7. California, Hawaii, Illinois, Maryland, Minnesota, New York, Ohio, Pennsylvania, Virginia, and Washington are among the twelve (NCSL 2008).

to the nineteenth century, when New York officials complained about bearing a disproportionate share of the costs of migration and were the leading advocates for the establishment of a federal reception center at Ellis Island. In addition to public services, high-immigration states bear greater costs of migration enforcement than the rest of the country, and since the 1980s a series of programs have reimbursed states for these costs and for border enforcement expenses. IRCA provided states with a four-year, $4 billion block grant to cover the costs of its legalization program. Even so, Arizona, California, Florida, New Jersey, New York, and Texas brought lawsuits during the 1990s demanding federal reimbursement for other migration-related expenses.

These two issues have intersected in the recent conflict between states and the federal government over the 2005 REAL ID Act. Under this law, which passed with limited debate as an amendment to an unrelated appropriations bill, state motor vehicle agencies and others responsible for issuing identification documents are required to verify that license holders are legally authorized to be in the United States and to incorporate a number of biometric and antifraud technologies in their licenses. As of January 2009, at least nineteen states had passed legislation or resolutions *against* complying with the law, citing public safety concerns associated with denying immigrants licenses and complaining about the absence of adequate federal funding to pay for new technology and personnel to implement the new requirements (ACLU 2009).

Finally, states have repeatedly clashed with the federal government on issues related to migrant workers. In the early twentieth century, South Carolina and other southern states saw in European immigrants an opportunity to develop a more skilled—and white—workforce; and several southern states established programs to recruit new immigrants, often paying for their passage, in violation of federal contract labor laws. In the 1940s, Mexico insisted that Texas be excluded from the bilateral Bracero Program because it feared the state would mistreat guest workers. The early history of the program was dominated by conflict between Texas growers and their congressional allies and the Roosevelt and Truman administrations, with the federal government blocking efforts by Texas growers to directly recruit workers in 1943 and 1948 (Calavita 1992; Rosenblum 2003). And when Truman finally persuaded Congress to pass legislation in 1952 making it illegal to harbor or abet unauthorized immigrants, the so-called Texas Proviso explicitly exempted employers from penalty under the act.

Two decades later, California was at the forefront of the migrant labor debate, passing the country's first law prohibiting the employment of unauthorized immigrants. A dozen other states followed suit, but none of the state laws was effectively enforced (Crewdson 1981). And during the debate over IRCA, it was the California delegation that led the drive to link federal employer sanctions to a new temporary worker program and to include employer protections (prohibition on non-warrant searches, tough standards for proving noncompliance), which have helped undermined the effectiveness of the current employer sanctions regime.

Given Congress's failure to pass comprehensive immigration reform between 2005 and 2007, states took the lead in crafting immigration-related legislation, with workplace enforcement as a priority. Widespread frustration over federal inaction to repair an outdated immigration system provoked states to spearhead reform at an unprecedented rate and scope. Immigration-related legislation (introduced and enacted) increased approximately five-fold during the same period. In 2005, for instance, state lawmakers introduced 300 immigration-related bills and resolutions, with 38 becoming law. Comparatively, in 2007 legislators sponsored 1,562 state bills, with forty-one states enacting 240 laws, and in 2008, forty-one states passed 205 immigration-related bills (NCSL 2008).[8] Employment was the top subject area for proposed immigration measures in 2007 (Migration Policy Institute and NYU School of Law 2007), and in 2008, nineteen employment-related laws were enacted in thirteen states (NCSL 2008), underlining state lawmakers' eagerness to address unresolved immigration concerns through workplace enforcement.

CONTEMPORARY CASES: ARIZONA, MISSISSIPPI, AND ILLINOIS

While states and localities have acted more quickly than Congress on a number of fronts, their actions to regulate immigrant employment are especially noteworthy. Thirteen states have passed laws that exceed federal penalties for the knowing employment of unauthorized immigrants and/or require some or all employers to participate in the nascent electronic eligibility verification system (EEVS), E-Verify.[9] Yet, as in the pre-IRCA period, these individual state-level policy efforts have produced mixed results and so far cannot be credited with improving employment conditions. Illinois has moved in the opposite direction, with policy makers expressing their concerns about E-Verify's design flaws by prohibiting state employers from enrolling in the system.

8. For more information on state responses after the collapse of federal comprehensive immigration reform efforts, also see the introductory chapter to this volume.

9. See note 1.

Arizona

Arizona, a state with a 350-mile border with Mexico and an economy tied to a growing low-wage Latino immigrant workforce, drew national attention in the summer of 2007 when both houses of the state legislature voted by four-to-one margins in favor of the Legal Arizona Workers Act (LAWA), considered the strictest workplace enforcement bill in the country. The bill required that all public and private employers authenticate the immigration status of their employees through E-Verify starting January 1, 2008. Employers who knowingly hired unauthorized immigrants would have their business license suspended for up to ten days for a first offense and revoked for a second violation.

A coalition of business owners led by the Arizona Chamber of Commerce and immigrant rights groups argued that the bill would lead to labor shortages in immigrant-dominated sectors like agriculture, construction, and services and to discrimination against Latino workers, and that it would weaken the state's economy. But the bill's proponents were frustrated by Congress's failure to pass immigration reform in 2006 and 2007, and increased undocumented immigration to Arizona fueled support for LAWA (Jordan 2007).[10] State Representative John Kavanagh (R), the bill's co-sponsor, disputed claims that the law would hurt Arizona's economy. Rather, he maintained, unauthorized immigrants are "a drain," receiving more in public services than they contribute economically. "People want a crackdown," added Kavanagh (Jordan 2007). LAWA's chief sponsor, State Representative Russell K. Pearce (R), believed that the bill would help Arizona fortify Anglo-American culture and language by eliminating the Arizona jobs magnet for tens of thousands of Mexican immigrants (Hockstader 2008).

Democratic Governor Janet Napolitano—who in 2009 became President Obama's secretary of homeland security, charged with enforcing the country's immigration laws—acknowledged concerns that E-Verify could overburden employers and discriminate against legal workers. But on July 2, 2007, Napolitano signed LAWA into law, arguing that Congress was currently "incapable" of addressing states' immigration needs and that reform at the state level was urgently warranted (Napolitano 2007). Conservative anti-immigrant attitudes, then, intersected with bipartisan concerns over the pressing task of tackling immigration reform in the absence of congressional action.

---

10. Even before the bill's implementation, Arizona served as a laboratory for restrictionist immigration reform. In 2004, voters approved Proposition 200, which required individuals to present proof of citizenship to be able to vote and receive state and local public benefits. In November 2007, another ballot initiative was introduced to deny U.S. citizenship to Arizona-born children of illegal immigrants.

As of March 2010, LAWA had survived constitutional challenges on pre-emption grounds, having been upheld by the U.S. District Court of Arizona and by the Ninth Circuit Court of Appeals. The legislature amended the law in May 2008 to exempt from the E-Verify requirements employees hired before 2008 as well as some subcontractors. But a business-backed ballot initiative (Proposition 202) to further limit the scope of LAWA was defeated by a 60–40 margin in November 2008.

Agricultural and other business groups immediately blamed the law for labor shortages and supported legislation to recruit more guest workers to the state. In March 2008, State Senator Marsha Arzberger (D) introduced SB 1508 to allow employers to certify to the Industrial Commission of Arizona their inability to find native workers to fill job vacancies. Under the proposal, companies would be eligible to recruit Mexican workers on two-year visas (versus ten months under federal H-2A guest worker rules), only good for work in Arizona. The bill garnered twenty-seven bipartisan sponsors, but it was attacked as a threat to local workers during an economic downturn and died in June 2008 without a floor vote (Bowers 2008a; Sunnucks 2008; Robbins 2008; Fischer 2008).

Mississippi

Mississippi followed in Arizona's footsteps in early 2008. Although Governor Haley Barbour had a record as a moderately pro-immigration and strongly pro-business Republican,[11] he supported tough immigration enforcement during the 2007 gubernatorial campaign. As election day approached, Barbour ran campaign ads promising to enforce federal immigration laws. In his successful campaign for the lieutenant governor position, Republican Phil Bryant also promised to crack down on unauthorized immigrant workers (Wagster Pettus 2008).

After Barbour's and Bryant's victories, the battle over employer sanctions heated up. Warning of Arizona-like worker shortages, critics of the proposed Mississippi Employment Protection Act (MEPA) highlighted additional expenditures the state could incur from undertaking immigration-related workplace enforcement (Northway 2008). The Mississippi Immigrant Rights Alliance cautioned that MEPA would burden taxpayers as incarceration rates

---

11. The governor broadly opposed government regulation of Mississippi businesses and had deferred to the federal government on immigration issues, and he had commended immigrant workers for their part in rebuilding the Mississippi Gulf Coast after Hurricane Katrina in 2005.

of immigrant workers and litigation costs from legal challenges rose.[12] Local law enforcement officials expressed concern over higher demand for jail space and immigration enforcement resources without corresponding budget increases (Lynch 2008). Business trade groups voiced their opposition as well (Northway 2008).

Yet broad-based anti-immigrant sentiment galvanized support for MEPA between the November 2007 election and the bill's passage in early 2008. The bill passed both chambers of the state legislature with bipartisan support and was signed into law by Governor Barbour on March 17. Barbour, acknowledging that E-Verify was problematic, signed the bill with the caveat that the state legislature would "add other reliable verification systems beyond E-Verify" to confirm the hiring eligibility of potential employees (Barbour 2008).

Under MEPA, all employers in Mississippi will be required in phases over the course of three years to enroll in E-Verify, with smaller companies given the most time to sign up.[13] Penalties for employers and workers exceed those of LAWA: employers who knowingly hire illegal immigrants can lose their business license for a year on the first offense and state contract work for up to three years. Unauthorized immigrants working in the state may face felony charges, punishable by prison terms of up to five years and fines of up to $10,000 (Wagster Pettus 2008; Verifications Inc. 2008b).

Illinois

The state of Illinois has moved in the opposite direction. Responding in part to publicity generated by the case of Fernando Tenocho, a U.S. citizen who was rejected from a Tysons Foods processing plant because of E-Verify inaccuracies (Schaper 2007), a coalition of unions, civil rights organizations, and the Illinois Chamber of Commerce supported legislation to prohibit employers from using E-Verify until the Department of Homeland Security significantly improves its accuracy (National Immigration Law Center 2008). Governor Rod R. Blagojevich (D) also questioned E-Verify's accuracy and its efficacy as an enforcement tool (Preston 2007).[14] Thus the state legislature passed a

---

12. Bill Chandler, of the Mississippi Immigrant Rights Alliance, letter to Governor Barbour, March 6, 2008.
13. Employers with 250 or more employees were to register by July 1, 2008; those with between 100 and 249, by July 1, 2009; those with between 30 and 99, by July 1, 2010; and employers with fewer than 30 employees, by July 1, 2011.
14. Abby Ottenhoff, a spokeswoman for Governor Blagojevich, said he had signed the bill because he "concurred with the General Assembly that the system now leaves too much room for mistakes and abuse."

pair of bills (Public Acts 95-0137 and 95-0138) amending the Illinois Human Rights Act and the Illinois Right to Privacy in the Workplace Act to make it a civil rights violation for an employer to refuse to hire a worker based on an E-Verify non-confirmation and requiring businesses not to enroll in E-Verify until its databases are certified to be 99 percent accurate.

The Department of Homeland Security sued Illinois in federal district court on preemption grounds, arguing that employers are authorized to participate in E-Verify under the 1996 Illegal Immigration Reform and Immigrant Responsibility Act (IIRIRA) (Preston 2007). In December 2007, the month before the law was to go into effect, the court stayed the federal lawsuit and the state's enforcement in order to permit lawmakers to amend the bill and address DHS concerns. In March 2009, the District Court in Central Illinois overturned the Illinois law as a violation of the Supremacy Clause and ruled that employers were free to participate in E-Verify. The state revised the law in August 2009 to require that participating employers complete the on-line E-Verify training materials and post a notice about the company's participation in the program; and it codified E-Verify's other worker protections into state law, imposing fees of between $500 and $1,000 for employer misuse of E-Verify (Meyer and Wald 2010).

THE PROS AND CONS OF STATE-LEVEL MIGRATION ENFORCEMENT

The transfer of immigration authority from the states (in the nineteenth century) to the federal government mirrors overall trends toward centralized policy making, especially following expansion of the federal government during the New Deal. Since the late 1960s, a large federal bureaucracy has been coupled with the explicit preemption of state policy making and the imposition of conditions on federal aid and other regulatory measures to ensure state and local compliance with federal policies (Bowman 2002; Kincaid 1993; Kincaid and Cole 2002). On worksite migration laws in particular, Section 274A(h)(2) holds that federal employment enforcement provisions "preempt any State or local law imposing civil or criminal sanctions (other than through licensing and similar laws) upon those who employ, or recruit or refer for a fee for employment, unauthorized aliens" (Immigration and Nationality Act 8 U.S.C. 1324a).[15] What, then, are the public policy implications when states make their own laws in this area?

---

15. The Ninth Circuit ruling on LAWA found that the Immigration and Nationality Act's "savings clause" allows states to make their own worksite enforcement laws as long as penalties are limited to state licensing restrictions.

Proponents of devolution make three primary arguments in favor of state-level (or local-level) policy making. First, in the often-cited words of Justice Louis Brandeis, federalism allows states to "serve as laboratories of democracy," testing out new political tools without running the risks or undertaking the costs of national reforms (Tarr 2001). Second, on a normative level, there is an important sense in which smaller administrative units are inherently more representative of their constituents, so that states may more accurately channel popular policy demands than does the federal government at a higher level of aggregation. Third, this is especially true where the fiscal and regulatory effects of a policy issue are unevenly distributed: on what basis can the federal government make taxing and spending or other regulatory decisions when the impact is concentrated in a particular region?

At first glance, these arguments would appear to be highly relevant to the question of immigration policy. Immigrants have always settled in discrete geographic regions, and the effects of migration and migration policy making are disproportionately borne by these gateway states and localities. Indeed, to a large extent the national policy debate is simply an aggregation of these more localized demands, and the episodically high salience of immigration as a national policy issue (despite its regional impact) is a function of the fact that the number of foreign-born residents in a state correlates fairly well with other measures of political influence (Skerry 1995).[16] And because the economics of immigration guarantee that these gateway states bear most of the costs of migration (both legal and unauthorized) while the federal government receives substantial fiscal benefits, non-gateway states have little incentive to federalize cost sharing or defer to their high-inflow neighbors (*Harvard Law Review* 1995).

There are also important practical arguments for states to take the lead on immigration policy making. The states-as-laboratories argument receives a degree of support from the empirical record: many of the most significant federal immigration policies—including head taxes and individual criteria for exclusion in the nineteenth century and employer sanctions and benefits restrictions in the twentieth—were originally pursued by gateway states before being adopted at the federal level. States have also consistently taken the lead in promoting English language classes and other programs for immigrant integration, though the federal government has been less ambitious in taking up this agenda. And with state and local enforcement personnel

---

16. As Skerry observes, immigrants are attracted to economically powerful states, which explains this convergence. Also see Money 1999.

outnumbering DHS and other federal law enforcement officers by a ratio of greater than ten to one, nonfederal governments bring important resources to the table, and their collaboration may make a vital contribution to successful policy implementation.[17]

On the other hand, there are several reasons to be wary of state policy making on immigration issues. First, migration is the "quintessential intermestic issue": policies made in the United States have a direct impact on migration countries of origin, and policy making abroad has an important effect on outcomes in the United States (Lowenthal 1999, 124; Manning 1977). Partly for this reason, immigration policy making has always been shaped— often decisively—by both diplomatic and national security considerations; and state-level policies may conflict with national and international strategic goals.[18] Border-state policies have been a particular, if episodic, source of tension in U.S.-Mexican relations.

A second, related point is that some aspects of migration policy, such as border control and measures combating terrorist mobility, require a national perspective and coordination with international partners. For all its staffing limitations, the federal government has far greater capacity than states or localities to alert a large number of citizens to the possibility of new terror threats and to prevent terrorism through surveillance, apprehensions of suspected terrorists, and overseas military action (Kincaid and Cole 2002). The issue of national coordination also matters at the domestic level: where states act on their own without national guidance, conflicting policies may cause perverse unintended consequences, with migrants and their employers "venue shopping" in a variety of ways to exploit variation among different policy regimes.

Theoretical arguments for and against states taking the lead on immigration policy would both appear to apply particularly well to worksite enforcement. We have already seen that high immigration states (especially California and Texas, and now Arizona) have taken the lead in demanding more or less restrictive worksite enforcement and temporary worker policies; and California's failed experiment with employer sanctions in the 1970s

---

17. Local police departments employed 580,749 full-time employees in 2003, and local sheriffs' offices employed an additional 330,274. This compares with about 75,000 federal law enforcement personnel (Department of Justice 2009; Kincaid and Cole 2002).

18. On the tension between domestic and international sources of migration policy making, see Rosenblum 2004, 2009; Salehyan and Rosenblum 2008; Rudolph 2006; Tichenor 2002.

should have offered important lessons for policy makers crafting IRCA's similar rules. State-level worksite enforcement also raises special concerns about policy coordination. Migrant labor markets are ultimately constrained by competitive forces, and pressure on employers to outsource immigrant jobs rather than raising wages and productivity will be greater when standards vary state to state, so that the costs of outsourcing are diminished.

Likewise, the effectiveness of worksite migration policies will be enhanced where policy is approached in a comprehensive way. On the one hand, this implies combining tougher enforcement of migration restrictions with improved access to legal sources of labor and/or increased productivity. Thus it is not surprising that Arizona lawmakers began exploring alternatives for expanding legal immigration to the state as LAWA went into effect, but (as the failed SB 1015 guest worker proposal conceded) states have far less capacity to generate additional legal visas than they do to impose new licensing restrictions. Only the federal government can enact comprehensive immigration reform.

On the other hand, state-level policy making also highlights the challenges associated with worksite enforcement in general. Most of the new pro-enforcement laws, including the two cases reviewed above, create incentives or mandates for employers to participate in E-Verify. Yet E-Verify has proven to be problematic because database errors cause the system to incorrectly screen out some U.S. citizens and other legal workers, while the system's vulnerability to identity fraud means that it incorrectly verifies some unauthorized immigrants (Westat 2010). And E-Verify relies exclusively on employers to manage this uncertainty, leaving workers vulnerable to employer misuse and abuse (Meissner and Rosenblum 2009).

EARLY LESSONS FROM ARIZONA AND MISSISSIPPI

Though it is too early to reach definitive conclusions about state-level worksite enforcement efforts in Arizona and Mississippi, preliminary evidence from the implementation of E-Verify laws in these states seems to confirm some of these concerns. While some employers describe the program as user-friendly and a useful tool for limiting unauthorized employment (Bowers 2008b), other data indicate that the program is costly and prone to mistakes (Pallack 2008). Partly for this reason, even though LAWA requires employers to verify all new workers through E-Verify, an independent analysis of the program commissioned by the Department of Homeland Security estimated that only about one-third of Arizona employers that should have been using E-Verify were doing so (Westat 2009, 87). Arizona employers also appeared more likely to violate the program's worker protections and less likely to be satisfied with how the program works (Westat 2009, 163, 186). The problem of "false negatives" is particularly worrisome. In one case, Abel Pacheco, a naturalized citizen of eight years, was denied work multiple times in 2008 because of "nonconfirmation" responses that prospective employers received from E-Verify (Boomer 2008). Such discrepancies have prevented a number of other legal workers from gaining employment in Arizona (Pallack 2008; Hansen 2008).

Employers in both states also worry that the system's design flaws undermine its purported benefits. The limitations of E-Verify were highlighted in the August 2008 Immigration and Customs Enforcement (ICE) raid of a Howard Industries electrical transformer plant in Laurel, Mississippi. Almost two months after MEPA took effect, ICE agents detained almost six hundred mostly Latino workers the agency alleged were illegally working at Howard. The immigration sweep was the largest in U.S. history (Department of Homeland Security 2008). Yet Howard had enrolled in E-Verify in 2007, and the company insists that it "runs every check allowed to ascertain the immigration status of all applicants for jobs." An ICE spokeswoman noted that their investigation of Howard commenced in 2006, before Howard joined E-Verify (Hsu, Lazo, and Fears 2008). As of January 2009, Howard had not been sanctioned or fined, but Mississippi Attorney General Jim Hood was conducting further investigations to determine whether Howard knowingly hired unauthorized workers after signing up for E-Verify (*Clarion-Ledger* 2008). The case, like the December 2006 raids at six Swift & Co. (now JBS Swift & Co.) meat-processing plants in North Carolina, illustrates that requiring employers to enforce immigration law is costly, especially in the absence of a reliable system for verifying workers' legal status.[19]

It is not possible to reach firm conclusions about LAWA's effects on Arizona's economy after such a short period and given that the law went into effect as the state and the country entered a recession, but there is anecdotal evidence that some employers—and some migrants—are leaving Arizona in search of a more friendly environment. Even before LAWA took effect, Jason Levecke, the grandson of the founder of the Carl's Jr. fast-food chain and the state's biggest franchisee, indefinitely postponed the opening of twenty new sites in the state, believing that "the risk is too great." Similarly, Sheridan

---

19. In the Swift case the company reported $53 million in losses due to production stoppages (Hsu, Lazo, and Fears 2008).

Bailey, president of steel-beam manufacturer Ironco, said he dismissed several Hispanic employees in anticipation of the sanctions law; and Ironco also planned to outsource some production to a Mexican company in anticipation of labor shortages (Jordan 2007). Richard Melman, a Chicago-based restaurant entrepreneur with seventy-five businesses across the country, scuttled plans for developing a multi-million-dollar Scottsdale restaurant, choosing instead to open it in suburban Washington, DC (Hansen 2008). Overall, while the two-thirds to three-quarters of small businesses in Arizona believed that LAWA had no impact on them, in three different surveys businesses were twice as likely to say that the law had a negative impact as to see it positively (Gans 2008, 11).

There is also evidence that unauthorized workers have responded to LAWA by shifting to the underground economy, depriving the state of tax revenue (González 2008). Others have exited the state, leaving the struggling economy without the workers it needs if it is to recover.[20] Still, as of December 2008, only about forty enforcement actions had been taken statewide in response to LAWA complaints.[21]

CONCLUSIONS

It is not surprising that states and even localities have passed their own migration laws in the last five years, including laws to regulate migrant workers and/or to protect immigrant and worker rights. Indeed, national policy makers have failed for decades to effectively manage labor migration, and recent efforts to do so as part of comprehensive immigration reform ran into partisan and legislative roadblocks in the 109th and 110th Congresses (Rosenblum 2009). In the absence of national solutions, traditional and "new gateway" immigration states have naturally filled the policy void.

There are both normative and public policy arguments in favor of state and local policy making. On a normative level, states are better attuned to the local circumstances of migration, which vary a great deal. The logic of states as "laboratories of democracy" may apply particularly well here given our uncertainty about the ability of E-Verify to accommodate the demands of a nationwide system. As employers in states like Arizona and Mississippi are compelled to register in the system, their experiences may reveal its

---

20. For more on LAWA-related labor shortages in Arizona, see INQUIRER.net 2008; Greene Sterling 2008.
21. Gans (2008) documents thirty-five to forty enforcement actions but was only able to collect data for fourteen of the state's fifteen counties.

limitations, giving federal policy makers the opportunity to make changes as they develop a national electronic eligibility verification system as part of broader reforms under the Obama administration.

Yet, on balance, the worksite enforcement experiences of Arizona, Mississippi, and Illinois seem to confirm that Congress is right to preempt state and local policy making in this area. The direct-democracy arguments in favor of local policy making are more than balanced by the risk that states and localities may overreact to changing circumstances. In Mississippi and other new gateways, rapidly changing migration flows have provoked a nativist response, and state and local policy making leave immigrants and their communities especially vulnerable to "tyranny of the majority" politics that are more easily checked at the national level.

The tension between national and local policy-making dynamics is further weighted toward a centralized response in the case of migration policy and immigrant labor markets because localized policy making is likely to be especially ineffective in these areas. As the case of Arizona has suggested, and as the U.S. experience since the 1990s confirms, increasing migration enforcement without rationalizing migrant admissions is more likely to create new underground markets and disrupt migrant-dependent industries than to stimulate native employment. Yet states simply lack the appropriate policy tools to address migration in a comprehensive way, a problem confronting supporters of a guest worker program for Arizona. Localized enforcement-only policies also seem particularly likely to export migration problems to neighboring states and regions.

State and local mandates to participate in E-Verify in particular raise an additional set of concerns in light of the ambiguous evidence about the program's accuracy and reliability. Independent evaluations of E-Verify confirm an alarming level of erroneous non-confirmations, and these errors disproportionately affect foreign-born individuals and other vulnerable populations. Although national policy makers have considered a number of additional due process protections as part of a package to expand E-Verify, worksite enforcement laws in Arizona and Mississippi fail to include such protections and will likely lead to discrimination against Latinos and other people of color—concerns that motivated policy makers in Illinois to put the program on hold.

The stakes are high, as both state- and national-level policy makers have often presented worksite enforcement and electronic eligibility verification as "silver bullets" in the management of labor migration. But even as E-Verify wrongly non-confirms work-authorized workers, it is also vulnerable to identity fraud and thus unable to reliably screen out unauthorized immigrants. Both types of problems are likely to increase as the system is scaled up to cover employers state- and nationwide. Mandatory participation in E-Verify may *not* be the right solution to the United States' immigration problems, but rather than serving as a useful "laboratory" to test this theory, the rush to make migration policy at the state and local levels may compel Congress to play catch-up and lock in a poorly designed system. If so, large-scale and well-publicized implementation of a flawed worksite enforcement system would further undermine confidence in immigration policy and could prove an obstacle to needed comprehensive reform.

WORKS CITED

ACLU (American Civil Liberties Union). 2009. "Anti–REAL ID Legislation in the States." http://www.realnightmare.org/news/105/.

Barbour, Haley (Office of Governor of Mississippi). 2008. "Statement of Governor Haley Barbour on Senate Bill 2988," March 17.

Boomer, Christina. 2008. "Some Valley Workers Having Trouble with E-Verify," ABC 15 TV, March 24. http://www.abc15.com/news/local/story/Some-Valley-workers-having-trouble-with-E-Verify/VdTlB1vZu0—Qy0e5zGJcg.cspx.

Bowers, Faye. 2008a. "Arizona Considers a Guest Worker Program of Its Own," *Christian Science Monitor*, March 31.

————. 2008b. "E-Verify: Worker Status with a Click of a Mouse," *Christian Science Monitor*, February 29.

Bowman, Ann O'M. 2002. "American Federalism on the Horizon," *Publius* 32, no. 2 (Spring): 3–22.

Calavita, Kitty. 1992. *Inside the State: The Bracero Program, Immigration and the I.N.S.* New York: Routledge.

Chae Chan Ping v. United States 130 U.S. 581 (1889).

Clarion-Ledger [Jackson, Mississippi]. 2008. "Hood to Decide if Howard Industries Broke Miss. Law," September 5.

Crewdson, John M. 1981. "Plan on Immigration," *New York Times*, July 31.

Department of Homeland Security/Immigration and Customs Enforcement. 2008. "595 Arrested in ICE and Department of Justice Joint Immigration Enforcement Action Initiated at Mississippi Transformer Manufacturing Facility: Approximately 106 Identified with Humanitarian Issues, Eight Charged Criminally." ICE News Release, August 26. http://www.ice.gov/pi/nr/0808/080826laurel.htm?searchstring=howard%20AND.

Department of Justice, Office of Justice Programs, Bureau of Justice Statistics. 2009. "State and Local Law Enforcement Statistics," January 15. http://www.ojp.usdoj.gov/bjs/sandlle.htm.

Fischer, Howard. 2008. "Arizona Guest-Worker Bill Dies without Floor Vote," *Arizona Daily Star*, June 28.

Gans, Judith. 2008. "Arizona's Economy and the Legal Arizona Workers Act." Phoenix, AZ: W.P. Carey School of Business, Arizona State University, and Udall Center for Studies in Public Policy, University of Arizona.

Gonzales, Roberto. 2007. "Wasted Talent and Broken Dreams: The Lost Potential of Undocumented Students," *Immigration Policy: In Focus* [Immigration Policy Center, American Immigration Law Foundation] 5, no. 13 (October).

González, Daniel. 2008. "Illegal Workers Manage to Skirt Ariz. Employer-Sanctions Law: Borrowed Identities, Cash Pay Fuel an Underground Economy," *Arizona Republic*, November 30. http://www.azcentral.com/news/articles/2008/11/30/20081130underground1127.html.

Greene Sterling, Terry. 2008. "Crossing the Line? The Economic Price of Arizona's Crackdown on Illegal Immigration," *Newsweek*, April 15. http://www.newsweek.com/id/132231/.

Hansen, Ronald. 2008. "Economy Serves Up Unhappy Meal: Worst Lull in 2 Decades Is Hurting Valley Restaurateurs," *Arizona Republic*, March 3.

Harvard Law Review. 1995. "Unenforced Boundaries: Illegal Immigration and the Limits of Judicial Federalism," 108, no. 7 (May): 1643–60.

Hockstader, Lee. 2008. "Arizona's Immigration Two-Step," *Washington Post*, April 21.

Hsu, Spencer S., Alejandro Lazo, and Darryl Fears. 2008. "Businesses Cite a Catch-22 after Miss. Immigration Raid," *Washington Post*, August 28. http://www.washingtonpost.com/wp-dyn/content/article/2008/08/27/AR2008082703931_pf.html.

INQUIRER.net. 2008. "U.S. Pays the Price for Absence of National Immigration Law," April 10. http://globalnation.inquirer.net/news/news/view_article.php?article_id=129490.

Jordan, Miriam. 2007. "Arizona Squeeze on Immigration Angers Business," *Wall Street Journal*, December 14.

Kincaid, John. 1993. "From Cooperation to Coercion in American Federalism: Housing, Fragmentation, and Preemption, 1789–1992," *Journal of Law and Politics* 9 (Winter): 333–433.

Kincaid, John, and Richard L. Cole. 2002. "Issues of Federalism in Response to Terrorism," Special Issue: Democratic Governance in the Aftermath of September 11, 2001, *Public Administration Review* 62 (September): 181–92.

LeMay, Michael C. 2006. *Guarding the Gates: Immigration and National Security.* Westport, CT: Praeger.

Lowenthal, Abraham. 1999. "U.S.–Latin American Relations at the Century's End: Managing the 'Intermestic' Agenda." In *The United States and the Americas: A Twenty-First Century View,* ed. Albert Fishlow and James Jones. New York: W. W. Norton.

Lynch, Adam. 2008. "Immigration Bill a Reality," *Jackson Free Press,* March 19.

Manning, Bayless. 1977. "The Congress, the Executive, and Intermestic Affairs: Three Proposals," *Foreign Affairs* 55 (January): 306–24.

Meissner, Doris, and Marc R. Rosenblum. 2009. "E-Verify: Evaluation and Recommendations for Worksite Enforcement." Washington, DC: Migration Policy Institute. http://www.migrationpolicy.org/pubs/Verification _paper-071709.pdf.

Meyer, Brandon, and Gregory Wald. 2010. "Illinois Blunts the E-Verify Juggernaut," *Immigration Daily,* February 10. http://www.ilw.com/ articles/2010,0210-meyer.shtm#13.

Migration Policy Institute and New York University School of Law. 2007. "State Responses to Immigration: A Database of All State Legislation." http:// www.migrationinformation.org/datahub/statelaws.cfm.

Money, Jeannette. 1999. *Fences and Neighbors: The Political Geography of Immigration Control in Advanced Market Economy Countries.* Ithaca, NY: Cornell University Press.

Napolitano, Janet (Office of Arizona Governor). 2007. "Governor Signs Employer Sanctions Bill," July 2.

National Immigration Law Center. 2008. "Continuing the Pioneer Tradition: Illinois' Basic Pilot/E-Verify Laws as a Model Policy," October.

NCSL (National Conference of State Legislatures) Immigrant Policy Project. 2008. "State Laws Related to Immigrants and Immigration," July 24. http:// www.ncsl.org/programs/immig/immigreportjuly2008.htm.

Northway, Wally. 2008. "With Immigration Grabbing Headlines, E-Verify Demands Attention," *Mississippi Business Journal,* February 25.

Pallack, Becky. 2008. "Small Businesses Bump into E-Verify Obstacles," *Arizona Daily Star,* April 8.

Plyler v. Doe, 457 US 202 (1982).

Preston, Julia. 2007. "U.S. Sues Illinois to Let Employers Use Immigrant Databases," *New York Times,* September 25.

Robbins, Ted. 2008. "Arizona Proposes Bill to Stop Loss of Migrant Workers," *Morning Edition,* NPR, April 1.

Rosenblum, Marc R. 2003. "The Intermestic Politics of Immigration Policy: Lessons from the Bracero Program," *Political Power and Social Theory* 17: 141–84.

———. 2004. *Immigration as Foreign Policy: U.S. Relations with Mexico and Central America since 1977*. Monograph No. 5. La Jolla, CA: Center for Comparative Immigration Studies, University of California, San Diego.

Rudolph, Christopher. 2006. *National Security and Immigration*. Stanford, CA: Stanford University Press.

Salehyan, Idean, and Marc R. Rosenblum. 2008. "International Relations, Domestic Politics, and Asylum Admissions in the United States," *Political Research Quarterly* 61 (March): 104–21.

Schaper, David. 2007. "Feds Sue Illinois over Worker-Verification Law," *All Things Considered*, NPR, October 3.

Skerry, Peter. 1995. "Many Borders to Cross: Is Immigration the Exclusive Responsibility of the Federal Government?" *Publius* 25, no. 3 (Summer): 71–85.

Sunnucks, Mike. 2008. "Proposed Arizona Guest-Worker Program Faulted," *Phoenix Business Journal*, February 18.

Tarr, G. Alan. 2001. "Laboratories of Democracy? Brandeis, Federalism, and Scientific Management," *Publius* 31, no. 1 (Winter): 37–46.

Tichenor, Daniel J. 2002. *Dividing Lines: The Politics of Immigration Control in the United States*. Princeton, NJ: Princeton University Press.

Verifications Inc. 2008a. "E-Verify Legislation Summary," November 14. http://www.verificationsinc.com/compliance-corner.html.

———. 2008b. "Mississippi E-Verify Legislation Guide," June 10. http://www.verificationsinc.com/mississippi-e-verify.html.

Wagster Pettus, Emily. 2008. "Miss. Governor Signs Bill Requiring Checks on Immigrants' Status," Associated Press State and Local Wire, March 17.

Westat Corporation. 2009. "Findings of the E-Verify Program Evaluation: Report Submitted to US Department of Homeland Security." Rockville, MD: Westat Corporation. http://www.uscis.gov/USCIS/E-Verify/E-Verify/Final%20E-Verify%20Report%2012-16-09_2.pdf.

7 City Ordinances as "Immigration Policing by Proxy": Local Governments and the Regulation of Undocumented Day Laborers

Monica W. Varsanyi

The federal government of the United States has long had sole authority over immigration enforcement and the formulation of immigration policy. Local and state governments are prevented by both the U.S. Constitution and a body of Supreme Court case law from formulating or enforcing policies that directly influence the admission, exclusion, or expulsion of noncitizens from the territory of the United States. Although federal legislation adopted in 1996 has offered city and state law enforcement agencies the opportunity to become local partners in federal immigration enforcement (that is, authority to arrest undocumented immigrants for immigration violations),[1] most local police forces have rejected this partnership, citing, among other concerns, the costs of implementing such a strategy and the public safety outcomes that might result if local police were also "La Migra."

While rejecting the opportunity to be *directly* involved in federal immigration enforcement, many subnational governments, at the urging of their constituents, have elected to do immigration policing "through the back door." As I detail in this chapter, an increasing number of cities and states are utilizing the tools at their disposal—local land use ordinances and ordinances that prevent certain behaviors in public spaces—to constrain the

---

1. The U.S. federal government enabled local immigration policing with the passage of the Illegal Immigration Reform and Immigrant Responsibility Act and the Antiterrorism and Effective Death Penalty Act in 1996.

opportunities and/or behaviors of the cities' undocumented residents and, essentially, "to get these people out of town" (Barry 2006). By invoking, formulating, and enforcing these local ordinances, cities are, in effect, doing local immigration policing by proxy.

In what follows, I explore one example that is illustrative of this phenomenon: the ways in which cities have deployed public space and land use ordinances to control the development and expansion of formal and informal day labor hiring sites within their jurisdictions. Because the vast majority of day laborers are recently arrived immigrants and a significant proportion are undocumented, I interpret the enforcement of these ordinances as, inter alia, locally scaled attempts to control "illegal immigration."

In the first section below, I describe the current landscape of undocumented immigration and day labor in the United States, as well as the federal legislative and enforcement context in which "local immigration policing by proxy" has emerged over the past decade. There has been a fair amount of scholarly research that profiles day labor markets and day laborers across the United States (España 2003; Fine 2006; Malpica 2002; Toma and Esbenshade 2001; Theodore, Valenzuela, and Meléndez 2006; Valenzuela 2000; Valenzuela et al. 2005, 2006). However, there is a dearth of research on both the responses of local communities to day laborers as immigrants and the recent florescence of "grassroots" immigration policies across the United States, even though these policies have taken center stage in many local governments and the mass media.[2] I therefore provide a national overview of these local ordinances in order to demonstrate the range of tactics cities employ to manage immigrant day laborers and day labor markets. Finally, I turn to three brief case studies of cities in the Phoenix metropolitan region that provide additional detail as to how day labor policies were developed in these localities.

IMMIGRANT DAY LABOR AND THE RISE OF LOCAL IMMIGRATION POLICING

Informal labor markets are a long-standing feature on the American landscape (Way 1993). Though native-born workers have been and continue to be an important presence in casual employment markets (Kerr and Dole 2005; Peck and Theodore 2001; Wallace 1965), immigrant laborers have long played a central role in filling the ranks of day labor markets (Kamber 2001; Wilentz 1984).

---

2. For early discussions of local policy responses to day laborers, see Esbenshade 2000 and Kornzweig 2000.

While once predominant mainly in traditional immigrant-destination cities like Los Angeles and New York, day labor markets now exist in communities throughout the United States. In collecting data for a recently released report, Abel Valenzuela and colleagues interviewed 2,660 randomly selected day laborers at 264 hiring sites in 139 cities across the country. They found that some 117,600 workers are either seeking employment or working as day laborers on any given day. The distribution of hiring sites still reflects traditional immigrants' settlement destinations to some extent, but a growing percentage of day labor markets are in regions not traditionally seen as "gateways," including the Midwest (3 percent of sites), Southeast (13 percent), and South (13 percent) (Valenzuela et al. 2006, 5). This changing distribution reflects a distinct and relatively rapid shift in immigrants' settlement choices over the past two decades, away from traditional gateway cities such as Los Angeles, Houston, and Tucson, to nontraditional settlement areas such as Georgia, Indiana, and North Carolina.[3]

Not all day laborers are unauthorized immigrants, though Valenzuela and colleagues found that the majority are both undocumented and recent arrivals; approximately three-quarters of the day labor workforce is estimated to be unauthorized, and 60 percent have been in the United States for five years or less. Furthermore, while a significant proportion (21 percent) of day laborers seek work from formal day labor hiring centers (Valenzuela et al. 2006, 27), the majority of hiring sites are informal. Given the nature of the hiring process, informal day labor markets are typically found in locations that are highly visible and highly accessible to potential employers, such as sidewalks at busy intersections and the parking lots of home improvement stores.

Over the past several decades, as the number of undocumented immigrants living in the United States has increased from an estimated three million in the early 1990s to some twelve million today (Passel 2006) and as informal day labor markets have proliferated in both traditional and nontraditional immigrant destinations, the term "day laborer" has become synonymous with "illegal immigrant" in popular discourse. And as such, tensions over undocumented immigration are increasingly being played out over day labor markets, which are often the most visible manifestation of "illegal immigration" on the local scale. The necessary visibility, presumed illegality, and sometimes large-scale nature of day labor markets have made them a focal point for local frustrations over unauthorized immigration in a growing number of communities across the country (Esbenshade 2000).

---

3. For a discussion of why this shift has occurred, see Zúñiga and Hernández-León 2005.

Different local stakeholders articulate various motivations for wanting to manage or eliminate day labor markets in their communities, but many native-born or naturalized city residents, homeowners, and local business owners connect their frustrations over undocumented immigration, broadly speaking, with the presumed illegal status of day laborers present in "their" communities (Esbenshade 2000).[4] To these local stakeholders, the workers' legal status is viewed as both the primary problem and the source of a potential solution. If day laborers are "illegal immigrants," so goes the argument, then they should be arrested by federal Immigration and Customs Enforcement (ICE) agents and deported.

As the federal government has pulled back from immigration policing and enforcement within the United States, residents concerned about day laborers and/or unauthorized immigration are turning to their local governments and police to take action on the perceived illegal immigration problem. Though the federal government has plenary power over immigration matters, starting in 1996 and continuing in the post–9/11 period, Congress and the executive branch have authorized local and state governments to do immigration policing if they choose to assume the responsibility (Coleman 2005; Decker et al. 2009; Waslin, this volume; Rodríguez, Chishti, and Nortman, this volume). Although legal scholars are still debating the fundamental constitutionality of this devolution of immigration policing powers (Hethmon 2004; Pham 2004), local immigration policing does not conflict currently with federal plenary power because it has been explicitly authorized by Congress.

Thus far, few subnational jurisdictions have accepted the offer to do federally sanctioned local immigration policing. However, this has not meant that cities are disinterested observers of undocumented immigration. On the contrary, there has been a recent proliferation of locally generated grassroots policies that engage with the presence of undocumented residents in cities, counties, and states across the United States (Wells 2004; Varsanyi 2006). Given the growing presence of unauthorized resident populations, myriad subnational governments are taking matters into their own hands by developing policies that in some cases protect their unauthorized residents and in others seek to constrain and expel those residents from their jurisdictions. In light of the federal government's plenary power over immigration, these local governments are walking a fine line when formulating these policies; constitutionally

---

4. I put "their" in quotation marks, because day laborers frequently live in the same communities as their critics and are thus local residents as well.

speaking, "local immigration policy" is an impossibility. While subnational governments do not have the constitutional power to formulate grassroots immigration policies as such, they *do* have explicit power to regulate and police public space within their jurisdictions via local land use and zoning ordinances, ordinances that regulate behavior in public space (for example, laws that criminalize loitering), and the enforcement of local and state laws (such as trespassing and traffic ordinances). As the local policies described in the next section illustrate, a secondary (and, I would argue, intended) effect of controlling and criminalizing certain behaviors in public space is policing the persons within those spaces—day laborers—who, by necessity of their livelihood strategy, participate in outlawed behaviors (Mitchell 1995, 1998a, 1998b, 2003).

IMMIGRATION POLICING BY PROXY: A NATIONAL OVERVIEW OF LOCAL POLICIES

There are no federal laws that speak directly to the prohibition or permission both to *work* as a day laborer and to *hire* day labor. Under the 1986 Immigration Reform and Control Act (IRCA), employers must verify that their potential employees are able to work legally in the United States, but this only applies to employees who are hired for more than three days, as opposed to casual labor, which is hired on a day-to-day, informal basis. The day-to-day nature of informal day labor, in combination with this "three-day loophole," provides contractors and employers a means by which they can regularly visit the same day labor sites and hire the same laborers, who, in effect, work for them on an informal but permanent basis. And because the hiring occurs on a daily basis, no federal law is broken as such, even if the *spirit* of the law is neglected.

In the absence of clearly enforceable federal laws regulating the hiring of day labor and day labor markets, on the one hand, and growing and various complaints by business owners and city residents over the presence of day labor hiring sites (and presumed "illegal immigrants"), on the other, city governments have turned to their own legislative toolkits in search of solutions. As I discuss below, these locally generated strategies are of four varieties: establishment of formal day labor hiring sites, enforcement of existing ordinances (such as housing, trespassing, and anti-solicitation ordinances), creation of new city ordinances (specifically, employer registration ordinances and Illegal Immigration Relief Acts), and the deployment of unofficial enforcement strategies, including harassment and intimidation.

Formal Day Labor Hiring Sites

A number of city governments have considered establishing formal day labor hiring sites to ease conflicts and complaints about (and from) day laborers. As Valenzuela et al. report (2006, 6–7), there are approximately sixty-three formal worker centers across the United States, over half of them established since 2000. Formal hiring centers are frequently the product of partnerships between various stakeholders, including "community organizations, faith-based organizations, law-enforcement agencies," and local governments. Valenzuela and colleagues found that the majority of these hiring centers provided a combination of services, such as space in which laborers can gather, a job allocation system that imposes a degree of organization and co-ordination on the hiring process, a requirement that laborers and employers register with the site, and a minimum wage requirement.

While a number of city governments have supported the establishment of formal hiring sites within their jurisdictions, others have considered and passed ordinances prohibiting these centers, either by restricting the use of taxpayer money to establish or run them or by restricting the use of public property for the centers. For example, debates over the establishment of a publicly funded day labor hiring center in Herndon, Virginia, gained national prominence in the summer of 2005. City officials proposed to build a day labor center using county funding in an effort to answer merchant and resident complaints about the expansion of an informal hiring site in the city. However, city residents and outside interest groups, such as the Minutemen Civilian Defense Corps (hereafter, the "Minutemen"), argued that it was illegal to build a hiring site with public money because this was tantamount to supporting the hiring of illegal immigrants, in violation of IRCA (Morello 2005; see also Wilson, Singer, and DeRenzis, this volume). Though the project was highly controversial, Herndon's city government ultimately decided to build a publicly funded day labor hiring center.

As noted above, there are currently no federal restrictions on the local establishment of formal day labor hiring centers, including those partially funded with taxpayer money. However, several cases currently making their way to the Supreme Court may set a federal precedent on this issue. Judicial Watch, a conservative think tank in Washington, DC, has filed a number of lawsuits against cities across the country, including Herndon and Laguna Beach, California, which use public funding to run day labor centers in their jurisdictions. The suits claim that these cities are breaking federal law by facilitating the hiring of illegal immigrants, in violation of IRCA (Delson 2006).

Enforcement of Existing City Ordinances

In seeking to manage or eliminate informal hiring sites (and, indirectly, un-documented immigrants) within their jurisdictions, many cities use ordi-nances that are already on the books and instruct their police departments to enforce them in the area of day labor markets.

Housing ordinances. Some cities use local housing laws to eliminate in-formal day labor markets. Immigrant day laborers, particularly recent arriv-als to suburban areas that lack affordable housing, often share rental units, and it is not uncommon for twenty to thirty individuals to live together in a single house. In indirect attempts to constrain day laborers' housing options and drive them out of town, cities are using anti-crowding or "anti-stacking" ordinances to eliminate cheap or illegal housing units that are viewed as a magnet for immigrant day laborers. For instance, Mayor Donald Cresitello, of Morristown, New Jersey, is a vocal critic of his city's informal day labor market and is aggressively employing the city's anti-stacking ordinance to target landlords who rent to day laborers. Since taking office in January 2006, Cresitello has hired additional city housing inspectors and increased the fines for landlords found in violation of the ordinance (Seman 2006).

Trespassing ordinances. Various cities and at least one state (Arizona) have attempted to use trespassing laws to manage day labor markets and, more broadly, the undocumented immigrants within their jurisdictions. In the summer of 2005, police in several New Hampshire towns arrested ten un-documented residents on criminal trespassing charges, arguing that their illegal presence in the United States also implied criminal presence within town boundaries (Belluck 2005). In the motion filed to dismiss the trespass-ing charges, the city prosecutor argued that state law defined someone guilty of criminal trespass if, "knowing that he is not licensed or privileged to do so, he enters or remains in any place" and that an immigrant's "omission to get permission to be in this country is his failure to act, just as a sexual offender who fails to register commits an omission to act when legally required to do so" (McLean 2005). More recently, eight laborers playing soccer on a pub-lic field were arrested on similar grounds in Brewster, New York (O'Conner 2006). Further, the Arizona state legislature passed a bill in 2006 authorizing city police departments to use state-level trespassing laws to arrest undocu-mented immigrants (Archibold 2006).

Thus far, these attempts to use trespassing ordinances to arrest undocu-mented migrants for simply being present within jurisdictional limits are not succeeding. A New Hampshire state judge rejected the strategy, arguing that the criminal trespassing charges were unconstitutional attempts at regulating immigration, an area in which the federal government has authority. On similar grounds, Arizona Governor Janet Napolitano vetoed the legislature's 2006 bill, and the Brewster case drew a legal challenge.

Anti-solicitation ordinances. Cities have also turned to anti-solicitation ordinances to regulate the activities of day laborers who congregate at informal hiring sites. Originally on the books as a means of cracking down on prostitution, anti-solicitation ordinances seek to restrict commercial transactions between a potential employer in a vehicle and potential employees on the sidewalk. The use of anti-solicitation ordinances in restricting day laborers has had mixed success in the courts. The city of Agoura Hills, California, adopted an ordinance in 1991 that prohibited individuals on sidewalks from seeking employment from someone traveling in a vehicle. The city claimed that day laborers and potential employers were conducting business in lanes of traffic, blocking the flow of traffic, and creating a safety hazard. The law, justified as a traffic safety measure, was ultimately upheld on appeal because the court found it did not violate the day laborers right to work, but only sought to restrict their activities in ways that increased safety and served the legitimate public interest (*Xiloj-Itzep v. City of Agoura Hills*, 1994; see also Kornzweig 2000). In contrast, in 2004, after police officers arrested sixty day laborers in Redondo Beach, California, under a similar anti-solicitation ordinance, U.S. District Court Judge Consuelo B. Marshall declared that this anti-solicitation law was not constitutional as it was too broad and "could conceivably restrict people from hailing taxis, or Girl Scouts from selling cookies outside of their school" (Gorman 2006).

Creation of New City Ordinances

Cities are also seeking ways to restrict or eliminate day labor markets and (presumed undocumented) immigrant day laborers from within their jurisdictions by creating new city ordinances, which are of two varieties.

Employer registration. The Southern California city of Vista achieved notoriety in summer 2006 by passing the nation's first day labor *employer* registration ordinance.[5] In the months leading up to the passage of the ordinance, the San Diego chapter of the Minutemen protested at a busy informal day labor hiring site within the city. According to Minutemen founder Jim Gilchrist, the goal of the protests was to "educate" potential employers that they were,

---

5. For more on Vista's ordinance, see Danielson, this volume.

according to the Minutemen's interpretation, breaking U.S. tax and labor laws by hiring undocumented day laborers (Klawonn 2006). As part of their protest, Minutemen photographed the license plates of drivers who hired day laborers and posted the photos on a Web site, www.wehirealiens.com. Responding to these pressures, the Vista City Council passed an ordinance in June 2006 (Ordinance No. 2006-8) that requires the employers of immigrant day laborers to register with the city, post proof of registration on their vehicles while hiring day laborers, and give the workers a "term sheet" which describes the job and wages and provides employer contact information. The ordinance is currently being challenged in court. The American Civil Liberties Union (ACLU) and California Rural Legal Assistance (CRLA) filed the suit, claiming that the ordinance is unconstitutional because it violates employers' free speech and equal protection rights and also has discriminatory intent (Rodríguez 2006).

Illegal Immigration Relief Acts. In summer 2006, a new variety of "anti–day labor/anti–undocumented resident" ordinance was added to the local toolkit. A number of U.S. cities have passed Illegal Immigration Relief Acts,[6] which do not target day laborers at hiring sites but rather, like the anti-stacking ordinances discussed above, restrict their broader living and working conditions with the intent of making the respective cities inhospitable for them.[7] Hazleton, Pennsylvania, was among the first—and perhaps the most publicized—cities to pass such an ordinance (Ordinance 2006-13) and served as a model for later ordinances elsewhere. The original Hazleton ordinance, passed in July 2006, included three major provisions: (1) it declared English as the official city language; (2) it required all tenants and potential tenants to apply for an "occupancy permit," which establishes their legal residency in the United States, and established fines for undocumented renters who lacked an occupancy permit and for landlords who rent property in the city to undocumented residents ($1,000 per day per undocumented resident); and (3) it denied permits or contracts to businesses that have "aided and abetted" (hired) undocumented immigrants, not only in Hazleton itself but *anywhere in the United States*, including by establishing a day labor hiring center that does not verify legal work status.

---

6. For more on IIRAs, see Esbenshade et al. and Fleury-Steiner and Longazel, this volume.

7. According to PRLDEF, as of September 2006, six U.S. cities had adopted these ordinances, four were in the preliminary stages of adopting them, twenty-six were considering these ordinances, and four had considered but rejected them (Preston 2006).

The ACLU and Puerto Rican Legal Defense and Education Fund (PRLDEF) filed a lawsuit two weeks after the ordinance was adopted, on the grounds that it was "riddled with constitutional flaws," clearly preempted federal authority over immigration, and would discriminate against any resident of the city who appeared to be foreign (Preston 2006). The city responded by adopting a revised version of the ordinance, which was slated to take effect in November 2006, but it, too, faces legal challenge by the ACLU and PRLDEF (Associated Press 2006). Many legal observers assume that the challenges being brought against these local ordinances will eventually make their way to the Supreme Court and establish a nationwide precedent.

Unofficial City Enforcement Strategies

Finally, it is important to note that not all locally scaled strategies are *official* policies sanctioned by legislative decree and circulated publicly. Harassment of day laborers by local police, private security guards, merchants, and/or citizens' groups (such as the Minutemen) also plays a role in attempts to manage, relocate, or eliminate informal hiring sites (Esbenshade 2000; Valenzuela et al. 2006). As Valenzuela and his colleagues recount, among day laborers surveyed nationally, 19 percent reported at least one instance of harassment by merchants, 16 percent reported harassment by local police officers, and 9 percent reported harassment or abuse by private security guards. Such harassment included verbal insults, threats or acts of violence, intimidation, and being photographed or videotaped. In one specific example, Joseph Turner, founder of the California anti-immigrant group Save Our State, was recently quoted as encouraging his group's members to bring baseball bats to an anti–day labor rally in Redondo Beach, noting, "if we're lucky, we're gonna need them" (Wall 2005).

Despite their undocumented status, day laborers and those representing them have successfully fought these unofficial harassment policies on equal protection grounds. A federal judge recently decided in favor of six day laborers represented by the National Day Labor Organizing Network and PRLDEF in a lawsuit against the city government of Mamaroneck, New York. The judge upheld the laborers' claim on equal protection grounds, stating that the village had used its police force in a "deliberate and coordinated" campaign to drive day laborers out of the city based solely on their Hispanic appearance (Santos 2006; Fitzgerald 2007).

ARIZONA CASE STUDIES

In Arizona, local attempts to manage informal day labor markets face an additional barrier. In May 2005, Governor Napolitano signed House Bill 2592 into law, making Arizona the only U.S. state to prohibit spending taxpayer money to establish or operate formal day labor hiring centers. This effectively denied Arizona communities one of the most successful means for managing their day labor markets, an approach that has been cited as having positive benefits for all stakeholders, including laborers, employers, business interests, and community residents. Though there is no state prohibition on the establishment of day labor centers as such, these must be wholly operated with private funding. As a result, there are currently only two formal day labor hiring sites in the Phoenix metropolitan area: the Macehualli Work Center in northeast Phoenix, and the Light and Life Day Labor Center in Chandler. Below, I discuss three case studies from the Phoenix area that provide further nuance and detail to the broader discussion of local immigration policing by proxy.

Chandler

Chandler is an incorporated city in the southeastern portion of the Phoenix metro area. Paralleling the rapid growth of the Phoenix area generally, Chandler was the seventh-fastest-growing city in the United States between 1990 and 2000. Its current population, just below 250,000, is 77 percent non-Hispanic white and 21 percent Latino.[8]

Because of the community's particular recent history, Chandler's government has had to strike a delicate balance in managing its informal day labor markets. The city was the site of the infamous "Chandler Roundups," a series of three multi-day raids in the summer of 1997 (Romero and Serag 2005; Romero 2006), in which the Chandler Police Department, working in tandem with agents from the Tucson sector of the Border Patrol, stopped and questioned thousands of Latino residents—citizens, legal residents, and undocumented residents alike—and entered their homes without warrants or probable cause. The Chandler police asked hundreds of Latino residents for their "papers" and ultimately detained 432 suspected undocumented immigrants and placed them in deportation hearings. Chandler's Latino community was understandably outraged by the racial profiling inherent to this local

---

8. www.chandleraz.gov.

immigration enforcement effort. A number of residents subsequently won a $400,000 settlement regarding the roundup.

The Chandler government now treads carefully when formulating strategies to manage and control its day labor markets. Day laborers congregate in two locations in Chandler: on a stretch of public sidewalk and in a public parking lot. Business owners are the most vocal critics of these informal hiring sites, complaining that the congregations of day laborers intimidate potential customers. Additionally, a recently completed freeway extension now brings most of the traffic flow into the city onto Arizona Avenue, the site of the day labor markets. According to prominent local citizens, government officials, and business owners, the fact that the first thing drivers see in Chandler is an informal hiring site tarnishes the city's image (*Arizona Republic* Southeast Valley Editorial Board 2006). The city government has also voiced concerns about traffic safety issues. As the volume of traffic along Arizona Avenue grows, city officials claim that day laborers and employers negotiating employment in traffic lanes endanger themselves and others.

Given Chandler's racially charged history, the City Council assigned the "day labor question" to the city's Human Relations Commission (HRC) in February 2005. The HRC then held meetings with key stakeholders, including small businesses and area residents, day laborers, contractors, and Hispanic community leaders, among others (Chandler Human Relations Commission 2005), incorporated comments from unsolicited e-mails and other communications from interested residents, and held a Regional Day Labor Forum, which brought various national and local experts together to discuss available options. Chandler is unique in the Phoenix metropolitan area in having a privately operated day labor hiring center within its jurisdiction, and the goal of many interested parties has been to move the day laborers from the informal hiring site on Arizona Avenue to the hiring center.

At the HRC's urging, the city adopted a traffic ordinance strategy. Drawing on existing state laws, the city developed a "no parking/no stopping or standing" zone at the site of the informal day labor market. From 4 AM through 9 AM, six days a week, parking and stopping are prohibited along designated stretches of Arizona Avenue; violators are issued $25 traffic tickets (Muench 2005). A hundred signs were posted in the enforcement area, and two police officers were initially assigned to it. For the first two weeks after the traffic restrictions went into effect in September 2005, the officers issued warnings to prospective employers, explained the new policy to them, and gave them information about the formal hiring site. Over the following two months, the officers issued thirty-four citations for illegal stopping and standing. At year's end the police returned to their regular patrol duty but continued random enforcement efforts along Arizona Avenue. Over a hundred citations have been issued since the beginning of the enforcement campaign.

Importantly, because of the racially charged nature of the Chandler Roundups, the city has followed HRC recommendations to target the demand side of day labor hiring. Therefore, it is prospective employers, not the laborers themselves, who are the focus of current enforcement efforts.[9]

The traffic ordinance strategy has been only partially successful in shifting the day labor market (Mulero 2006; Powell 2006). For one thing, Chandler police feel that the fine is not high enough to convince employers that the convenience of hiring workers along Arizona Avenue is not worth the risk of being ticketed. More problematically, anecdotal evidence suggests that employers are simply passing the fines onto the laborers by docking their wages. Therefore, the city is exploring other options, including a higher fine (county ordinances permit fines up to $85) or amending its ordinances so that fines can increase with each successive violation.[10]

Phoenix, Arizona

Even though Phoenix has one of the two formal day labor hiring sites in the metro region (the Macehualli Worker Center), a number of informal sites still operate throughout the city. In November 2005, an informal site at 36th Street and Thomas Avenue, in front of a Home Depot store, became the focus of anti–day labor, anti–illegal immigration demonstrations by the Minutemen, which then caught the attention of local media (Meléndez 2006) and the Phoenix Police Department, and made the location a test case for city and police responses to the day labor "problem."[11]

For several years in the late 1990s the Home Depot management had set up a rudimentary day labor hiring site in the store's parking lot. The store provided rental toilets and trash pickup, but it shuttered the facilities when local residents and business owners complained about the growing presence of day laborers and "illegal immigrants" in the community.[12] However, because the demand for day labor persisted, the laborers continued to gather on the sidewalk in front of the store in an informal hiring site. On any given

9. L. Powell, interview by the author, September 25, 2006.
10. Ibid.
11. S. O'Connell, interview by the author, October 12, 2006.
12. Jeff Hynes, commander of the Central City Precinct, interview by the author, 2006.

day, between seventy-five and two hundred day laborers would gather in this location.

In response to continued complaints by local residents and business owners along with organized and regular demonstrations by the Minutemen, in the fall of 2005 the Phoenix Police Department—in conjunction with business owners, day laborers (including representatives from the Macehualli), and residents—developed a strategy that relied on the enforcement of several local ordinances in tandem. First, because the day laborers were gathering on private property (the Home Depot parking lot), the police started to enforce "no trespassing" ordinances, giving citations and arresting repeat offenders (Meléndez 2006). Second, "no stopping or standing" signs were posted, enabling police to cite potential employers for traffic violations if they stopped to pick up workers. And third, at the outset of the enforcement campaign, police made three arrests under a "no solicitation" ordinance, but given the constitutional ambiguity of anti-solicitation ordinances, the Phoenix city prosecutor dismissed all three cases.

This enforcement strategy has had mixed success in moving day laborers from the informal hiring site at Thomas Avenue and 36th Street. According to the Phoenix Police Department, only about twenty day laborers now gather at the site, down from a previous population of up to two hundred. But as Commander Hynes of the Central City Precinct admitted, enforcement has merely "squeezed the balloon," and day laborers and their potential employers have simply gone elsewhere in the city.[13]

Mesa

Mesa, like Chandler, is located in the southeastern portion of the Phoenix metro area. Mesa is now the third-largest city in Arizona, after Phoenix and Tucson, numbers fortieth in size among U.S. cities (Juozapavicius 2005a), and has a population larger than St. Louis, Miami, or Pittsburgh. The Latino share of the population is also rising, from 20 percent in 2000 to 25 percent in 2003.[14]

In the late 1990s, Mesa's city government began receiving complaints from several constituencies about day laborers. First, business owners complained that congregations of day laborers (numbering between fifty and seventy-five, on average) were negatively affecting their business, as laborers seeking work harassed potential customers. Second, community residents sent

13. Ibid.
14. www.cityofmesa.org.

e-mails, phoned members of city government, and attended City Council meetings to complain about illegal immigration and changes they perceived in their neighborhoods, such as residential overcrowding, excessive numbers of cars parked on the street, loud music playing late into the night, beer cans discarded on the street, and so on. Importantly, these city residents made a direct connection between the day laborers and undocumented immigration, thought that the federal government was not doing enough about "illegal aliens," and urged the city to do something about the perceived problem (Juozapavicius 2005b).

Mesa presents several important features. First, though Mesa police have never participated in a roundup, many members of the Minutemen live in the community, and the city has been represented in the Arizona House of Representatives by Russell Pearce, who recently called for a resurrection of the 1950s INS "Operation Wetback" deportation campaign. Second, the city government was the first in the region to commission a task force engaging with the presence of informal day labor markets and seeking alternatives (Mesa Day Labor Task Force 2000). With the input of a wide range of stakeholders, including three day laborers appointed to the commission and a number of day laborers who participated in a commission-led survey, the study concluded that a formal day labor center was the best solution to perceived problems. However, given Mesa's anti-immigrant climate, there was no political support for building a center, and there is currently no formal hiring site in the city. The city government says it will only consider a center if it is privately funded and there is a guarantee that all laborers are legally present in the United States. Third, unlike Chandler, where day laborers congregate on the public sidewalk, the two informal day labor markets in Mesa are on private property (the parking lots of two strip malls), requiring the city government to draw on different legal tools and ordinances in its efforts to manage the day labor hiring sites (Jensen 2005).

After consulting with business owners and representatives of the Mesa Police Department, the city government chose a "no trespassing" strategy based on extant city trespassing laws. Business owners who wanted to participate in the program signed an agreement with the police force, and signs reading "Day labor pick-up prohibited" were posted on their properties. Starting in July 2005, police spent three weeks warning laborers and employers about the new policy and urging them to find alternative pickup spots, such as the laborers' apartment buildings. After the warning period, Mesa police began enforcing the ordinance, with police officers assigned to observe the day laborers and potential employers. If employers and laborers used the private parking lot to arrange employment but did not patronize the business, the police cited both the laborers and employers for trespassing. During the initial enforcement period, approximately 110 citations were issued; each entailed a $500 fine, a requirement to appear in court, and a potential thirty days in jail. The police did not make any effort to contact ICE and were concerned only with discouraging the gathering of day laborers at the informal hiring site. To date, the city is only partially satisfied with the outcome of the enforcement campaign and is seeking additional options.

CONCLUSION

For many local government officials, city residents, and police officers, the formulation of local ordinances is not explicitly about controlling "illegal immigration" at the local scale. With the notable exceptions detailed above, many city government officials and police officers echo the opinion of Supreme Court Justice Brennan: the federal government has responsibility for immigration enforcement, and the hands of local government are tied in these matters. City government representatives and police officers explicitly state that they are not seeking to do immigration enforcement with these ordinances. Rather, they justify passage and enforcement of the ordinances by referring to traffic safety, public nuisance issues, and complaints that informal day labor hiring sites hurt local businesses. Nonetheless, city officials are responsive to city residents, especially voting and highly vocal city residents, who draw connections between day laborers and undocumented immigration and, frustrated with declining federal enforcement efforts, demand action from local governments.

WORKS CITED

Archibold, Randal C. 2006. "Arizona Governor Vetoes Bill Aimed at Illegal Immigration," *New York Times*, June 7.

Arizona Republic Southeast Valley Editorial Board. 2006. "Arizona Avenue Fix-up Should Move Laborers," *Arizona Republic*, August 17.

Associated Press. 2006. "Lawsuit Challenges Illegal Immigrant Crackdown," *International Herald Tribune*, October 30.

Barry, Ellen. 2006. "It's 'Get These People Out of Town': As More Communities Consider Measures Aimed at Expelling Illegal Immigrants, One Group Files Suit in Hopes of Stopping Such Laws," *Los Angeles Times*, August 16.

Belluck, Pam. 2005. "Towns Lose Tool against Illegal Immigrants," *New York Times*, August 12.

Chandler Human Relations Commission. 2005. "Downtown Chandler Day Laborer Issues: A Report from the Chandler Human Relations Commission: Tangible Next Steps for the City, the Existing Day Labor Center, and the Community." On file with the author.

Coleman, Mathew. 2005. "U.S. Statecraft and the U.S.-Mexico Border as Security/Economy Nexus," *Political Geography* 24: 185–209.

Decker, Scott H., Paul G. Lewis, Doris Marie Provine, and Monica W. Varsanyi. 2009. "Immigration and Local Policing: Results from a National Survey of Law Enforcement Executives." In *The Role of Local Police: Striking a Balance between Immigration Enforcement and Civil Liberties*, ed. Anita Khashu. Washington, DC: Police Foundation.

Delson, Jennifer. 2006. "Laguna Beach Is Sued over Day Labor Center," *Los Angeles Times*, October 4.

Esbenshade, Jill. 2000. "The 'Crisis' over Day Labor: The Politics of Visibility and Public Space," *WorkingUSA* 3, no. 6 (Spring): 27–70.

España, Mauricio A. 2003. "Day Laborers, Friend or Foe: A Survey of Community Responses," *Fordham Urban Law Journal* 30: 1979–2005.

Fine, Janice. 2006. *Worker Centers: Organizing Communities at the Edge of the Dream*. Ithaca, NY: ILR Press/Cornell University Press.

Fitzgerald, Jim. 2007. "Westchester Hiring Site Opens after Village, Day Laborers Settle," Associated Press, June 12.

Gorman, Anna. 2006. "Judge Blocks Arrests of Day Laborers; the Ruling States that a Redondo Beach Law That Bars People from Gathering on Sidewalks while Seeking Work Is Unconstitutional," *Los Angeles Times*, May 3.

Hethmon, Michael M. 2004. "The Chimera and the Cop: Local Enforcement of Federal Immigration Law," *University of the District of Columbia Law Review* 8: 83–140.

Jensen, Edythe. 2005. "Day-Labor Trespass Citations Unlikely," *Arizona Republic*, July 29.

Juozapavicius, Justin. 2005a. "Mesa Latino Town Hall Will Focus on Change," *Arizona Republic*, October 14.

———. 2005b. "Racial Tensions Erupt at Meeting: Town Hall Forum Shows Culture Gap," *Arizona Republic*, April 8.

Kamber, Michael. 2001. "New York's Undocumented Day Laborers Fight for Their Piece of the Big Apple," *Village Voice*, July 25–31.

Kerr, Daniel, and Chris Dole. 2005. "Cracking the Temp Trap: Day Laborers' Grievances and Strategies for Change in Cleveland, Ohio," *Labor Studies Journal* 29: 87–108.

Klawonn, Adam. 2006. "Counterprotest Expected at Minutemen Event in Vista," *San Diego Union-Tribune*, February 4.

Kornzweig, Gabriela Garcia. 2000. "Commercial Speech in the Street: Regulation of Day Labor Solicitation," *Southern California Interdisciplinary Law Journal* 9: 499–519.

Malpica, Daniel Melero. 2002. "Making a Living in the Streets of Los Angeles: An Ethnographic Study of Day Laborers," *Migraciones Internacionales* 1: 124–48.

McLean, Dan. 2005. "Police Outline Prosecution of 'Trespassing' Alien," *New Hampshire Union Leader*, June 29.

Meléndez, M. 2006. "Patrols Keep Day Laborers Away from Business Area," *Arizona Republic*, May 24.

Mesa Day Labor Task Force. 2000. "Final Report." www.cityofmesa.org/humansvc/pdf/FinalReportEnglish.pdf.

Mitchell, Don. 1995. "The End of Public Space? People's Park, Definitions of the Public, and Democracy," *Annals of the Association of American Geographers* 85: 108–33.

———. 1998a. "Anti-Homeless Laws and Public Space I: Begging and the First Amendment," *Urban Geography* 19: 6–11.

———. 1998b. "Anti-Homeless Laws and Public Space II: Further Constitutional Issues," *Urban Geography* 19: 98–104.

———. 2003. *The Right to the City: Social Justice and the Fight for Public Space.* New York: Guilford Press.

Morello, Carol. 2005. "Shouts, Signs over Day Laborers: Hundreds Crowd Herndon Hearing on Gathering Spot," *Washington Post*, August 2.

Muench, Sarah. 2005. "Day Labor Center Use Up 50%," *Arizona Republic*, September 30.

Mulero, Eugene. 2006. "Day Laborers Still Seek Jobs near Chandler Intersection: City Crackdown on Stopped Cars Loses Traction," *Arizona Republic*, January 19.

O'Conner, A. 2006. "In Brewster, a Backlash against Day Laborers," *New York Times*, February 5.

Passel, Jeffrey S. 2006. "The Size and Characteristics of the Unauthorized Migrant Population in the U.S.: Estimates Based on the March 2005 Current Population Survey," March 7. http://pewhispanic.org/files/reports/61.pdf.

Peck, Jamie, and Nik Theodore. 2001. "Contingent Chicago: Restructuring the Spaces of Temporary Labor," *International Journal of Urban and Regional Research* 25: 471–96.

Pham, Huyen. 2004. "The Inherent Flaws in the Inherent Authority Position: Why Inviting Local Law Enforcement of Immigration Laws Violates the Constitution," *Florida State University Law Review* 31: 965–1003.

Preston, Julia. 2006. "Pennsylvania Town Delays Enforcing Tough Immigration Law," *New York Times*, September 2.

Rodriguez, M. 2006. "Vista Sued over Day-Laborer Law by Rights Groups," *San Diego Union-Tribune*, July 19.

Romero, Mary. 2006. "Racial Profiling and Immigration Law Enforcement: Rounding Up of Usual Suspects in the Latino Community," *Critical Sociology* 32, nos. 2–3: 447–73.

Romero, Mary, and Marwah Serag. 2005. "Violation of Latino Civil Rights Resulting from INS and Local Police's Use of Race, Culture and Class Profiling: The Case of the Chandler Roundup in Arizona," *Cleveland State Law Review* 52: 75–96.

Santos, Fernanda. 2006. "Day Laborers' Lawsuit Casts Spotlight on a Nationwide Conflict," *New York Times*, September 17.

Seman, R. 2006. "Cresitello's Day Worker Vow Raises Concerns: Illegal Morristown Immigrants Fear Deportation Could Be Ahead," *Daily Record*, January 7. http://www.dailyrecord.com/apps/pbcs.dll/article?AID=/20060108/NEWS01/601080346/1005.

Theodore, Nik, Abel Valenzuela, Jr., and Edwin Meléndez. 2006. *"La Esquina* (The Corner): Day Laborers on the Margins of New York's Formal Economy," *WorkingUSA* 9: 407–23.

Toma, Robin S., and Jill Esbenshade. 2001. *Day Labor Hiring Sites: Constructive Approaches to Community Conflict.* Los Angeles, CA: Los Angeles County Commission on Human Relations.

Valenzuela, Abel, Jr. 2000. "Controlling Day Labor: Government, Community, and Worker Responses." Working Paper. Los Angeles, CA: Center for the Study of Urban Poverty, University of California, Los Angeles.

Valenzuela, Abel, Jr., Ana Luz González, Nik Theodore, and Edwin Meléndez. 2005. "In Pursuit of the American Dream: Day Labor in the Greater Washington D.C. Region." Los Angeles, CA: Center for the Study of Urban Poverty, University of California, Los Angeles.

Valenzuela, Abel, Jr., Nik Theodore, Edwin Meléndez, and Ana Luz González. 2006. "On the Corner: Day Labor in the United States." Los Angeles, CA: Center for the Study of Urban Poverty, University of California, Los Angeles.

Varsanyi, Monica W. 2006. "Interrogating 'Urban Citizenship' vis-à-vis Undocumented Migration," *Citizenship Studies* 10: 224–44.

Wall, Stephen. 2005. "Anti-Migrant Groups Clash over Name Use," *San Bernardino Sun*, January 15.

Wallace, Samuel E. 1965. *Skid Row as a Way of Life*. Totowa, NJ: Bedminster Press.

Way, Peter. 1993. *Common Labor: Workers and the Digging of the North American Canals, 1780–1860*. New York: Cambridge University Press.

Wells, Miriam. 2004 "The Grassroots Configuration of US Immigration Policy," *International Migration Review* 38: 1308–47.

Wilentz, Sean. 1984. *Chants Democratic: New York City and the Rise of the American Working Class, 1788–1850*. New York: Oxford University Press.

Xiloj-Itzep v. *City of Agoura Hills*, 1994, 24 Cal.App.4th 620, 29 Cal.Rptr.2d 879.

Zúñiga, Víctor, and Rubén Hernández-León, eds. 2005. *New Destinations: Mexican Immigration in the United States*. New York: Russell Sage Foundation.

SECTION THREE

Tracing the Evolution of Local Policy Activism

8 Neoliberalism, Community Development, and Anti-Immigrant Backlash in Hazleton, Pennsylvania

BENJAMIN FLEURY-STEINER AND JAMIE LONGAZEL

In today's global political economy, immigrant workers are increasingly conceived of as "useful invaders," providing economic benefits to employers and political capital to elites while simultaneously being seen as a threat to dominant cultural values (Ambrosini 1999; Calavita 2005). This ideology of the "useful invader" has become fundamental to understanding contemporary immigration law and policy. Whereas immigration law has historically functioned to maximize the profits that immigrant work provides while minimizing the cultural threat accompanying demographic change (Calavita 1992), recent and far-reaching shifts in the global economic order have problematized this conception of the so-called immigration crisis.

The rise of neoliberal economic policies has tended to transfer state power upward to global institutions (such as the WTO) and responsibility downward to local communities.[1] This has resulted in a localization of conflicts over immigration, where communities simultaneously include and exclude

---

1. Throughout this chapter our use of the term "neoliberalism" stresses both economic and social functions of the reemergence of market-centered political regimes. This conception is best explained by Bourdieu (1998): "The neoliberal programme draws its social power from the political and economic power of those whose interests it expresses: stockholders, financial operators, industrialists, conservative or social-democratic politicians who have been converted to the reassuring layoffs of laisser-faire, high-level financial officials eager to impose policies advocating their own extinction because, unlike the managers of firms, they run no risk of having eventually to pay the consequences. Neoliberalism tends on the whole to favour severing the economy from social realities and thereby constructing, in reality, an economic system conforming to its description in pure theory, that is a sort of logical machine that presents itself as a chain of constraints regulating economic agents."

immigrant workers into and from the economy. The backlash[2]—with local public officials constructing their immigrant "problems" as akin to an "alien invasion"—has received most of the attention in the scholarly literature (see, for example, Welch 2003). This largely one-dimensional focus has been driven by highly visible cases involving local political elites who play on the nativist fears of whites, thereby deflecting attention away from the fundamental economic shifts that brought immigrants to their locales in the first place.

Our focus on Hazleton, a small, former coal-mining city in rural Pennsylvania that has been at the center of a high-profile localized immigration debate, illuminates the nexus of neoliberalism and anti-immigrant backlash at the community level. By focusing specifically on Hazleton's primary community development organization—the Community Area New Development Organization, or CAN DO—we show how recent shifts in the region's economy have driven a dramatic reconfiguration of its approach to community development. CAN DO has attracted large, pro-employer firms like Cargill Meat Solutions,[3] which have reputations for both hiring undocumented workers and treating them inhumanely. Moreover, CAN DO has taken advantage of aggressively pro-business state laws such as the Keystone Opportunity Zone Initiative (KOZ) as a primary means to spur economic development in Hazleton.

THE POLITICS OF "USEFUL INVADERS"

Kitty Calavita's recent study of the politics of immigration in Spain and Italy advances a nuanced understanding of how immigrant workers are simultaneously included and excluded in the global economy (Calavita 2005). This research demonstrates that policies in place in these countries create a class of immigrants constructed by political elites and employers as what Ambrosini (1999) first termed "useful invaders." Strong unions and active state regulation created a labor pool in Italy that economic analysts have deemed "inflexible" and identified as the cause of Italy's declining viability in the global economy. In response, employers began hiring temporary and part-time employees, following a pattern not uncommon in America's post-Fordist economy (Calavita 2005, 46, 57). Calavita finds that the most "useful"

---

2. Quotes like the following, from Hazleton's mayor, are common in immigration backlash: "Unfortunately, it's become a problem . . . they cross the border . . . they come into cities such as Hazleton. It's like a cancer" (Jackson 2006).

3. The Cargill meatpacking plant was formerly known as the Excel plant, a primary Cargill subsidiary. For simplicity's sake, we refer to it as Cargill throughout.

of these exploited labor populations is not Italians, however, but African immigrants, who willingly endure low wages and poor working conditions. Indeed, similar to the experiences of other exploited immigrant groups, these jobs represent an improvement from what is offered in their impoverished homeland.

Calavita persuasively shows how both Italy and Spain have embraced exploitable immigrant labor as a way to respond to changing global economic conditions and to improve their overall economic standing in the world. In contrast to the nativist politics of exclusion currently popular in the United States, the Italian and Spanish governments have both heralded "integrationist" policies as inclusive and pro–human rights. This utility is contingent, however, upon the pool of immigrant labor remaining "flexible" and willing to work for significantly lower wages and under significantly worse conditions than the native workforce.

Calavita shows, moreover, how legal documentation is elusive for new immigrants, a hurdle that creates a host of problems. Immigrant laborers in Italy and Spain are not able to attain citizenship and thus suffer an attendant marginality as the dominant culture begins to perceive immigrant laborers as an unaesthetic underclass that is subsequently criminalized and racialized (Calavita 2005, 144–56).

We argue that the simultaneous inclusion and exclusion that is fundamental to a politics of useful invaders is ever more pervasive at local levels in the United States. On the one hand, locales with struggling economies adapt to the neoliberal environment by encouraging pro-employer legislation and attracting corporations that exploit immigrant labor. On the other hand, immigrant laborers "pulled" by these new development tactics find themselves "suspect for their Otherness" (Calavita 2005, 75).

A POLITICAL ECONOMY OF HAZLETON'S IIRA

Hazleton has been at the epicenter of the movement against undocumented immigrants. The city's mayor, Louis Barletta,[4] spearheaded a controversial Illegal Immigration Relief Act (IIRA) in 2006, which proposed to punish landlords and businesses that rented to or hired illegal immigrants and to

---

4. Barletta has emerged as a major figure in the national movement to criminalize illegal immigrants, appearing numerous times on national television with pundits such as Lou Dobbs, engaging in fund raising on the Internet (www.smalltowndefenders.com), and receiving invitations to debate the immigration issue at a variety of venues (such as the 2007 Notre Dame immigration forum).

make English the city's official language.[5] Similar ordinances soon began appearing across the country. While many resembled the Hazleton IIRA and even borrowed directly from its language, others followed their own unique approach. For example, in Pahrump, Nevada, residents were prohibited from flying foreign country flags at a height above that of the U.S. flag (Lazos Vargas 2007). Officials in Danbury, Connecticut, considered an ordinance that would give police more leeway in controlling "repetitive outdoor activities" in order to curtail volleyball playing among the community's new Ecuadorean immigrants (Yardley 2005). Perhaps Alex Kotlowitz best captured the spirit of the times in his 2007 *New York Times Magazine* cover story. "All immigration politics is local," he noted, continuing:

> We may be witnessing the opening of a deep and profound fissure in the American landscape. Over the past two years, more than 40 local and state governments have passed ordinances and legislation aimed at making life miserable for illegal immigrants in the hope that they'll have no choice but to return to their countries of origin. Deportation by attrition, some call it. (Kotlowitz 2007)

Mayor Barletta has suggested that he welcomes the arrival of new immigrants to his city, noting that it is only *illegal* immigrants he wishes to deter.[6] However, echoing Kotlowitz's words, the Hazleton IIRA reportedly drove many recent immigrants out of the city regardless of legal status (Kroft 2006). Moreover, a number of city officials declared that the ordinance was passed as a result of a crime wave perpetrated by illegal immigrants; Hazleton's city council president went so far as to assert that the main purpose of the ordinance was crime prevention. Media coverage suggests, however, that claims making prior to the IIRA's passage was more indicative of a moral panic. Such claims linked negative images of drugs and crime to illegal immigrants (Longazel 2008), effectively criminalizing Hazleton's new immigrant population with a broader law-and-order rhetoric (Beckett 1997).

5. The ordinance has since been ruled unconstitutional by a U.S. District Court in *Lozano et al. v. the City of Hazleton* (2007). This ruling has been appealed, and the appeal had yet to be heard at the time of writing (see Varsanyi n.d.).

6. On a Web site devoted to fund raising for Hazleton's legal defense of the IIRA, Barletta makes the following remarks: "To our recently arrived legal immigrants, I say welcome to our city. I wish you all the best and hope the United States and Hazleton can be a place where your dreams come true. I am proud to represent you as your mayor. And to illegal immigrants and those who would hire or abet them in any way, I say your time is up. You are no longer welcome" (www.smalltowndefenders.com).

Situating Anti-Immigrant Backlash in Hazleton's Broader Economic Order

The politics surrounding the passage of the IIRA constructed Hazleton's im-migration "problem" as akin to an "alien invasion." But what of the policies that attracted the immigrant labor pool to Hazleton in the first place? As discussed by Danielson and by Wilson, Singer, and DeRenzis in this volume, demographic change is often understood as a primary catalyst behind local anti-immigration political activism.[7] And it is true that Hazleton's popula-tion has changed dramatically in a short time.[8] What is frequently left unex-amined, however, are the policies and broader economic circumstances that produced these demographic changes. In the remainder of this chapter, we situate the anti-immigrant backlash in Hazleton's broader economic history and context. We do this by considering why Hazleton's primary economic development organization, CAN DO, abandoned its grassroots approach to community development in favor of a neoliberal approach that supported pro-employer legislation, attracted firms with dubious reputations for ex-ploiting immigrant labor, and successfully detached itself from the "immi-gration crisis" by touting its policies under the guise of a hegemonic pro-growth rhetoric.

Hazleton's history is fraught with conflict between labor, capital, and im-migration. Sitting atop an abundance of anthracite coal, Hazleton attracted thousands of European immigrant workers to its coal mines prior to the turn of the twentieth century. Despite a history of tensions between locals and immigrants (Aurand 1986), there were also signs of ethnic cohesion. By 1974, Hazleton's residents pointed to the city's ethnic diversity as one of its pri-mary strengths (Rose 1981). However, as oil quickly replaced coal as the na-tion's primary energy source in the twentieth century, economic troubles hit Hazleton and the surrounding towns very hard (Dublin and Licht 2005).

In 1954, members of the Hazleton Chamber of Commerce created a grass-roots organization, CAN DO, in an attempt to attract industry to the area. CAN DO's original mission was to "involve the entire community, raise mon-ey, represent all facets of the public on its board of directors, and . . . acquire land for industrial park development" (CAN DO 1991, 5). The organization's founders would tout their inclusive, grassroots approach in the local press, declaring in 1956 that they "would like to have every facet of community life

---

7. See Ramakrishnan and Wong, this volume, for a competing explanation.
8. In 2000, 95 percent of Hazleton's approximately 24,000 residents were white. In 2006, city officials estimated that 30 percent of Hazleton's 31,000 residents were Latino (Savage and Gaouette 2007). The Latino population in Hazleton's Luzerne County has increased at the fourth-fastest rate of all large U.S. counties (El Nasser and Heath 2007).

represented" (CAN DO Archives, Book 1).[9] Indeed, CAN DO's community-centered approach was consistent with that of other organizations emerging in the 1950s and 1960s as part of the "first wave" of community development (Fisher 1994).

CAN DO's early efforts are characteristic of its original mission. Its "Dime a Week" campaign encouraged residents to donate ten cents per week to the cause of attracting industry to the area; lunch pails were strategically placed as collection points in the town's restaurants and workplaces to symbolize the community's determination to attract jobs. Likewise, in the "Miles of Dimes" campaign, strips of tape placed along downtown streets encouraged donations. Such events both raised funds and revived community spirit (CAN DO 1991).

Other local organizations played an important role in supporting and encouraging these campaigns. Local unions published statements in CAN DO pamphlets, assuring local residents that their union affiliates were supportive of the donations that residents were asked to make (Dublin and Licht 2005, 129). Area social clubs began competing to see which could drum up the most financial and community support for redevelopment (CAN DO 1991). The efforts attained a level of success far beyond original expectations. Sufficient funds were collected to purchase land and build an industrial park that is still attracting industry to the area into the present day. In 1964, CAN DO's efforts received national attention when Hazleton was granted the All-American City Award.

CAN DO as "Community Development Industry System"

Despite the early successes of community development corporations (CDCs) like CAN DO, observers have documented a move away from their original grassroots-centered community development imperatives (Fisher 1994; Newman and Ashton 2004). Beginning in the 1980s, many CDCs became far more market-oriented (Fisher 1994), with many forming partnerships with corporations. Operating within the confines of a complex "community development industry system" (Yin 1998), CDCs have largely abandoned their

---

9. The CAN DO office in downtown Hazleton archives a collection of local newspaper articles and other materials that pertain to the organization. This expansive file contains documents from 1956 to the present. One of the authors of this chapter was granted access to this file in December 2007 and July 2008, and we draw from that investigation extensively in this chapter. Previous research on the Hazleton area has also utilized CAN DO's archival records (Dublin and Licht 2005).

historically grassroots approach that involved the community directly in their fund-raising objectives.

Such changes are evident in the recent history of Hazleton's CAN DO. Rather than understanding these changes as a function of increased technical capabilities and greater bureaucratization, we argue that CAN DO has been transformed by the broader political-economic climate. That is, we seek to understand the increasing corporatization of contemporary CDCs, as well as the state's aggressive role in implementing pro-employer legislation, as a product of the intense competition between cities that has been driven by more macro-level shifts in the global economic order.

Reflecting the national trend, in the 1980s CAN DO began to depart from its original community-based approach to economic development. Recognizing that it would need to "change its way of thinking in order to compete," CAN DO relinquished its community-based approach in favor of a "more aggressive" approach in its effort to attract industry (CAN DO Archives, Book 7). CAN DO heightened its attention to marketing, advertising, and public relations, and this often meant making decisions that would defy broader community sentiment[10] and attracting corporations to the area by any means available. Recently, for example, it was reported that when representatives of potential firms visited Hazleton, CAN DO officials strategically routed the prospective clients through the more scenic parts of the community and avoided the "eyesores" that are Hazleton's abandoned coal fields (Dino 2007).

One might argue that CAN DO's transformation merely indicates a shift to a business model of community development and is not part of a broader neoliberal transformation. But how, then, to explain why CAN DO enticed Cargill Meat Solutions to Hazleton, especially when one considers Cargill's record of antilabor practices and exploitation of undocumented immigrant labor (De Jesús 2006)? Cargill's Hazleton plant employs between eight hundred and one thousand workers, and as many as 70 percent of them are Latino immigrants.[11] Thus Cargill's entry into Hazleton's economy

---

10. The legal case *Association of Concerned Citizens of Butler Valley v. Butler Township Board of Supervisors* (1990) is a prime example of this. Here, a grassroots community group emerged to oppose CAN DO's application to rezone conservation land for industrial use.

11. The "Community Profile" on the Hazleton Chamber of Commerce's Web site (http://www.hazletonchamber.org) numbered Cargill's employees at eight hundred. Other reports note that city officials put the plant's workforce at one thousand, and estimates suggest that as many as 70 percent of the workforce is Latino, although Cargill has refused to verify these statistics (Sheehan and Cárdenas 2005).

produced an ever-growing immigrant labor pool that is subject to backlash (as confirmed by the passage of the IIRA in 2006).[12] So the question remains: why would CAN DO bring Cargill to Hazleton? As a corollary, why would a corporation like Cargill choose Hazleton as a location for one of its meat-packing plants?

The Economic Disciplining of Hazleton and the Myth of Community Control

For well over five decades, CAN DO has been the primary institution dedicated to the revitalization of Hazleton's economy. Yet despite its efforts, it is increasingly clear that the city and surrounding region have not fully recovered from the demise of the coal industry (Dublin and Licht 2005). Manufacturing's recent decline in Pennsylvania as a whole, with 207,300 jobs lost since 2001 (McMillion 2008), has devastated Hazleton. Between January 2001 and January 2008, Hazleton and nearby cities such as Wilkes-Barre and Scranton lost just under 28 percent of their manufacturing jobs.

Given this dramatic downturn, CAN DO's ability to attract corporations like Cargill is less surprising. A growing literature highlights neoliberalism's tendency to place localities like Hazleton in a position where they are forced to adopt a market-based economic development approach. Neoliberal processes of devolution, privatization, and "glocalization" (Swyngedouw 1997) have exerted "economic discipline" (Harvey 1985) on locales, disillusioning them with a "myth of community control" (Stoecker 1997, 8). Moreover, the absence of federally mandated redistributive economic policies leaves communities like Hazleton on their own to compete for scarce resources, including industry and jobs. Even a highly entrepreneurial city is not guaranteed economic success given the fierce competition that takes place among, rather than within, municipalities (Cox and Mair 1988).

Under these circumstances, organizations like CAN DO become less discriminating and may turn a blind eye when trying to attract companies that have a reputation for exploiting immigrant labor, dramatically altering the approach to "community development." When asked about Cargill's questionable practices, CAN DO's current president, W. Kevin O'Donnell, remarked, "We are a private organization; we're not a public entity" (Tarone 2003, 4). This suggests that the community-oriented, public approach upon

---

12. Though Cargill serves as a strong illustration of neoliberal policy in action, CAN DO has also recruited large warehouse firms, such as OfficeMax, that also employ a predominately immigrant workforce.

which CAN DO was founded is no longer part of the organization's philosophy, and CAN DO's current mission statement reflects this: "Our mission is to improve the quality of life in the Greater Hazleton Area through the creation of employment opportunities" (CAN DO 2007). This exhibits a profound departure from the organization's original mission—that CAN DO would "involve the entire community, to raise money, to represent all facets of the public on the board of directors" (CAN DO 1991, 53).

Explaining Cargill's Arrival to Hazleton

Communities and their development organizations are struggling for economic survival in the neoliberal environment, and state law tends to reflect this struggle. In the case of Hazleton, the Keystone Opportunity Zone Initiative (KOZ) played a vital role in attracting Cargill to the area. Pioneered by Pennsylvania Governor Tom Ridge (R), KOZ allows municipalities across the state to designate certain properties within their jurisdictions as "opportunity zones." According to Ridge, this approach represents "the most powerful market based incentive: no taxes" (Argall 2006, 78).[13] State Representative Joseph Gladeck (R) echoed these neoliberal imperatives: "Rather than pumping millions of state funds into various state and local run programs, [KOZ] gets the government out of the way" (Argall 2006).

When KOZ was first introduced, Pennsylvania municipalities were invited to compete for "opportunity zones" by demonstrating the magnitude of their economic need, and the five counties that were ultimately awarded the most KOZ acreage all suffered from high unemployment rates. Hazleton's high unemployment, coupled with an abundance of abandoned coal fields, put the city, guided by CAN DO, among the locales to receive important KOZ recognition. In fact, Hazleton's Luzerne County won more "opportunity zone" acreage than any other county in Pennsylvania (Argall 2006).

The KOZ initiative played a direct role in attracting Cargill to Hazleton. When queried about the company's decision to locate in Hazleton, Cargill representatives declared, "they would not be building here if not for Gov. Tom Ridge's Keystone Opportunity Zone program" (CAN DO Archives, Book 19). Importantly, despite the deleterious effects of this type of legislation—both for immigrant populations and for economically deprived rural

---

13. Legislation such as this, it should be noted, is not unique to Pennsylvania. Similar programs have been initiated elsewhere at both the state (Michigan's renaissance zones) and federal (supplemental opportunity zones) levels.

communities like Hazleton—there has been little resistance to such initiatives.[14] The linkages between neoliberal legislation, immigration, and anti-immigrant backlash were never laid out in the public debate. The reason for this, we argue, derives from one of the defining characteristics of neoliberalism, which has allowed it to dominate the modern political economy: it has become hegemonic. Neoliberal policies like KOZ have come to be taken for granted as the appropriate solutions to economic problems.

Fundamentally, neoliberal hegemony is accomplished by ignoring the complexities of local economic issues and instead presenting "reforms" as stark moral dichotomies. Laws like KOZ are driven by a zero-sum rhetoric of community growth versus total community breakdown. Because of the pervasiveness of "neoliberal common sense" (Goode 2006, 205), citizens, CDCs, public officials, and, ultimately, the implementation of law are driven by a denial or ignorance of the complex and potentially economically debilitating outcomes of aggressive corporate welfare policies like KOZ. Unfortunately, the complexities that are ignored often involve racial and ethnic minorities, given that "neoliberal common sense" is driven by a color-blind mentality which, frankly, ignores these issues (see, for example, Delgado 2004).[15]

The KOZ initiative serves as a useful example to highlight how neoliberal policy is framed as an "either/or" predicament that promotes neoliberalism as though there is no alternative and that neglects the complexities of racially diverse communities in the United States today. The neoliberal common sense at the core of KOZ is this: if the economic initiative were not carried through, blight would prevail. With the situation presented in these terms, the decision is not difficult; advocating for blight over economic development would be absurd. Unfortunately, other grounds on which to contest the initiative were virtually absent from the public discourse.

The recent tendency of CDCs to adopt a pro-growth rhetoric that emphasizes job creation and the elimination of undesirable circumstances is well documented in the literature (see, for example, Weber 2002). Cox and

---

14. In analyzing CAN DO's archives, we found plenty of criticism of KOZ, but this criticism failed to make the connection between CAN DO, KOZ, and immigration (the IIRA). Instead, the criticism focused on the bill's tendency to hurt the local tax base (as in a lack of funding for schools) or environmental concerns (CAN DO Archives, Book 19, "CAN DO's KOZ status irks environmentalists," February 22, 2001).

15. Even when these policies are resisted, inattention to race and ethnicity persists. Ansley's (2001) work on the plant closings in Tennessee is instructive here. Originally Ansley was critical of the globalizing forces that limited local control over economic decisions, only later to realize that such globalizing forces also created negative attitudes toward the now large population of Latino workers in Tennessee.

Mair (1988) note the tendency of locally dependent organizations like CDCs to exploit the working class's need for gainful employment. Developers attempt to gain support by emphasizing job growth with the rhetoric of "community worthiness," which makes citizens feel that they deserve the jobs local development groups have awarded them. In Hazleton's case, media outlets announced Cargill's arrival with hyperbolic pronouncements: "Meat plant eyes up to seven-hundred jobs for Hazleton" and "New jobs for area . . . 'Excel'-lent" (CAN DO Archives, Book 19).

The position of Hazleton's Mayor Barletta on immigration and economic development is instructive. After spearheading the anti-immigrant backlash in Hazleton, Mayor Barletta has applauded CAN DO's efforts and has employed his administration in the struggle for economic growth in Hazleton. In defense of the IIRA, for example, Mayor Barletta:

> increased industry within the city with the CAN DO project. This project encouraged unskilled laborers to move into the city where housing prices were low and quality of life was increasing. (*Lozano et al. v. the City of Hazleton*, 4)

Not only did Mayor Barletta effectively criminalize the Latino population, he encouraged the development policies that attracted this population to Hazleton in the first place. By framing the invitation to immigrants as "economic growth" on the one hand and by criminalizing immigrants by touting a crackdown on "illegals" on the other, Barletta and other Hazleton elites (including CAN DO) adhered to an approach that simultaneously includes and excludes immigrant workers in the city's economy.

Following the influx of Latino residents to Hazleton, a number of Latino-based businesses, such as grocery stores, cropped up to meet the new residents' demand for goods. With the passage of the IIRA, however, this demand was cut drastically, leaving a host of Latino-owned and Latino-focused businesses with a much-reduced Latino clientele. In hopes of retaining their customer base, local Latino business owners asked the Chamber of Commerce to speak out against the ordinance, but the Chamber refused to take a position on the issue (Tarone 2007).[16] Eduardo Rodríguez, a prominent Latino business owner in Hazleton, described the relationship between

---

16. Despite the refusal of Hazleton's Chamber of Commerce to take a stand against the IIRA, the U.S. Chamber of Commerce filed a brief in opposition to the ordinance (*Lozano et al. v. the City of Hazleton*).

local development organizations and Latino business owners in Hazleton as follows:

> CAN DO and the Chamber of Commerce are more receptive to chain stores, which leaves Latino small business owners forced to go their own way. So it makes no sense now to open a business when you can make more money working in a factory.[17]

Despite his criticism of CAN DO and the city's Chamber of Commerce, Rodríguez realizes that "without CAN DO the city would be a ghost town." Yet the negative impacts on Latinos cannot be ignored. Indeed, with CAN DO focused on attracting large firms like Cargill and, by implication, neglecting small businesses, Latino businesspeople have limited options. The decline in their (now-criminalized) customer base (Longazel 2008) that resulted from the passage of the IIRA dramatically reduced their chances to succeed.

CONCLUSION: FROM NEOLIBERALIZED COMMUNITY DEVELOPMENT TO CRIMINALIZATION

The notion of immigrant workers as "useful invaders" is increasingly applicable at the local level in the United States. While most of the attention on the localization of the immigration problem in the United States has gone to exclusionary laws and anti-immigrant backlash, we have considered in detail the dialectical processes that simultaneously *include* and *exclude* immigrants in the local economy. Focusing on community development in one small U.S. city, we argue that this city's community development corporation has been transformed into what might best be called a *neoliberal conduit*. Broader shifts in policies (that is, antilabor practices) that echo the current global economy have functioned to place communities like Hazleton in a position where adherence to such policies is not only a necessity but also part of an increasingly "taken-for-granted" common sense.

We believe the Hazleton case points to a fundamental transformation of the meaning of "community development" in the United States more broadly. Hazleton provides a clear opportunity to discuss the politics of anti-immigrant backlash. However, our focus on local institutions such as CAN DO and state initiatives such as KOZ reveals the pervasive political, ideological, and legal

---

17. Eduardo Rodríguez (pseudonym), telephone interview conducted by the authors, April 30, 2008.

dynamics that are fundamental to understanding the roots of the immigration crisis in the city. We have shown that CAN DO played a crucial role in driving the crisis, not out of animus but out of an attempt to adapt to sharp downturns in Hazleton's economy. By embracing KOZ (a pro-employer/antilabor policy), by attracting corporations like Cargill, with long-standing reputations for exploiting undocumented workers, and by approaching these issues as taken-for-granted solutions to economic problems, CAN DO exemplifies the changing nature of community development and thus the increasingly hostile environment facing immigrant workers in the United States today.

Though we believe that neoliberalism has dramatically altered the local economic landscape, it is important to note that some case studies tell a different tale about neoliberalism's effect (see, for example, Jaffe and Quark 2006). It may be that a neoliberal political economy is actually beneficial for some communities (Kondras 1997).[18] Other U.S. municipalities may be less dependent on their community development corporation than is Hazleton. Obviously, not all communities are served by corporations that rely on low-wage immigrant labor, nor are most of them active in the anti-immigration movement. As Hackworth suggests, "the rollback/destruction of Keynesian interventions and the roll-out/creation of more proactively neoliberal policies are thus highly contingent, incremental, uneven, and largely incomplete" (2007, 12). Nevertheless, the rise of a neoliberal economic order has dramatically altered the consciousness of community institutions. By claiming that "pro-growth" legislation is a panacea for a volatile local economy and scapegoating "illegal immigrants" as somehow responsible, politicians make the economic exploitation of workers—ethnic minorities in particular, and increasingly marginalized U.S. workers and communities more broadly—invisible.

WORKS CITED

Ambrosini, Maurizio. 1999. "Utili Invasori: L'inserimento degli Immigranti nel Mercato del Lavoro." Milan: FrancoAngeli.

Ansley, Fran. 2001. "Inclusive Boundaries and Other (Im)Possible Paths toward Community Development in a Global World," *University of Pennsylvania Law Review* 150, no. 1: 353–417.

---

18. Absent an exclusionary rhetoric, immigrant populations can also serve to boost local economies. In Hazleton, many have argued that small Latino businesses have revitalized the city's downtown. Moreover, in places like Riverside, New Jersey, exclusionary statutes have been revoked once a full understanding was reached of the devastating consequences a fleeing immigrant population would have on the community (Belson and Capuzzo 2007).

Argall, David G. 2006. "A Policy Analysis of the First Six Years of Pennsylvania's Keystone Opportunity Zone Program, 1998 to 2004: Enlightened Economic Development of Corporate Welfare?" PhD diss., School of Public Affairs, Pennsylvania State University.

Association of Concerned Citizens of Butler Valley v. Butler Township Board of Supervisors, 135 Pa. Commw. 262 (Pa. Commw. 1990).

Aurand, Harold. 1986. *Population Change and Social Continuity: Ten Years in a Coal Town.* London: Associated University Press.

Beckett, Katherine. 1997. *Making Crime Pay: Law and Order in Contemporary American Politics.* Oxford: Oxford University Press.

Belson, Ken, and Jill P. Capuzzo. 2007. "Towns Rethink Laws against Illegal Immigrants," *New York Times,* September 25.

Bourdieu, Pierre. 1998. "Utopia of Endless Exploitation: The Essence of Neoliberalism," *Le Monde Diplomatique,* December.

Calavita, Kitty. 1992. *Inside the State: The Bracero Program, Immigration, and the I.N.S.* New York: Routledge.

———. 2005. *Immigrants at the Margins: Law, Race, and Exclusion in Southern Europe.* Cambridge: Cambridge University Press.

CAN DO. 1991. "Upon the Shoulders of Giants: The CAN DO Story." Hazleton, PA: CAN DO.

———. 2007. "What Vision, Drive and a Community CAN DO." CAN DO Pamphlet. Hazleton, PA: CAN DO.

Cox, Kevin R., and Andrew Mair. 1988. "Locality and Community in the Politics of Local Economic Development," *Annals of the Association of American Geographers* 78, no. 2: 307–25.

De Jesús, José. 2006. "Employees at Meatpacking Plant Allege Mistreatment," *Des Moines Register,* April 12.

Delgado, Richard. 2004. "Locating Latinos in the Field of Civil Rights: Assessing the Neoliberal Case for Radical Exclusion," *Texas Law Review* 83, no. 2 (December): 489–524.

Dino, Jim. 2007. "Dodging Mines: Economic Developers Must Downplay Past to Secure Future," *Standard-Speaker* [Hazleton], December 16.

Dublin, Thomas, and Walter Licht. 2005. *The Face of Decline: The Pennsylvania Anthracite Region in the Twentieth Century.* Ithaca, NY: Cornell University Press.

El Nasser, Haya, and Brad Heath. 2007. "Hispanic Growth Extends Eastward," *USA Today,* August 9.

Fisher, Robert. 1994. *Let the People Decide: Neighborhood Organizing in America.* New York: Twayne Publishers.

Goode, Judith. 2006. "Faith-based Organizations in Philadelphia: Neoliberal Ideology and the Decline of Political Activism," *Urban Anthropology* 35, nos. 2–3: 203–36.

Hackworth, Jason. 2007. *The Neoliberal City: Governance, Ideology, and Development in American Urbanism.* Ithaca, NY: Cornell University Press.

Harvey, David. 1985. *The Urbanization of Capital: Studies in the History and Theory of Capitalist Urbanization.* Baltimore, MD: Johns Hopkins University Press.

Illegal Immigration Relief Act Ordinance 2006-18. Hazleton, Pennsylvania.

Jackson, Kent. 2006. "Ferdinand: Time to Seal Off Border," *Standard-Speaker* [Hazleton], May 17.

Jaffe, JoAnne, and Amy A. Quark. 2006. "Social Cohesion, Neoliberalism, and the Entrepreneurial Community in Rural Saskatchewan," *American Behavioral Scientist* 50, no. 2: 206–25.

Kondras, Janet. 1997. "Restructuring the State: Devolution, Privatization, and the Geographic Redistribution of Power and Capacity in Governance." In *State Devolution in America: Implications for a Diverse Society*, ed. L. A. Staeheli, J. E. Kodras, and C. Flint. Urban Affairs Annual Reviews, 48. Thousand Oaks, CA: Sage.

Kotlowitz, Alex. 2007. "Our Town," *New York Times Magazine*, August 5.

Kroft, Steve. 2006. "Welcome to Hazleton: One Mayor's Controversial Plan to Deal with Illegal Immigration," *CBS News*, November 19.

Lazos Vargas, Sylvia R. 2007. "Emerging Latina/o Nation and Anti-Immigrant Backlash," *Nevada Law Journal* 7: 685–712.

Longazel, Jamie. 2008. "The Straw That Broke the Camel's Back: Illegal Immigration and Moral Panic in a Rural Pennsylvania City." Presented at the Eastern Sociological Society Annual Meeting, New York, February 23.

Lozano et al. v. the City of Hazleton, 496 F. Supp.2d 477 (M.D. Pa. 2007). Findings of Fact and Legal Brief.

McMillion, Charles M. 2008. "Pennsylvania's Jobs Market 2001–2008: Trading Down in a Debt-Driven, Weak Economy." Prepared for the American Manufacturing Trade Action Coalition.

Newman, Kathe, and Phillip Ashton. 2004. "Neoliberal Urban Policy and New Paths of Neighborhood Change in the American Inner City," *Environment and Planning* 36: 1151–72.

Rose, Dan. 1981. *Energy Transition and the Local Community: A Theory of Society Applied to Hazleton, Pennsylvania.* Philadelphia, PA: University of Pennsylvania Press.

Savage, David G., and Nicole Gaouette. 2007. "Judge Rejects Hazleton Law on Immigrants—A City Cannot Take Such a National Issue into Its Own Hands, He Says," *The Nation*, July 27.

Sheehan, Dan, and José Cárdenas. 2005. "New Culture in Old Coal Town," *Morning Call*, July 25.

Stoecker, Randy. 1997. "The CDC Model of Urban Redevelopment: A Critique and an Alternative," *Journal of Urban Affairs* 19, no. 1: 1–22.

Swyngedouw, Erik. 1997. "Neither Global nor Local: 'Glocalization' and the Politics of Scale." In *Spaces of Globalization: Reassessing the Power of the Local*, ed. K. Cox. New York: Guilford Press.

Tarone, L. A. 2003. "Has CAN DO Lowered Its Standards?" *Standard-Speaker* [Hazleton], August 14.

———. 2007. "U.S. Chamber of Commerce against IIRA," *Standard-Speaker* [Hazleton], March 5.

Varsanyi, Monica W. n.d. "Neoliberalism and Nativism: Local Anti-Immigrant Policy Activism and an Emerging Politics of Scale." Manuscript.

Weber, Rachel. 2002. "Extracting Value from the City: Neoliberalism and Urban Redevelopment," *Antipode* 34, no. 3: 519–40.

Welch, Michael. 2003. "Ironies of Social Control and the Criminalization of Immigrants," *Crime, Law and Social Change* 39: 319–37.

Yardley, William. 2005. "Volleyball and Violations: Immigrants' Pastime Is Out of Bounds in Danbury," *New York Times*, August 2.

Yin, Jordan S. 1998. "The Community Development Industry System: A Case Study of Politics and Institutions in Cleveland, 1967–1977," *Journal of Urban Affairs* 20, no. 2: 137–57.

9 Localized Immigration Policy: The View from Charlotte, North Carolina, a New Immigrant Gateway

OWEN J. FURUSETH AND HEATHER A. SMITH

In 2002, Charlotte, North Carolina, and surrounding Mecklenburg County were identified as the fourth-fastest-growing Hispanic "hypergrowth" metro area in the United States (Suro and Singer 2002). This label was as unprecedented as it was unexpected. Charlotte has long been viewed as a quintessential southern city, defined largely by its black/white dichotomy. Although Charlotte is emblematic of what James Cobb labeled the progressive "New South," it was not until the mid-1980s that Latino immigrants began settling in large numbers in the city's older, middle-ring, suburban neighborhoods (Smith and Furuseth 2008). What began as a largely shadow workforce of pioneering young men has turned into a conspicuous and mature transnational community.

The shift has been dramatic, with the most fundamental impacts redefining social and economic relations. Given the city's absence of any significant international immigration experience and its traditional biracial class structure, Charlotte's status as a "new pre-emerging immigrant gateway" (Singer, Hardwick, and Brettell 2008) has created extraordinary and unanticipated challenges.[1] Indeed, Latino migration to, and settlement within, the city and its surrounding communities has required reconsideration of the racial constructs and associated norms and structures embedded within many southern communities.

---

1. The preemerging immigrant gateway is an archetype for the twenty-first-century American urban immigrant destination. Preemerging gateways are urban areas with little or no immigration history, where immigrant populations grew rapidly in the 1990s and are expected to continue to grow as important immigration destinations (Singer 2008).

For new Latino immigrants, the processes of identity formation and place connection must be navigated through a racially organized context and conducted within an increasingly fraught national and local discourse around immigration and belonging (Winders 2005). Juxtapose the speed and scale of the inflow of Latino newcomers (many of whom are undocumented) with the anti-immigrant rhetoric of national and state-level political discourse, and the outcome has been struggle and tension around community receptivity and the place of Latinos in Charlotte. At the center of these tensions are public policy debates focused on the availability of public services for immigrants and the translation of public signage and documents into Spanish.

Within this setting, the localization of immigration has played out in disjointed policy guidelines and practices and in increasing divisiveness across the community. For example, corporate and governmental practices and policies, traditionally in alignment, have increasingly been at odds. In a similar fashion, social spaces and place-making intrusions by newcomers have activated new racial and class hostilities, especially, but not exclusively, evident between working-class African-Americans and Latino newcomers.

The political turmoil and social tensions evidenced in Charlotte echo broader-scale trends. According to Nguyen (n.d.), North Carolina, along with Pennsylvania, had the highest total number of anti-immigrant local ordinances proposed between 2005 and 2006. National-level analysis by Cornelius (2008) found that anti-immigrant/exclusionary policies were more likely in places where immigrants are physically isolated from native populations and newcomers play a small role in the local economy. Additionally, these places displayed conservative political cultures and prevailing Republican voting patterns. Complementary research by Ramakrishnan and Wong (this volume) discovered that restrictionist activities are linked to the partisan (Republican) composition of a locality and the intensity of local activity around national immigration reform as reflected in protests and rallies.

In North Carolina, local anti-immigrant initiatives are linked to places with dominant conservative cultures and Republican partisan orientation. Examples include Beaufort, Gaston, and Johnston counties. Immigrant settlement patterns and economic participation are also salient. In this regard, high levels of Latino immigration were found in nearby counties or municipalities but not in the locality attempting to pass the ordinance. In these instances, anti-immigrant political actions might be viewed as a preventative measure—in other words, as a way to keep out or discourage new, spillover Latino settlement. Alamance and Cabarrus counties, which sit on the edge of

Hispanic "hypergrowth" metropolitan regions, illustrate this strategy (Suro and Singer 2002).

The focus of our chapter is the city of Charlotte and surrounding Mecklenburg County, twin urban jurisdictions with both distinctive and shared government functions. In addition to Charlotte, Mecklenburg County contains six other municipal governments (map 9.1), all of which have struggled with regard to localized immigrant policy and ordinances. Their collective experiences demonstrate that neither pro-immigrant nor anti-immigrant positions are politically sustainable. As the balance of this chapter details, indecision about where to fall on the spectrum has resulted in tension, missteps, and contradictions as this new immigrant gateway has sought to localize immigration policy during a period of considerable political tension and rapid demographic adjustment.

Map 9.1 Mecklenburg County Municipalities

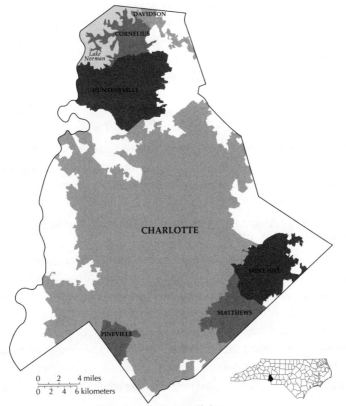

Cartography Lab, Department of Geography & Earth Sciences, UNC Charlotte.

Drawing from research that incorporates quantitative assessment of local and census-based data, content analysis of major print news media, and key informant interviews with over a dozen community leaders and advocates working in various capacities with Charlotte's Latino population, our analysis is framed by a four-phase typology. The phases are as follows:

- Phase I: "Welcome, amigos": incipient Latino immigration, early 1980s–early 1990s;

- Phase II: The Bank of America phenomenon: early immigration maturity, mid-1990s–2000;

- Phase III: "Honk if you hate Spanish": mature and sustained immigration, post 2001;

- Phase IV: Charlotte at the immigration crossroads: the present.

This framework is built upon the changing rate and composition of Latino immigration to the city and county, along with associated adjustments in community and government responses. Indeed, the speed and scale of Latino immigration is the most fundamental driver in the current turmoil and confusion surrounding where Charlotte can (should) be positioned along the anti- versus pro-immigrant continuum. Thus, shifts in the immigration stream have provoked critical changes in public discourse, accompanying public policy adjustments, and an increasing splintering of the private-public alliance. Though the corpus of this research is local, state-level policy and broader political processes have strongly affected the city and county ethos. And, in turn, the national debate and localized immigration activities in other states and regions inform and spur the process in Charlotte-Mecklenburg. We also incorporate these exogenous influences into our analysis.

PHASE I: "WELCOME, AMIGOS": INCIPIENT LATINO IMMIGRATION, EARLY 1980s–EARLY 1990s

In the late 1980s, Charlotte enjoyed unprecedented economic and population growth. There was a boosterish enthusiasm about Charlotte's emergence as the vanguard city for a contemporary "New South." The large and increasingly powerful banking and financial services cluster, anchored by Bank of America (formerly Nations Bank) and Wachovia (formerly First Union), actively rebuilt the city center with office towers and cultural icons. Rapid population expansion, primarily a function at this point of in-state and regional migration, sparked neighborhood revitalization and greenfield suburbanization across Mecklenburg County. In the midst of vigorous economic expansion, Latino laborers were recruited, formally and informally, to meet critical employment shortages. Most of the earliest Latino migrants were secondary immigrants drawn from other parts of the United States. During the 1980–1990 decade, the census recorded a modest 2,170-person increase in Hispanic Charlotteans. But, with a small base, this translated into a 70 percent jump in the Hispanic population.

Following the pioneer immigration model, the newcomers were primarily young men, many of whom occupied low-wage and low-skill jobs in employment sectors associated with city building, the construction trades in particular. Representing an invisible labor force, the newcomers toiled at job sites across the community and retreated to anonymous apartment complexes in the aging middle-ring suburbs during their free time. Their physical presence was concentrated in these areas, which were literally and figuratively far away from the more prosperous, high-profile parts of the city. Further contributing to the fledgling community's invisibility was a seasonal form of transnational commuting, with men returning to their homes (predominantly in Mexico) for an extended period over the winter months and reappearing again with the early spring upswing of construction-related opportunities.

Latino community leaders half-jokingly refer to this early immigration phase as the "welcome, amigos" period. Latino immigrant labor was lauded and much sought after by business interests. Stereotypes and mythmaking presented the immigrants as hardworking and uncomplaining. In Charlotte's free market–oriented business scene, immigrant Latinos were also viewed as cheaper than native workers. As such, there was both the perception and the reality that Hispanic labor was replacing black and white labor in certain building trades and industrial sectors.

The public policy realm was largely unaffected during this period of incipient Latino settlement and community building. The workforce was young, healthy, and required only minimal public services. The primary impacts of newcomers were focused on the North Carolina Department of Motor Vehicles, where driver's licenses are issued and automobiles are registered; on the Charlotte-Mecklenburg Police Department (CMPD), concerned about increasing rates of Hispanic victimization during this period; and on county-funded emergency medical facilities, provided by Carolinas HealthCare System (CHS), where sick and injured Latinos often sought health care. All three service providers were ill prepared to handle Spanish language requests for services. Additionally, the CMPD and CHS encountered fear and/or reluctance among their Latino service users to provide full disclosure of information and a limited or erroneous understanding of service practices. These culturally based challenges were particularly evidenced with international immigrants from rural Mexico, who were adjusting not only to life in the United States but also to life in an urban setting.

Although the Latino newcomers elicited some public complaints, largely because natives perceived that immigrants were straining public services and causing service funding shortfalls, community and government leaders were generally positive and articulated their support for the Latino newcomers. Overall, the growing numbers of multicultural immigrants were providing critical labor services and offered evidence of Charlotte's ascendancy as a "globalizing city."

One example of this broad public support is the Charlotte-Mecklenburg Police Department's International Relations Unit (IRU). The IRU was established in 1993 to meet the needs of non-English-speaking immigrants and to build trust and collaborative relationships with groups that distrusted or feared public safety officers. Following a community policing model, culturally and linguistically trained police officers were assigned to work exclusively with immigrant communities, offering assistance with service provision and settlement processes, as well as police services. Citizenship status was not a consideration. The IRU's success was measured in strong levels of immigrant support and customer service activity. In a 2006 countywide Latino Needs Assessment Study, the community identified the CMPD's International Relations Unit as a top-ranked public service program (UNC Charlotte Urban Institute 2006).

PHASE II: THE BANK OF AMERICA PHENOMENON: EARLY MATURITY, MID-1990s–2000

In the mid-1990s, Charlotte and Mecklenburg County experienced an accelerating rate of domestic and international Latino in-migration. U.S. Census Bureau estimates for this period, based on the 1990 population count, projected significant annual rates of population increase. These ranged from 12.3 percent in 1994–95 to 10.7 percent in 1998–99. Although these estimates were substantial, they severely undercounted the pace of growth. Consider that the 1999 estimate for Hispanics in Mecklenburg County was 17,651, while the 2000 census count was 44,871. Indeed, Latino community leaders recount that this inter-censal period coincides with the largest increase in new Latino residents to the community. Beyond the quantity of immigrants, the demographic characteristics of the newcomers were also changing. More women, families, and Central Americans were settling, as opposed to single men of Mexican origin. Direct international immigration was also widespread. Whereas formerly most migrants had relocated to Charlotte-Mecklenburg from other U.S. locations, a growing number of arrivals were coming directly from their countries of origin. Through channels of social and economic networking, North Carolina, and Charlotte specifically, had emerged as a key destination for Hispanic immigrants coming from Mexico and Central America.

Why Charlotte? Why the early to mid-1990s? Our interviews in the community point to the crucial role that the construction of the Bank of America headquarters tower played. This building, located in the city's business core, was completed in 1993. The general contractor for the construction project was based in Houston, Texas. Beyond bringing project managers, the manager recruited subcontractors and tradespeople from Texas, where Latinos were a central component of the building trades. While up on the sky-high scaffolding, Latino laborers were treated to a panoramic view of the city's transitioning landscape. It was apparent that this was a place where there was work in the construction, landscaping, personal services, and processing trades, all anxious for labor. Sending word back to friends and colleagues in Texas and to families and communities in Mexico, these workers forged the first substantive link in the Charlotte-Mecklenburg migration chain.

As friends and families began to join the pioneering men, processes of household formation and community building began to mature, and what had been more of a sojourner community was becoming a permanent one. Indeed, the incipient suburban settlement processes were reinforced and expanded as Latino settlement continued to focus on the multifamily apartment complexes in the aging and middle-ring suburbs. The Eastside and Southwest sections of Charlotte offered abundant, well-maintained, low-cost housing stock, plus vacant business space. These geographies also provided proximity to job sites. The combination of incipient social networks and locational advantages steered the new immigrant streams to these subgeographies.

The growing number of Latinos, enhanced by larger numbers of families and female immigrants, began to remake social space and fostered Latino place-making processes. The earlier invisible Latino immigrant moved into the private and public realms. Small-scale entrepreneurship revitalized declining strip malls and filled empty spaces along suburban arterial roadways. Between 1997 and 2002, the number of Hispanic-owned businesses in Charlotte grew by 195 percent, from 570 to 1,681 (U.S. Census Bureau 2002).

The overwhelming majority were small, with no paid employees. Vibrant signage in Spanish attracted Latino shoppers. Public parks and soccer fields increasingly became destinations for the newcomers.

This visible and rapidly changing presence of Latino immigrants in Charlotte and Mecklenburg County triggered a challenge to the equilibrium of the post-racist "New South" image. For a community that boasted it had moved past class constructs and prejudice based on race, the seemingly "overnight" arrival of Latinos occupying and laying claim to community spaces was powerful. Public discourse began to revolve around the newcomers' lack of assimilation and sensitivity to local customs and traditions, as well as the down-market appearance and perceived lack of safety in neighborhoods where Latinos were settling. Concurrently, tensions between Latinos and African-American communities were beginning to surface. At the root of this foreboding lay economic competition.

Within the Charlotte business community, the penetration of Latino labor in selected employment sectors deepened. As a consequence, certain construction trades and landscaping activities were increasingly dominated by Hispanic workers. In a parallel fashion, Hispanic women were rapidly moving to housekeeping, food service, and personal service sectors.

Despite the experiences of the late 1980s, public and nonprofit service providers remained unprepared for the expansive growth in demand for education, health care, and social service provision. Language and cultural differences, as well as the increased demand for scarce resources, led service providers into reactive response modes. Public service organizations affected during the first wave of settlement continued to be on the front line of service needs. The early success of the International Relations Unit within the Police Department enabled public safety services to expand and respond effectively to an extended set of immigrant needs. However, the state-run Department of Motor Vehicles' auto registration and driver-licensing operations were overwhelmed and received widespread public criticism. In contrast to the municipal police department, the state had failed to hire adequate staff and resisted printing Spanish language materials. Customer service for all clients suffered as a result.

The Carolinas HealthCare System also responded directly to their new Latino users in this period. CHS recruited bilingual staff, trained medical and support staff in culturally sensitive practices, translated materials and educational information, and redeployed services for targeted programs and service delivery. Although these initiatives have not always been successful and there is clear recognition that similar efforts need to be implemented more deeply and broadly across the system, the metrics for measuring health care delivery to Latinos in Mecklenburg County are generally positive.

Paralleling the efforts of CHS, the Charlotte-Mecklenburg Schools (CMS) was similarly proactive in addressing the needs of a rapidly expanding Latino student population. In the 1995–96 school year, Hispanic students represented 1.9 percent of CMS enrollment. By 2000, this group had grown to 4.4 percent. Spanish language and cultural awareness initiatives, combined with health care and other community services, were launched concomitant with the rapid rise in the number of immigrant students across the school system. Public backlash against providing specialized services to Latino children was insignificant. CMS had traditionally embraced multicultural education, and at this stage a renewed focus on Spanish language and cultural awareness was viewed as an extension of this education approach.

PHASE III: "HONK IF YOU HATE SPANISH": MATURE AND SUSTAINED IMMIGRATION, POST 2001

As Charlotte and Mecklenburg County moved into the twenty-first century, the expansion of the regional economy and bustling urban growth and redevelopment continued unabated. Both locales were experiencing unprecedented increases in income and population levels. Prosperity, in turn, made the community an even stronger destination magnet for Latino immigrants. The 2000 population census counted 44,871 Hispanic residents in Mecklenburg County and 39,800 in Charlotte. Four years later, census estimates of Hispanic residents had jumped to 66,043 and 58,789, respectively. Owing to the census undercount, community leaders suggest that the real Latino population in Mecklenburg County in 2004 was closer to between 75,000 and 85,000 (Smith and Furuseth 2006).

While the rate of immigration to Charlotte-Mecklenburg and the absolute size of the immigrant population continued to pressure service providers to keep pace with growing demand, growth-related economic sectors, especially construction and services, absorbed new Latino labor with ease. In the robust economic climate of the early 2000s, and pre-9/11, checks for legal documentation were only casually enforced, and when they were an impediment to employment, undocumented workers had other job options.

Following a decade of maturing immigration streams, the role and importance of Latinos in Charlotte's and the regional economy were unambiguous. By 2004, the economic impact of Latinos on the Charlotte metropolitan region was estimated to be $1.9 billion and included the creation of 16,900 new jobs (Kasarda and Johnson 2006). Between 1997 and 2002, the number of Hispanic business owners in the metro area jumped from 1,372 to 3,013, with one-third of these entrepreneurs of Mexican origin (U.S. Census Bureau 2002). On the city landscape, Eastside Charlotte and Southwest Charlotte were increasingly imprinted with Latino images, place-making activities, and ethnically specific services and entrepreneurial enterprise. At least outwardly, the Eastside in particular was beginning to show the hallmarks of an enclave.

Concurrently, the local communications media were "discovering" Charlotte-Mecklenburg's Latino immigrant residents and increasing their coverage of Latino and immigrant-themed stories. Although some news coverage was positive and included a focus on the role of Latinos in the booming local economy and their cultural contributions to the community, an analysis of print media content revealed that immigration-related challenges and crime-themed stories were the most frequent topics and that a majority of stories reflected negatively on the Latino newcomers (Furuseth, Smith, and Cook 2007).

At the state level, the national political debate around the impact of immigrants increasingly politicized policy making. In 2002, a state-level version of the DREAM Act,[2] which would offer in-state tuition at state-supported institutions of higher education for children of undocumented immigrants in North Carolina, was introduced in the legislature, but it was never moved to a vote. Over the following six years, subsequent proposals met the same fate or failed to find a sponsor. The Republican leadership in Raleigh assailed illegal immigration and warned that North Carolina was at risk of being overrun by dangerous, welfare-dependent aliens.[3] Limited in their options by federal preemption, the minority Republicans and allied conservative Democrats passed highly restrictive rules for obtaining driver's licenses and registering automobiles in North Carolina. In February 2004, the Department of Motor Vehicles was directed by legislative act to stop accepting most international birth certificates and identification cards (*matrículas consulares*) issued by the

---

2. The Development, Relief, and Education for Alien Minors (DREAM) Act has been pending in Congress since 2001. The legislation would permit states to offer in-state tuition rates to undocumented students who have lived in the United States for five years and are under the age of twenty-one. It would repeal a federal provision that discourages states from providing in-state tuition based upon immigration status. It also provides students who have grown up in the United States greater opportunity to apply for citizenship. The DREAM Act was most recently defeated in 2007.

3. See, for example, Americans for Legal Immigration 2006.

Mexican federal government as proper documentation for driver's licenses. At the time, community leaders and safety specialists pointed out that the change in the law would not stop Latino drivers. Rather, it translated into more untested drivers behind the wheel and more uninsured cars on the highways. Republican attempts to take stronger, direct punitive actions aimed at undocumented Latinos were diverted to dead-end committees by the Democratic leadership in the legislature. Still, the new licensing rules played out with the anticipated consequences.

The construction of a "Latino menace" as a theme in state-level politics reactivated the "Old South" political strategy built around racism and nativist ideology. The late Senator Jesse Helms perfected this brand of politics, and it earned him thirty years in the U.S. Senate. During his career, Helms built a grassroots political organization that spread this brand of politics across the state into local GOP structures. And indeed, before his death in 2008, Helms publicly railed against Latino immigrants, comparing them to burglars breaking into your house and taking up residence (Morrill 2005). At the local level, perspectives were more balanced but still undoubtedly influenced by state and national viewpoints.

The political terrain of Charlotte-Mecklenburg is dynamic and actively contested between Republicans and Democrats. Within the GOP, the ideologically right wing controls the party leadership, but business-oriented Republicans tend to represent the party in elected positions. As Latino immigration became more visible and place-identifiable, local GOP campaigns have taken up state and national themes. Congresswoman Sue Myrick (R), representing North Carolina's 9th Congressional District, centered in Mecklenburg County, has served as a conduit for infusing national anti-immigration policies and discourse into the local scene. Over the past decade, Myrick has emerged as a congressional leader against immigration reform. She has authored a series of anti-immigrant proposals, including legislation to summarily deport undocumented immigrants convicted of drunk driving, impose $10,000 fines on employers for hiring undocumented workers, and force local police to check the immigration status of persons during normal policing activities (Funk 2005). Myrick was a strong advocate for building ICE 287(g) partnerships across the region as a way to identify and remove "terrorists" and "criminals" from the community (Myrick 2008).

Representative Myrick's highly visible leadership has complemented and encouraged localized political action on immigration. Ultimately, the combination of leadership from Raleigh and from Washington, in concert with local activism, precipitated the unsuccessful attempts to pass restrictionist local ordinances in two small Mecklenburg County towns (Mint Hill and Pineville) and fostered persistent anti-immigrant debate within the Mecklenburg County Commission. Conservative Republican Commissioner Bill James, for example, has offered a string of unsuccessful proposals to limit immigrant access to public facilities and services in the county. At one point James proposed that users of county facilities provide proof of citizenship or documented status before admittance.

Although localized immigration actions have been overwhelmingly unsuccessful, two initiatives stand out for their impact and their success. In 2002, County Sheriff Jim Pendergraph, a conservative Democrat and ally of Representative Sue Myrick, joined the ICE 287(g) program.[4] The Sheriff's Office boasted that it was the only local or state agency in North Carolina to participate in the program and the only Sheriff's Office to check the immigration status of every arrestee. Subsequent efforts to pressure the Charlotte-Mecklenburg Police Department to check for undocumented status in the course of routine policing actions were rebuffed. Sheriff's Office data compiled in 2006 indicate that 15 percent of the Mecklenburg County jail population were "illegal immigrants who are accused of committing a crime other than immigration violation" (Mayor's Immigration Study Commission 2007). But community groups and others offer that most of the immigrants arrested and deported under the county's program are not violent criminals, but rather are charged with DWI, traffic, and petty crimes (HELP 2008; Kirkpatrick 2008; Ovaska 2008).

The county's participation in the 287(g) program has been politically controversial. Based on his leadership and experience, Sheriff Pendergraph was recruited to Washington as ICE's first executive director for state and local coordination. He later resigned. The selection of a new sheriff by the Democratic Party leaders resulted in a racially charged contest in which the future of the 287(g) program was challenged. Ultimately, a white deputy sheriff and 287(g) supporter was chosen over an African-American candidate who opposed 287(g). Commissioner James and other advocates for localized anti-immigrant policies view Mecklenburg County's leadership in this program as a small victory. However, this "victory" has not led to further restrictions or a significant reduction in new immigration to the community, which is a secondary goal of the program. Rather, Latino immigrants, at risk

---

4. For more on 287(g) agreements, see the chapters by Waslin and by Rodríguez, Chishti, and, Nortman, this volume.

of arrest and deportation, have changed their lifestyle and behaviors, becoming more clandestine or "going underground."

The second highly visible localized initiative was Charlotte Mayor Pat McCrory's Immigration Study Commission. McCrory, a Republican, appointed the Commission in 2005. Its purpose was to help "the Charlotte community and region have a better understanding of the growing immigration issues facing the community and nation." Earlier, President George W. Bush had appointed McCrory to the Homeland Security Advisory Council (HSAC). McCrory offered that his exposure to border issues and illegal immigrant flows in San Diego, California, which he had gained as a member of HSAC, prompted his decision to establish the Commission.[5]

The 28-person Commission was split between immigrant critics and advocates. Their final report contained four recommendations, with minority dissenting opinions. The contentious findings centered around anti- and pro-immigrant perspectives. Opponents to immigration advocated for aggressive expansion of 287(g)-type checks for immigration status by all local police and for more local 287(g) funding to augment federal resources. Another recommendation urged local support for federal legislation to make first-time DWI offenses deportable offenses for illegal immigrants. In contrast, the advocacy faction proposed local lobbying for the creation of a program to enable immigrant workers who have contributed to the U.S. economy through employment to earn a pathway to lawful status. And they continued to advocate for a North Carolina DREAM Act.

The Commission presented its recommendations to the public but included no implementation strategy. Anti-immigrant leaders in the community immediately threw their support behind the expanded 287(g) and deportation policy recommendations. Immigrant advocates, meanwhile, applauded the path to citizenship proposal and in-state tuition for undocumented North Carolina students, but they were not in a position to affect either proposal, both of which required federal and state-level support. Ultimately no localized action resulted. On a broader level, however, the Commission did legitimize and add to the public discourse language that

---

5. In May 2008, Mayor McCrory was chosen as the Republican candidate for governor. Candidate McCrory identified enforcing laws to control illegal immigration as a top issue. He proposed new state funding to expand 287(g) throughout the state, eliminating state benefits to illegal immigrants, and punishing companies that hire illegal immigrants with loss of eligibility to state contracts (http://www.patmccrory.com/docs/ issue/Policy-Statement-Illegal-Immigrants). McCrory was defeated in the November 2008 election.

positioned Latino immigration as threatening to the community. During their deliberations, Commission members worked to identify areas or policies where immigration impacts could be localized (Mayor's Immigration Study Commission 2007).

In sharp contrast with traditional public–private sector cooperation, the Charlotte-Mecklenburg corporate community displayed little interest in targeting undocumented immigrants or designing strategies to punish or remove them from the area. The Charlotte Chamber of Commerce, a powerful agent in local policy making and political processes, ignored the efforts to localize the enforcement of federal immigration rules. Rather, the Chamber staff has worked to organize and recruit Latino entrepreneurs into the Chamber structure. Moreover, the Charlotte Chamber identifies the expansion of bilingual skills among the labor force and the recruitment of new businesses that cater to Latino customers as business success stories. Large, locally based financial institutions—notably, Bank of America and Wachovia—have aggressively marketed products and services to the Latino community and appointed Hispanic professionals to highly visible leadership positions at the local level.[6] Both banks have earned public rebukes and, in some cases, lost public sector accounts because of their perceived sympathetic and pro-immigrant business practices (see, for example, Rothacker and George 2007).

While Charlotte-Mecklenburg's business community's lack of interest in pursuing localized anti-immigrant actions may be viewed as enlightened self-interest, the disconnect between private interests and public policy on the issue is very important. Traditionally, an alliance between business interests and local government has been a quintessential element of this community context. Public policies and financial decision making are crafted with input and agreement from the business leadership. The corporate community's unwillingness to endorse localized anti-immigrant themes reflects a growing awareness that Charlotte-Mecklenburg's future competitiveness is linked to internationalization of the workforce and success in national and global markets. Nativist political trends and the accompanying policy directions are counterintuitive to economic growth and directly erode the city's positionality as a *New* South city with a promising and lucrative globalized future.

---

6. On October 3, 2008, San Francisco–based Wells Fargo Bank bought Wachovia Corporation. Rebranding of the Charlotte operations is still in progress. Corporate communications and activities signal no change in the bank's active pursuit of expanding markets to local and statewide Latino populations.

PHASE IV: CHARLOTTE AT THE IMMIGRATION CROSSROADS: CURRENT PERIOD

Following its fifteen-year transition from a community that welcomed Latino newcomers as hardworking, trailblazing laborers to one in which Latino and Hispanic have become increasingly synonymous with illegal immigrant, Charlotte-Mecklenburg finds itself today at an immigration crossroads. Both perspectives vie to shape public discourse as well as concrete policy initiatives. There is recognition, especially on the part of local business leadership, that an anti-immigrant stance is not good for a city determined to hold on to and permanently entrench its hard-won globalizing status.[7] But there are also growing and valid concerns about the realities and challenges for service providers and everyday citizens as the migration stream to the city continues to expand and mature.

Even in the midst of increasing anti-immigrant rhetoric and localized policy attempts, the notion of Latino migrants as a potentially temporary phenomenon is unrealistic. Hispanic newcomers—native and foreign born, documented and undocumented—are now visible and permanent members of Charlotte's workplaces, neighborhoods, churches, schools, and citizenry. Indeed, census data record that 27 percent of Charlotte's Hispanic residents were born in North Carolina. Responses and policies that were formulated through the lens of reaction need to be reconsidered. Traditional, preexisting service structures and policy frameworks must be reconfigured.

The weight of this responsibility and Charlotte-Mecklenburg's reluctance to embrace this reality were evidenced in the 2008 election cycle. Though immigration was a powerful theme in the state-level campaigns, with both Democratic and Republican Senate and gubernatorial candidates aspiring to the most extreme anti-immigrant positions, no local candidate conveyed either a pro- or anti-immigrant message.[8] And in terms of services, although some agencies work to solidify their commitment to Latino newcomers by enhancing the depth and range of their service (such as Carolinas HealthCare System), others, like the Sheriff's Office, working through its ICE 287(g) enforcement, pursue actions that discourage immigrant arrival or promote a

---

7. For a similar discussion of Phoenix, Arizona, and Vancouver, Canada, see Provine, this volume.
8. "AS MANY AS 500,000 ILLEGAL ALIENS FROM ALL OVER THE WORLD LIVING IN NORTH CAROLINA," screams an anti–Kay Hagan flyer distributed to Mecklenburg residents by the Washington, DC–based Freedom's Watch. The flyer also notes, "Kay Hagan AGAINST making it easier to find, track, and kick out violent illegal immigrants."

reconsideration of settlement. It should be added that following the recent hiring of a new Charlotte-Mecklenburg police chief, the once-lauded IRU is slated to be disbanded as a cost-saving measure.

Charlotte's ambiguous stance on the immigration issue translates into confusion and disengagement among the immigrants themselves. In interviews with local Latino outreach workers, we heard their concerns about a growing number of clients who were altering their daily routines to become less visible, less engaged, and less likely to access services. There is escalating fear of encountering hostility, aggressive enforcement of immigration status, or being reported to authorities. Actions like the recent ICE raids on House of Raeford poultry plants in South Carolina are widely reported in the local English and Spanish media. The uptick in federal immigration enforcement follows the *Charlotte Observer*'s extensive coverage of labor abuses in that company's plant, further confusing community members about where Charlotte falls on the pro- versus anti-immigrant spectrum (Hall, Alexander, and Ordóñez 2008; Alexander and Ordóñez 2008).

In many ways, Charlotte-Mecklenburg's immigrant advocates and Latino newcomers seem to be waiting to see which path political, business, and community leadership will follow. In the absence of leadership, the city's course is heavily influenced by exogenous forces, particularly those at work at the state and national levels. The national economy is certainly one of those factors. Prior to the 2008 economic crisis, Hispanic Charlotteans were increasingly represented among home owners, bank account holders, public school enrollees, and new business owners and entrepreneurs—the classic channels and hallmarks of integration and assimilation.

It is too soon to tell whether the convergence of economic downturn and anti-immigrant sentiment will translate into altered migration decisions. Preliminary evidence does suggest, however, a slowing in Latino settlement. Specifically, after years of steady and marked growth, the pace of Latino enrollment in the Charlotte-Mecklenburg schools eased in the fall of 2008. The 6 percent increase seen between fall 2007 and fall 2008 was the smallest in over eight years (Frazier 2008). In addressing the reasons for the drop-off, school administrators and Latino advocates speculated that the county's tougher enforcement of immigration laws might play a minor role. More importantly, they offered a sharp decline in economic growth, especially in sectors that most directly affect the Latino labor market (construction and services). "In large part, it's the economy," the head of planning and placement noted. "Jobs drive families coming into the area, which of course drives enrollment gains.

Certainly [Hispanics] can be hit just as badly as any other [group] with the slowdown in the economy" (Frazier 2008). The executive director of the Latin American Coalition was even more specific. "Right now people are spending less on landscaping. There's less construction going on. People are moving back [to their home countries] or to other parts of the country" (Frazier 2008).

While officials and community advocates highlight economic forces, reader responses to the *Charlotte Observer*'s coverage suggest that immigrant foes assign far greater credit to aggressive immigrant prosecution activities and policies. As one letter writer commented in response to the paper's school enrollment story, "If you are not here legally, move on. GO drain the system resources of your HOME country" (Frazier 2008).

CONCLUSIONS

As a preemerging immigrant gateway, Charlotte-Mecklenburg lacks a long-standing history of welcoming immigrants and aligning service structures and policy frameworks to meet their settlement and integration needs. Nor in the context of the scale and speed of this growth has Charlotte-Mecklenburg had time to thoughtfully consider "best practice" approaches. Accordingly, the various responses of government, nonprofit, and private sector service-providing agencies have to date been largely reactive, not proactive. This reactive approach, particularly in the absence of strong local leadership, leaves the city open to spillover impacts from the national and state-level debates that shape policy making and actions at the local level.

In this context, even after more than two decades of Hispanic immigrant growth, Charlotte continues to struggle to understand immigrant processes and their long-term impacts. This is made even more complicated when framed by a growing anti-immigrant, anti-Latino discourse, which forces uncomfortable rethinking about what it really means to be a globalizing New South city. Without its Latino immigrants, Charlotte quite simply would not be the city it is today, and its view from the crossroads would be far less promising.

WORKS CITED

Alexander, Ames, and Franco Ordoñez. 2008. "More than 300 Arrested in S.C. Raid at Poultry Plant," *Charlotte Observer*, October 8.

Americans for Legal Immigration. 2006. "NC Republican Candidates Make Fighting Illegal Immigration Central Issue!" http://www.alipac.us/article1654.html.

Cornelius, Wayne A. 2008. "Welcome and Introductory Comments." Paper presented at "State and Local Immigration Policy in the U.S.: An Interdisciplinary Workshop," University of California, San Diego, May 9.

Frazier, Eric. 2008. "Increase in Latino Student Slowing," *Charlotte Observer*, September 26.

Funk, Tim. 2005. "Myrick Introduces Two Immigration Bills," *Charlotte Observer*, September 15.

Furuseth, Owen J., Heather A. Smith, and David B. Cook. 2007. "Discovering Charlotte's Latino Community: Coverage and Representations in the Local Print Media." Paper presented at the meeting of the Southeastern Division of the Association of American Geographers, Charleston, SC, November 19.

Hall, Kerry, Ames Alexander, and Franco Ordoñez. 2008. "The Cruelest Cuts," *Charlotte Observer*, February 10.

HELP (Helping Empower Local People). 2008. "Hola Charlotte! Latino Civic Engagement in Charlotte-Mecklenburg and the Impact of Immigration in Charlotte." Charlotte, NC: HELP.

Kasarda, John D., and James H. Johnson, Jr. 2006. "The Economic Impact of the Hispanic Population on the State of North Carolina." Chapel Hill, NC: Frank Hawkins Kenan Institute of Private Enterprise, Kenan-Flagler Business School, University of North Carolina at Chapel Hill.

Kirkpatrick, Christopher D. 2008. "New Tool Speeds ID of N.C. Illegal Immigrants," *Charlotte Observer*, November 24.

Mayor's Immigration Study Commission. 2007. "Immigration: Legal and Illegal, Local Perspective–Charlotte, NC," January.

Morrill, Jim. 2005. "Helms Reflects on the Past, Present, and Future," *Charlotte Observer*, August 31.

Myrick, Sue. 2008. "Hot Topics: Immigration." http://myrick.house.gov/hot_topics_immigration_issues.shtml.

Nguyen, Mai Thi. n.d. "Anti-Immigrant Ordinances in North Carolina: Consequences on Local Communities and Governance." Manuscript. Chapel Hill, NC: Department of City and Regional Planning, University of North Carolina at Chapel Hill.

Ovaska, Sarah. 2008. "DWIs Ensnare Many Illegal Immigrants, Inmates Slated for Deportation," *News and Observer*, September 18.

Rothacker, Rick, and Jefferson George. 2007. "Gaston Spurns Bank Deal over Card: County Board Unhappy Illegal Immigrants Can Obtain Credit from BoA," *Charlotte Observer*, April 14.

Singer, Audrey. 2008. "Twenty-First-Century Gateways: An Introduction." In *Twenty-First-Century Gateways: Immigrant Incorporation in Suburban America*, ed. Audrey Singer, Susan W. Hardwick, and Caroline B. Brettell. Washington, DC: Brookings Institution Press.

Singer, Audrey, Susan W. Hardwick, and Caroline B. Brettell, eds. 2008. *Twenty-First-Century Gateways: Immigrant Incorporation in Suburban America*. Washington, DC: Brookings Institution Press.

Smith, Heather A., and Owen J. Furuseth. 2006. "Making Real the Mythical Latino Community in Charlotte, North Carolina," In *Latinos in the New South: Transformations of Place*, ed. Heather A. Smith and Owen J. Furuseth. London: Ashgate.

———. 2008. "The 'Nuevo South': Latino Place Making and Community Building in the Middle-ring Suburbs of Charlotte." In *Twenty-First-Century Gateways: Immigrant Incorporation in Suburban America*, ed. Audrey Singer, Susan W. Hardwick, and Caroline B. Brettell. Washington, DC: Brookings Institution Press.

Smith, Heather A., and William Graves. 2005. "Gentrification as Corporate Growth Strategy: The Strange Case of Charlotte, North Carolina and the Bank of America," *Journal of Urban Affairs* 27, no. 4: 403–18.

Suro, Roberto, and Audrey Singer. 2002. "Latino Growth in Metropolitan America: Changing Patterns, New Locations." Survey Series, Census 2000. Washington, DC: Center on Urban and Metropolitan Policy and Pew Hispanic Center, July.

UNC Charlotte Urban Institute. 2006. "Mecklenburg County Latino Community Needs Assessment Report." Charlotte, NC.

U.S. Census Bureau. 2002. "Hispanic-Owned Firms: 2002." 2002 Economic Census, Survey of Business Owners, Company Statistics Series.

Winders, Jamie. 2005. "Changing Politics of Race and Region: Latino Migration to the U.S. South," *Progress in Human Geography* 29, no. 6: 683–99.

10 Growing Pains: Local Response to Recent Immigrant Settlement in Suburban Washington, DC

JILL H. WILSON, AUDREY SINGER, AND BROOKE DERENZIS

In 2007, Congress failed for the second time in two years to pass comprehensive immigration laws. Many states and localities across the country have responded to the lack of federal action by proposing and often passing legislation that attempts to control immigration locally. Virginia has been at the vanguard in the number of pieces of legislation introduced, the majority of which are designed to be restrictive of immigrants, particularly unauthorized immigrants (Migration Policy Institute 2007). However, because animosity toward unauthorized immigrants tends to be localized, few of the state bills have made it into law. Indeed, in preceding years, two high-profile Virginia political races were lost by candidates that campaigned with a hard-line approach toward immigration: Republican Jerry Kilgore lost the governor's seat to Tim Kaine in 2005, and in his 2006 Senate reelection bid, George Allen narrowly lost to Democrat James Webb.

By contrast, local measures have had some success, with Prince William County—an outer suburb of the nation's capital—emerging as an important focal point. Though there have been anti-immigrant flare-ups across the Washington region, usually around day labor issues (Price and Singer 2008), a sense of urgency developed in Prince William County to "do something" to control what county residents perceived as an invasion of

We are grateful to the public and private individuals we consulted during this project. We appreciate their frankness and their desire to have Prince William's story told. Our thanks also go to Roberto Suro, Cristina Rodríguez, Marie Price, Caroline Brettell, Alan Berube, and the staff of the Greater Washington Research at Brookings, who reviewed earlier drafts of this chapter.

unauthorized immigrants (Kumar 2008). Starting with a December 2006 directive that mandated county staff to calculate the total cost of providing county services to unauthorized immigrants, the Prince William Board of County Supervisors has repeatedly introduced and revised restrictive policies aimed at the unauthorized population. The campaign for the November 2007 Board of Supervisors elections produced an outpouring of anti–illegal immigrant rhetoric and intense pressuring of candidates for local offices to take a stand against illegal immigration. County leaders portrayed the presence of unauthorized immigrants as an affront to the rule of law and a public safety issue. "What part of illegal don't you understand?" became a slogan for those running for office. Together, officials and residents used legal status to frame their words and actions against immigrants. In July 2007 the Board of Supervisors unanimously passed a resolution that ordered local police to check the residency status of those in violation of county or state law if there was "probable cause" to believe they were present illegally. It also required county staff to deny certain public benefits to persons unable to prove legal residency. Over the course of ten months, the policy underwent revisions that resulted in a more moderate enforcement strategy, but the initial crackdown had immediate and lasting effects.

There were local precedents for restrictive policies. In August 2005, the nearby town of Herndon, Virginia (Fairfax County) attracted national attention when it approved a publicly funded day labor center, over protests by many residents. Less than a year later, Herndon voters ousted the mayor and council members who supported the day labor center and elected new leaders who shut it down. In December 2005, Manassas, an independent city within the geographic boundary of Prince William County, passed an ordinance restricting the definition of "family" as a way to address residential overcrowding among immigrants. A month later, the ordinance was repealed under pressure from the ACLU and residents.

Though the wave of restrictive policy making on immigration in Prince William seemed to have emerged with little forewarning, the concerns that lay behind it had been building among residents over a long period marked by intense demographic change. The Washington region experienced an economic and population boom in the 1990s and early 2000s. Faced with skyrocketing home prices, longer-term residents and newcomers alike settled farther out, drawn by affordable homes, good schools, and safe neighborhoods. During the past several decades, the region has grown rapidly and now encompasses twenty-two local jurisdictions in Maryland, Virginia, and West Virginia, as well as the District of Columbia (see map 10.1).[1]

Map 10.1 Washington, DC Metro Area

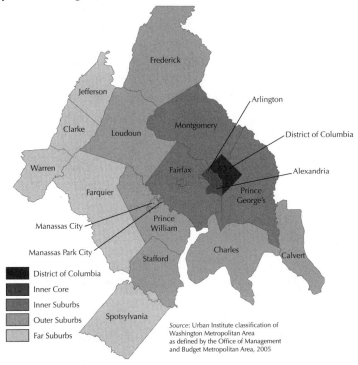

Source: Urban Institute classification of Washington Metropolitan Area as defined by the Office of Management and Budget Metropolitan Area, 2005

Simultaneously, in the last three and a half decades, the Washington metro area has emerged as a major immigrant gateway. Many know the region as a cosmopolitan place that prides itself on racial and ethnic diversity, a thriving knowledge-based economy, and relative affluence. As such, the Washington region generally has been characterized as a welcoming place for immigrants and refugees from nearly every country in the world. The region's

---

1. We use "Washington region," "Washington metro," and "Washington area" interchangeably to refer to the federal government's 2007 definition of the Washington, DC, metropolitan area. For analytical purposes, we aggregate the twenty-two jurisdictions into five areas: the District of Columbia, the inner core, inner suburbs, outer suburbs, and far suburbs (see map 10.1). Although the cities of Manassas and Manassas Park are geographically surrounded by Prince William County, our analysis treats them separately from the county since they are independent municipalities.

one million immigrants now make up a fifth of a population that was almost completely native-born in 1970. Among all metropolitan areas in the United States, Washington now ranks seventh for its number of immigrants.

In this chapter we describe the metamorphosis of Prince William County within this rapidly transforming metropolitan area. Prince William County's policy is recognized as one of the most restrictive enforcement strategies regionally and nationally, and it has attracted much national and local media attention. Mainstream media have tended to focus on the opposing extremes of the debate, but most residents feel caught somewhere in the middle, overwhelmed by the growth and change happening around them and conflicted about how to respond to the challenges they present.[2] What factors hurtled Prince William County to the front lines of local immigration battles within the region and across the nation? This chapter examines how population growth, demographic change, and economic development combined with politics, grassroots activism, and media attention to produce Prince William's very restrictive immigration policy.

FINDINGS

The Washington metro area has experienced high population growth over the past twenty-five years, fueled by its burgeoning job market. Between 1980 and 2006, when the United States grew by 32 percent, the metro area's total population increased by 56 percent. By 2005 the Washington area had the fourth-largest number of jobs and the eighth-largest population of all metro areas in the nation.[3]

Population growth has not been even across the region, and Washington, like other fast-growing immigrant gateways, has seen higher growth rates

---

2. We followed events in Prince William County over the course of a year. We reviewed local and national media coverage. We witnessed Board of County Supervisor meetings, sometimes by video provided by 9500Liberty and sometimes by live audio via the Board's Web site. We reviewed documents from the Board of County Supervisors, the Police Department, and the County Executive's office regarding county immigration policies. We toured the county, especially neighborhoods with the highest immigrant growth. We interviewed a select group of residents, members of community-based organizations, business and community leaders, and county officials from the Board of Supervisors, the Police Department, Neighborhood Services, and the school district.

3. Job ranking from Bureau of Economic Analysis 2005 Wage and Salary Employment. Population ranking from Population Division, U.S. Census Bureau, "Table 5. Estimates of Population Change for Metropolitan Statistical Areas and Rankings: July 1, 2005 to July 1, 2006," www.census.gov/population/www/estimates/metro_general/2006 /CBSA-EST2006-05.xls.

in the suburbs. The most striking changes have occurred in the outer sub-urbs.[4] While the total population in the outer suburbs increased 150 percent between 1980 and 2006, the immigrant population grew more than fourteen-fold (table 10.1). The foreign-born share of the population increased dramati-cally in the outer suburbs—from 2.6 percent in 1980 to 7.3 percent in 2000 to 14.2 percent in 2006, the largest gain in the region.[5]

Explosive Growth and Change in Prince William County

Prince William was once perceived as a somewhat rural, southern, small-town county. Though bedroom communities for Washington's commuters started to crop up there after World War II, Prince William's status as a cos-mopolitan suburb of Washington is much more recent. Growth in the county has been particularly strong since 2000. With gains of over 11,000 residents each year, annual population increases from 2000 to 2005 were nearly double the annual average for the 1990s, and the county population in 2006 num-bered over 357,000.[6]

Prince William's swift growth was accompanied by an increase in racial and ethnic diversity.[7] The non-Hispanic white share of the county's popula-tion fell from 87 percent in 1980 to 52 percent in 2006. Hispanics accounted for 31 percent of Prince William County's total population growth over this period, outpacing both whites (28 percent) and blacks (25 percent). While Hispanics made up only 2 percent of the county's population in 1980, by 2006 they accounted for 19 percent (figure 10.1).[8]

---

4. The analysis in this paragraph does not include Manassas and Manassas Park because 2006 data are not available for them.
5. We use "foreign born" and "immigrant" interchangeably to refer to anyone born out-side the United States who was not a U.S. citizen at birth. This population includes naturalized citizens, legal permanent residents, temporary migrants, refugees, asylum seekers, and, to the extent to which they are counted, unauthorized immigrants.
6. Calculations based on Population Estimates data from Census Bureau, available at factfinder.census.gov.
7. While race/ethnicity, nativity, and birthplace are separate characteristics, we present data on all three categories because they are often undifferentiated in the public's view. In Prince William County, half of all immigrants are Hispanic, compared to only one-third of the metropolitan area's immigrants. Likewise, immigrants from Latin America represent 54 percent of the county's foreign-born population, compared to 39 percent in the Washington metro area. At the same time, the proportion of Hispanics in Prince William County who are foreign born is 58 percent, statistically the same as that for the Washington metro area.
8. Data from 1980, 1990, and 2000 decennial censuses and the 2006 American Com-munity Survey.

Table 10.1 Foreign-born Population in the Washington Metro Area, by Jurisdiction, 1980–2006

	Foreign-born Population				Percent Change			
	1980	1990	2000	2006	1980–90	1990–2000	2000–2006	1980–2006
District of Columbia	40,559	58,887	73,561	73,820	45.2	24.9	0.4	82.0
Inner Core	33,205	54,514	85,293	78,619	64.2	56.5	-7.8	136.8
Arlington County, VA	22,337	36,516	52,693	46,614	63.5	44.3	-11.5	108.7
Alexandria city, VA	10,868	17,998	32,600	32,005	65.6	81.1	-1.8	194.5
Inner Suburbs[a]	164,273	338,481	581,154	703,416	106.0	71.7	21.0	328.2
Montgomery County, MD	70,128	141,166	232,996	273,227	101.3	65.1	17.3	289.6
Prince George's County, MD	40,036	69,809	110,481	159,468	74.4	58.3	44.3	298.3
Fairfax County, VA	54,109	127,506	237,677	270,721	135.6	86.4	13.9	400.3
Fairfax city, VA	1,461	2,900	5,451	NA	98.5	88.0	NA	NA
Falls Church city, VA	907	1,008	1,667	NA	11.1	65.4	NA	NA
Outer Suburbs[b]	12,000	26,162	67,907	170,771	118.0	159.6	151.5	1323.1
Loudoun County, VA	1,840	4,880	19,116	56,378	165.2	291.7	194.9	2964.0
Prince William County, VA	***5,741***	***13,447***	***32,186***	***78,371***	***134.2***	***139.4***	***143.5***	***1265.1***
Manassas city, VA	460	2,129	4,973	NA	362.8	133.6	NA	NA
Manassas Park city, VA	107	368	1,543	NA	243.9	319.3	NA	NA
Stafford County, VA	734	1,833	3,713	9,625	149.7	102.6	159.2	1211.3
Calvert County, MD	515	847	1,643	1,856	64.5	94.0	13.0	260.4
Charles County, MD	1,441	2,082	3,470	5,104	44.5	66.7	47.1	254.2
Frederick County, MD	1,729	3,073	7,779	19,437	77.7	153.1	149.9	1024.2
Total Washington Metro Area[c]	255,439	488,283	829,310	1,063,033	91.2	69.8	28.2	316.2

Sources: 1980 data from printed census volumes; 1990 data from Geolytics Census CD; 2000 and 2006 data from American FactFinder.

NA: Data not available at smaller geographic levels

[a] Subtotals for inner suburbs exclude independent cities of Fairfax and Falls Church

[b] Subtotals for outer suburbs exclude independent cities of Manassas and Manassas Park

[c] Totals for the metro area include the Far Suburbs, not listed on this table

Figure 10.1 Hispanic Population Change by Jurisdiction, 1980–2006

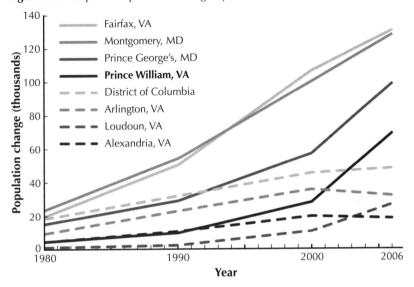

Most of the growth in the county's Hispanic population over the past quarter-century occurred from 2000 to 2006, putting Prince William County among the top fifteen counties in the nation for Hispanic growth rates during that period.[9] Not surprisingly, population change by nativity shows the same trend. In 2006, 22 percent of Prince William's population was foreign born, compared to only 12 percent just six years earlier (table 10.2). In 2006, immigrants from Latin America made up 54 percent of the foreign-born population, nearly double their share in 1990 (28 percent).

Immigrants moving to Prince William County are not all recent newcomers to the United States; many are established immigrants who have moved out of the inner core to Prince William. For example, the inner-core county of Arlington had a higher-than-metro-average share of its immigrant population who entered the United States in the most recent period, 2000–2006 (41 percent), compared to 27 percent in Prince William County (table 10.3). Conversely, 38 percent of Arlington's immigrant population present in 2006 entered the United States in the 1990s, while 66 percent of Prince William's

9. Other counties in the area that ranked among the top fifteen were Frederick, Fauquier, Spotsylvania, Stafford, and Loudoun in Virginia, Berkeley, WV, and Frederick, MD (based on data from the 2006 American Community Survey and Census 2000). Counties with fewer than 65,000 people (not covered in this analysis) may outrank larger counties in growth rate due to their smaller initial populations.

did. According to journalistic accounts, affordable housing was a primary motivator for immigrants moving from the inner core to Prince William County (Cohn 2004; Layton and Keating 2006).

Table 10.2 Percent Foreign Born in the Washington Metro Area, by Jurisdiction, 1980–2006

	Percent Foreign Born			
	1980	1990	2000	2006
District of Columbia	6.4	9.7	12.9	12.7
Inner Core	13.0	19.3	26.8	23.3
Arlington County, VA	14.6	21.4	27.8	23.3
Alexandria city, VA	10.5	16.2	25.4	23.4
Inner Suburbs[a]	8.9	14.7	22.0	25.3
Montgomery County, MD	12.1	18.6	26.7	29.3
Prince George's County, MD	6.0	9.6	13.8	19.0
Fairfax County, VA	9.1	15.6	24.5	26.8
Fairfax city, VA	7.5	14.8	25.4	NA
Falls Church city, VA	9.5	10.5	16.1	NA
Outer Suburbs[b]	2.6	3.9	7.3	14.2
Loudoun County, VA	3.2	5.7	11.3	21.0
Prince William County, VA	**4.0**	**6.2**	**11.5**	**21.9**
Manassas city, VA	3.0	7.6	14.2	NA
Manassas Park city, VA	1.6	5.5	15.0	NA
Stafford County, VA	1.8	3.0	4.0	8.0
Calvert County, MD	1.5	1.6	2.2	2.1
Charles County, MD	2.0	2.1	2.9	3.6
Frederick County, MD	1.5	2.0	4.0	8.7
Total Washington metro area[c]	7.5	11.8	17.3	20.1

Sources: 1980 data from printed census volumes; 1990 data from Geolytics Census CD; 2000 and 2006 data from American FactFinder

NA: Data not available at smaller geographic levels

[a] Subtotals for inner suburbs exclude independent cities of Fairfax and Falls Church

[b] Subtotals for outer suburbs exclude independent cities of Manassas and Manassas Park

[c] Totals for the metro area include the far suburbs, not listed on this table

Rapid population growth and ethnic change have contributed to residents' sense of social upheaval, but the characteristics of immigrants have also influenced the ways in which people have reacted to their arrival. Less educated immigrants and those with lower English proficiency are generally perceived as more of a "burden to society" than are highly educated, English-speaking immigrants. In Prince William County in 2006, more than half (55 percent) of immigrants had limited English proficiency (LEP),[10] the highest in the region (table 10.3). It could also be the case that the dominance of a single non-English language in a county (combined with high levels of LEP) supports the perception of a "foreign invasion." Spanish speakers made up 70 percent of the immigrant LEP population in Prince William County in 2006.

Immigrants' education level is another characteristic that affects how local residents perceive their arrival. In Prince William County, immigrants are less likely to have high school degrees than are immigrants in the metro area as a whole (table 10.3). Immigrants are also much less likely than native-born residents of the county to have high school degrees.

The most controversial characteristic of immigrants in the Prince William County debate has been legal status. Ironically, this is the trait for which data are least available, especially for smaller geographies like counties. However, the most widely used method of approximating the unauthorized population estimates that one-third of immigrants in both the Washington metro area and the state of Virginia are in the United States illegally (Fortuny, Capps, and Passel 2007).

Housing and Jobs as Drivers of Population Growth

Although direct evidence of motivations is sparse, data on the housing and labor markets suggest that home ownership and job opportunities in Prince William and nearby counties have been major draws for immigrants and native-born residents alike.

Relatively stable during the 1990s, home sales prices in the Washington area soared from 2000 to 2005, with the median sales price doubling in many of the region's suburbs, even after adjusting for inflation. Squeezed by rising home prices, many first-time home buyers were willing to "drive to qualify," that is, move farther from the urban core in order to meet the criteria for a home mortgage. Others, looking to upgrade, found newer, larger homes

---

10. Limited English proficiency (LEP) is defined (for the population age five and over) as speaking English less than "very well." Thus the LEP population includes those who indicate that they speak English "well," "not well," or "not at all."

Table 10.3 Period of Entry, Language, and Educational Attainment among Immigrants, 2006

	Percent of Immigrants Who Entered U.S. between 2000 and 2006	Percent of Immigrants Who Are LEP	Percent of LEP Immigrants Who Speak Spanish	Percent of Immigrants with Less than HS Degree	Percent of Native Born with Less than HS Degree
District of Columbia	32.8	35.3	65.1[x]	25.9[x]	13.9
Inner Core					
Arlington County, VA	42.3	40.5	52.8	23.0	2.7
Alexandria city, VA	40.7	33.0	60.9[x]	23.3[x]	2.3
	44.8	51.1[x]	45.4	22.5[x]	3.2
Inner Suburbs[a]					
Montgomery County, MD	29.9	43.4	44.5	18.5	5.3
Prince George's County, MD	29.4	41.9	38.1	16.6	3.8
Fairfax County, VA	35.2	36.9	69.8[x]	27.3[x]	9.4
	27.4	48.7	38.6	15.4	3.0
Outer Suburbs[b]					
Loudoun County, VA	27.1	46.3	57.7	21.1	6.9
Prince William County, VA	28.2	41.8	40.3	15.8	3.6
Stafford County, VA	***26.6***	***55.0***	***70.0***	***29.1***	***5.7***
Calvert County, MD	24.5	30.6	63.7[x]	24.0[x]	
Charles County, MD	9.5	11.9	NA	8.8	8.0
Frederick County, MD	22.2	15.0	0.0	11.8	10.7
	29.9	40.4	46.5	8.0	8.6
Total Washington metro area[c]	30.9	43.3	49.7	20.2	7.2

Source: ACS 2006 data from American FactFinder

NA: Data not available at smaller geographic levels

[x] Not significantly different from Prince William County

[a] Subtotals for inner suburbs exclude independent cities of Fairfax and Falls Church

[b] Subtotals for outer suburbs exclude independent cities of Manassas and Manassas Park and, in the case of LEP immigrants who speak Spanish, Calvert County

[c] Totals for the metro area include the far suburbs, not listed on this table

within their budget in farther-flung suburbs, a trend that accelerated the de-velopment of "exurbs."[11] Indeed, at the height of the housing boom in 2005, the outer suburbs contained a third of all regional single-family home sales under $250,000 (affordable to a family with an annual income of $76,000).[12]

The county was not immune to the region's skyrocketing housing prices. The median sales price in Prince William County increased in real terms by 144 percent over this period (Turner et al. 2007). Yet even with this tremen-dous increase, the median sales price in Prince William was significantly low-er than those in other Northern Virginia jurisdictions, including Arlington, Fairfax, Falls Church, and Loudoun, strengthening Prince William's status as an affordable bedroom community to the "beltway." Indeed, two-thirds of Prince William's residents commute outside of the county for work, with a large number employed in places with more expensive housing.

Movement to the outer suburbs was also facilitated by regional job de-centralization. The outer suburbs held 16 percent of the region's jobs by 2006, a substantial increase from their 1990 share. Not surprisingly, jobs in population-serving industries accompanied Prince William's population and housing boom. The number of jobs in Prince William County nearly doubled—from 55,000 in 1990 to 104,000 in 2006. The overwhelming major-ity of the county's jobs are in the private sector. In 2006, the trade, transpor-tation, and utilities super-sector accounted for the largest share of jobs (28 percent), the vast majority of them in retail. Not surprising given the local housing boom, construction provided the second-largest share of jobs in the county, at 19 percent. Likewise, 14 percent of the county's jobs were in leisure and hospitality, heavily dominated by accommodations and food services. These sectors are more predominant in Prince William County than in any of the other Northern Virginia jurisdictions.[13]

In combination with relatively affordable housing, the high proportion of jobs in these population-serving industries may have attracted immigrants, particularly Latin Americans, to Prince William County. Indeed, census data from 2006 show that Washington's Latin American immigrants are more heavily represented in these industries, particularly construction and lei-sure/hospitality (Singer 2007).

---

11. For a national comparative analysis of exurban areas, see Berube et al. 2006.
12. Metropolitan Regional Information Systems, Inc. We borrow our affordability thresh-old from Turner et al. 2007.
13. We use the Quarterly Census of Employment and Wages (QCEW), a Bureau of Labor Statistics survey, to review total employment from 1990 to 2006 and super-sector em-ployment among private establishments in 2006.

Growing Pains, Neighborhood Change, and Sense of Place

The county's rapid population changes resulted in challenges typical of fast-growing communities: traffic congestion, crowded schools, and heavy demand on public services. More subtly but just as importantly, they also aroused anxiety among some of Prince William's longtime residents about the county's changing identity and their place within it.

Although incoming home buyers of different income levels and races found housing to meet their needs in Prince William, they did not necessarily settle next door to one another. Affluent, mostly white home buyers settled in new and sometimes gated developments, while many Latinos and other minorities with more moderate incomes bought homes in older neighborhoods.[14] Recent Hispanic settlement was particularly concentrated in two areas—"up-county" neighborhoods contiguous to Manassas and Manassas Park, such as Bull Run, Sudley, Loch Lomond, Westgate, and Yorkshire, and "down-county" neighborhoods such as Dale City, Woodbridge, and parts of Dumfries, Triangle, and Lake Ridge. The Hispanic share of loans for owner-occupied home purchases in both of these areas was above the county average of 37 percent in 2006 (map 10.2). Indeed, in the down-county neighborhoods, 56 percent of home purchase loans were made to Hispanics in 2006, compared to only 8 percent in 1997. Even more striking, three-quarters of 2006 home purchase loans in up-county areas were to Hispanics, up from 11 percent just nine years earlier.

A change in the "feel" of older neighborhoods long inhabited by native-born residents accompanied these settlement patterns.[15] These differences included changes in outward appearance of houses and property (trash, debris, tall grass, parking on lawns, inoperative vehicles, and, on occasion, the raising of chickens or corn), overcrowding as evidenced by multiple vehicles and the apparent presence of unrelated people sharing homes, more Spanish being spoken, less personal interaction among neighbors, increases in outdoor activities and noise levels, and in some cases a rise in street crime, hit-and-run driving accidents, gang activity, and the appearance of graffiti.

---

14. Based on our analysis of HMDA data by race and income for census tracts (provided by Dataplace).
15. Spatial analysis of 1980, 1990, and 2000 census data shows that census tracts in these up-county neighborhoods were majority-white and native-born during those years. The most affected down-county tracts had a longer history of minority (black and Hispanic) settlement, as well as settlement by military personnel.

Map 10.2 Percent of Owner-Occupied Home Purchase Loans to Hispanics in Prince William County, by Census Tract, 2006

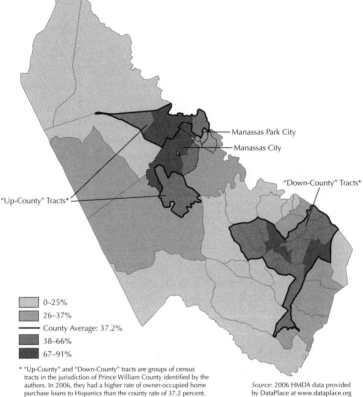

Manassas Park City

Manassas City

"Down-County" Tracts*

"Up-County" Tracts*

- ☐ 0–25%
- ☐ 26–37%
- — County Average: 37.2%
- ☐ 38–66%
- ☐ 67–91%

* "Up-County" and "Down-County" tracts are groups of census tracts in the jurisdiction of Prince William County identified by the authors. In 2006, they had a higher rate of owner-occupied home purchase loans to Hispanics than the county rate of 37.2 percent.

Source: 2006 HMDA data provided by DataPlace at www.dataplace.org

Without home owner associations to turn to, residents in older neighborhoods reported problems to the county's Property Code Enforcement (PCE) Group in the Neighborhood Services Division. Complaints jumped from 2,271 (including 128 overcrowding complaints) in 2004 to 3,977 (460 overcrowding complaints) in 2007. The PCE group could not keep up, even after adding more staff. In order for PCE to investigate overcrowding complaints, county staff must receive the resident's permission to enter a home and must have evidence of unrelated individuals living together. Because of these constraints, most violations identified by the PCE were not for overcrowding per se,[16] but

---

16. The county's zoning ordinance does not distinguish by level of family relationship, so multiple nuclear families who are related to each nother are permitted to live together,

reflected symptoms thereof: outside storage, dump heaps, inoperative vehicles, and parking on lawns. Nevertheless, PCE identified fifty-seven occupancy violations in FY 2007 (up from five in FY 2004), which were clustered in the older neighborhoods identified above. In all, there were more than 3,600 PCE violations in the county in 2007, compared to 972 in 2004.[17]

Initially, the Prince William County government was not equipped to respond to the soaring number of complaints, nor was it prepared to communicate with new residents who were often the target of such complaints. When Prince William's growth boom began in 2000, the county's Property Code Enforcement Group had five members, none of whom spoke Spanish. In response to a mounting number of complaints about community maintenance, the county doubled the PCE staff and hired a neighborhood coordinator in 2005. By 2006 the county had formed the Neighborhood Services Division, which includes Property Code Enforcement, a litter and landscaping crew, and a single neighborhood coordinator; two of the staff spoke Spanish fluently. The county increased its staff responsible for enforcing property code and distributed compliance information in Spanish through radio, mail, and leaflet distribution. It did not, however, hire more neighborhood coordinators to expand education campaigns on property code compliance. PCE was still understaffed for the number of complaints it received, violations that were initially dealt with often recurred, and long-term residents in older neighborhoods were frustrated by the lack of progress. Long-term residents resented the fact that the neighborhoods they had known and loved—and invested their money in—were showing signs of distress.

In addition, some long-term residents complained that their neighborhood schools were overcrowded (a phenomenon occurring throughout the county as a result of overall population growth) and that resources were being diverted to the growing number of students requiring ESOL classes (English for Speakers of Other Languages). ESOL enrollment in Prince William County schools experienced a 31-fold increase, from 421 students in September 1990 to 13,409 students in 2007. Further, the proportion of county students enrolled in ESOL increased from 1 percent in 1990 to 18 percent in 2007. The schools with the highest proportions of ESOL students are in many of the same neighborhoods that submitted complaints to PCE. Some

---

with up to two unrelated boarders. Some long-term residents were shocked when they discovered the permissiveness of the ordinance.

17. Data in this paragraph refer to fiscal years (October–September) and were provided by the Department of Neighborhood Services.

residents associated these trends with the presence of unauthorized immigrants. In the 2007–2008 school year, 61 percent of the county's ESOL students were native born (and therefore U.S. citizens), but it is not known what proportion of their parents were illegally present.[18]

In essence, long-term residents of the affected areas perceived a decline in their quality of life, and many expressed concerns about declining property values. Some reacted by moving to the newly developed parts of the county where homes were more expensive and association rules prohibited many of the "blight" issues of the older neighborhoods. Others, whether because they could not afford to move or wanted to take a stand to preserve their former way of life, became politically active around the issue of immigration.

A Call to Action

Faced with an initial tide of complaints, followed by increasingly organized demands for action, county supervisors first deferred responsibility to the federal government, but when Congress failed again to reform immigration policy in late 2006, pressure on local officials mounted. In December 2006, the Board of Supervisors directed staff to study the cost of and regulations regarding the provision of human services to unauthorized immigrants. A month later, county staff reported back on services legally available or unavailable to unauthorized immigrants.[19] In response to the Board's request for the total cost of illegal immigrants to the county, staff, noting the lack of data on the size of the unauthorized population among other methodological limitations, concluded, "we cannot give you an accurate or dependable answer."[20]

Nevertheless, residents continued to pressure the Board to act, spurred by events in nearby Herndon, where in summer 2005 the Town Council had authorized use of public funds for a day labor hiring site. Two grassroots organizations quickly formed in opposition: Help Save Herndon and the Herndon Minutemen. By May 2006, and in time for a local election, these groups had raised the visibility of the issue, the Town Council was voted out, and the center was subsequently closed (Price and Singer 2008). Prince William County residents who had been told for years that immigration was

---

18. Data in this paragraph were provided by the county's ESOL program.
19. Specifically, the staff produced a list of the services already being denied to illegal immigrants, services that may not legally be denied, and services that have no regulation governing their provision to illegal immigrants.
20. January 19, 2007, memo from Prince William County Executive to Board of County Supervisors, http://www.pwcgov.org/docLibrary/PDF/008284.pdf.

the responsibility of the federal government alone felt empowered to work for change through their local government. They had to look no further than neighboring jurisdictions to find models of community organizing, and in March 2007, Help Save Manassas (HSM) was formed to "reduce the number of illegal aliens living in our community."[21]

Focusing on the legal status of immigrants provided a means to justify targeting the people seen as responsible for neighborhood decline, despite the absence of authoritative data on the size of the local unauthorized immigrant population. In the minds of some residents, it was obvious that the problems they were experiencing in their neighborhoods were associated with unauthorized immigration. Others acknowledged that legal status was secondary to behavior, but given the failure of property code enforcement, they nevertheless focused on legal status as a more expeditious means to enact change. Help Save Manassas grew quickly, from just forty members to over fifteen hundred six months later.

In June 2007, the county supervisor from the district encompassing some of the most heavily impacted neighborhoods, and where many HSM members lived, introduced draft legislation to deny public services to unauthorized immigrants and mandate police checks of legal status for anyone caught breaking the law. By design, the legislation had not been previously discussed with the rest of the supervisors, and only a handful of people knew about it. These included the leaders of HSM, who had put their county supervisor in touch with the Immigration Reform Law Institute (IRLI), a nonprofit law firm dedicated to controlling illegal immigration and reducing legal immigration. IRLI provided "boilerplate" language for the initial legislation.

After the legislation was introduced, the county supervisors received mass e-mails and phone calls in support of it, though it was later alleged that many of these communications came from outside the county. With few public voices to speak against the proposal, there was no initial counterbalance to the groundswell of support for the introduced legislation. Unlike localities with long-standing immigrant communities, Prince William County did not have a professional nonprofit infrastructure to advocate on the behalf of immigrants. The resolution took the county's more informal network of immigrant advocates by surprise, leaving them with little time to organize a public response. The Board members (all of whom are native-born whites) seemed swayed by the grassroots campaign organized by HSM, the likes of which they had never seen. Coincidentally, seven of the eight county

21. http://www.helpsavemanassas.org/index.php/about.

supervisors were up for reelection in November 2007, and HSM members (approaching two thousand by election time) made clear their intention to use immigration as a litmus test. The Board chair ran his reelection campaign based solely on an anti–illegal immigration platform. Although the stated purpose of the policy was to deter illegal immigration and its effects, fear spread among the broader immigrant and minority communities about the process and implications of the legislation.[22]

On July 10, 2007, the Board voted unanimously in favor of Resolution 07-609, a somewhat softened version of the measure introduced the previous month. It directed police to ascertain a person's legal status only when they had probable cause to believe the person was illegally present (rather than inquire of everyone they encountered). It also ordered a report by county staff in ninety days on the legal grounds for restricting unauthorized immigrants from receiving benefits. It ordered the Police Department to enter into a 287(g) agreement with Customs and Immigration Enforcement (ICE).[23] Finally, it stated that the Board of County Supervisors would send letters to President Bush, the Virginia congressional delegation, and Governor Tim Kaine, clarifying their position and asking for help in addressing the problem of illegal immigration.

By the time the resolution passed, however, some people had begun to raise concerns about its implications. Most notable were the remarks made on July 10 by Prince William's well-respected police chief, on the force since its founding in 1970 and chief since 1988.[24] He argued that the proposed legislation would have "significant unintended consequences," including the underreporting of crime by minority populations as well as perceptions of the county "as a racist community intent on driving out a single population." The chief also worried that the resolution would result in a polarized population, with "residents in solid pro and con camps," and would require higher taxes to pay increased operating costs for police and detention facilities.

A small group of local activists also came together following the July 10 vote to express their opposition. In September 2007, a resident erected a twelve-by-forty-foot sign in the city of Manassas that demanded, "Prince

---

22. In September 2007, the Ku Klux Klan distributed an anti-immigrant appeal to "white, Christian Americans" to some households in Manassas. Klan officials claimed that local residents had asked for the literature to be distributed, but officials and activists on both sides of the issue condemned the leafleting (Constable 2007).

23. For more on 287(g) agreements, see the chapters by Waslin and by Rodríguez, Chishti, and Nortman, this volume.

24. http://www.pwcgov.org/docLibrary/PDF/006635.pdf.

William County stop your racism to Hispanics." The sign's site became a gathering place for demonstrations against the resolution, as well as a flash-point for debate. It was defaced multiple times before being firebombed. Activists replaced the ruined sign with another that more severely criticized the resolution and the County Board that adopted it.[25]

Residents, both for and against the resolution, set their sights on the October 16 meeting at which the Board of County Supervisors was to re-spond to the staff and police proposals for implementing the resolution. Board members received mass e-mails, phone calls, and faxes urging them to continue to back the resolution. Again, some of these communications came from outside the county but were interpreted by county supervisors as constituent support. The leader of HSM acknowledged that national or-ganizations, such as NumbersUSA, were helping inundate Board members. In addition, the Board chair—who was criticized for electioneering from the dais—used $30,000 of his discretionary budget to send a postcard to all county residents urging them to appear at the October 16 meeting to lend their support to the policy.

On October 16, 2007, the Board held a marathon fifteen-hour meeting that included spirited public comment both for and against the resolution. Following the debate, Resolution 07-894 passed unanimously, restricting unauthorized immigrants from receiving business licenses and accessing eight social service programs.[26] In addition, the October 16 version of the resolution reflected recommendations the police chief had made earlier: it created a new criminal alien unit within the Police Department, directed po-lice to engage in outreach on the new police policy, and directed the county to hire an independent consulting firm to evaluate it. The Board also voted to install video cameras in the county's 250 police cars to record traffic stops in order to defend the department against accusations of racial profiling if necessary.

Election Day, November 6, came just weeks later. Corey Stewart, the Board chair who had campaigned almost exclusively on his anti–illegal immigration stand, took 55 percent of the vote against his Democratic ri-val, who campaigned on a broader range of issues. In his acceptance speech,

---

25. Amid growing pressure from the city's zoning enforcement division, the sign was removed on September 9, 2008.

26. In January 2008, staff reported back with the recommendation to remove two of the programs from the list of restricted services. The revised resolution came into effect on July 1, 2008.

Stewart asserted that his reelection was evidence of widespread support for the county's new immigration policies.[27]

After the election, the Board turned its attention to implementing the immigration resolution—and paying for it. The estimated cost was $6.4 million, with half slated for the purchase of the video cameras for police cars. In a tight budget year, when home values were dropping, supervisors balked at raising property taxes, particularly as the resolution and its price tag became less popular with residents. Nonetheless, the Board did not want to leave police officers without protection against possible claims of racial profiling. Their solution was to modify the resolution on April 29, 2008, so that the legal status of *all* persons arrested would be checked *after arrest*. This eliminated the "probable cause" standard and the risk of accusations of racial profiling, obviating the need to purchase the cameras. Thus, less than a year after taking the toughest stance possible for a local jurisdiction, the leaders of Prince William County curtailed the role that local police would play in enforcing federal immigration law within the county. Many police departments that do not have 287(g) agreements or directives for enforcing immigration law now have policies similar to the one passed by the Prince William Board of County Supervisors in April 2008.[28]

The Perfect Storm

Although we have stressed the centrality of demographic change in creating Prince William County's anti-immigrant policy activism, a number of additional factors multiplied the impacts of demographic change and further explain how the county rose to the forefront of local immigration enforcement.

First, the emergence of local immigration policy activism was spurred on by Congress's failure to pass comprehensive immigration reform. When Congress failed to act in 2006 and 2007, leaders in many areas with fast-growing immigrant populations sought to address the issue at a local level, and, as discussed throughout this book, a number of ordinances were passed in localities around the country. Much of the appeal of this approach, especially for local lawmakers, was that it placed the blame for Prince William

---

27. The chairman received 30,334 votes, which represented 16 percent of the registered voters in the county at the time of the election.
28. Discussed by police chiefs and others at the Police Foundation conference "The Role of Local Police: Striking a Balance between Immigration Enforcement and Civil Liberties," Washington, DC, August 21–22, 2008.

County's problems squarely on the federal government's inability to keep unauthorized immigrants out of the United States.

Second, the sharpness of the national and local public debates permeated and was perpetuated by talk radio, new forms of media (blogs and Web postings of videos), television personalities like Lou Dobbs, a new county television channel that aired Board meetings, and public forums, both governmental and nongovernmental. This discourse covered various dimensions of the immigration debate but focused most prominently on the unauthorized population living in the United States. Newer forms of media in particular gave anti-immigrant groups an amplified voice. In Prince William County, the animus was further fueled by the significant extent of local public discussion in the aforementioned county forums, community gatherings, and the blogosphere.

Third, immigration control, traditionally under the authority of the federal government, has only recently become an issue that local areas have sought to control. Prince William County, along with other unseasoned local governments searching for solutions, seemed to pursue the most forceful options available. Prince William's Board of County Supervisors looked to other jurisdictions that had taken on immigration control, consulted with legal advocates, and aimed to improve on existing policies. Indeed, they intentionally sought to outdo other efforts.

Fourth, the electoral calendar amplified the issue's importance. Seven of the eight county supervisors were up for reelection in the fall of 2007, and the chairman pushed to have the immigration resolution implemented before Election Day. Further, the chairman was accused of seeking media attention to bolster his future political career beyond the county's borders.[29]

Fifth, Prince William County lacked a mature immigrant service and advocacy infrastructure. In areas with a more established immigrant population, well-developed constellations of community- and faith-based organizations often serve as buffers between immigrant communities and local governments by providing information and advice about local laws and ordinances, referring immigrant residents to services, and providing outreach to immigrants who speak languages other than English. In some areas, local governments themselves reach out to immigrants, often with staff members serving a liaison role with immigrant constituents.[30] However, Prince William

---

29. In February 2008, he announced his intention to run for lieutenant governor of Virginia in 2009. But when the incumbent decided to seek reelection, the Board chairman put his plans on hold.

30. For more, see Mitnik and Halpern-Finnerty, this volume.

County's immigrant population cropped up quickly, without time for these kinds of organizations and services to develop.

These issues—the federal-local debates, an unprepared local government, imported policy ideas, and the heightened pressures due to media attention and local political races—combined with rapid population change to create the "perfect storm" that led to the much-publicized local crackdown.

CONCLUSION

"Clouds" still hang over the perfect storm, and there is continued disagreement in Prince William County about whether the costs—direct and indirect—have been worth the outcomes—intended and unintended. Some residents are angry that the legislation was rushed through without a proper public hearing or research regarding the contention that unauthorized immigrants were causing "economic hardship and lawlessness" in the county.[31] Some are angry that special interest groups from outside the county appeared to have such a strong influence over county policy. Some are angry that the issue was used as a partisan election tactic. And some are angry that the county's reputation was sullied by sensationalized media reports. Yet, others are pleased with the improvements they believe resulted from the immigration policy: less neighborhood blight, fewer ESOL students, and shorter lines at emergency rooms.[32] Above all, proponents of the legislation are pleased that a clear message was sent: illegal immigration will not be tolerated in Prince William County.

Although not enough time has passed to assess long-term effects, some evidence demonstrates the more immediate civic costs of the policy. Immigrants, particularly Latin American immigrants, feel they have become targets of the new policy regardless of their legal status. An annual survey of Prince William County residents in 2008 revealed that, for the first time in fifteen years, Hispanic residents rated the "quality of life" in the county significantly below other residents' evaluations. Perhaps more importantly, survey results showed a plunge in satisfaction with the performance and attitudes of the Police Department among Hispanic residents but not among other residents.

31. Quote from resolution passed July 10, 2007, by the Board of County Supervisors, http://www.pwcgov.org/documents/bocs/briefs/2007/0710/res07-609.pdf.
32. Recent reports from the county present some data to support these perceptions, though more time is needed to determine a trend. See September 9 report to Board of County Supervisors from County Executive's office, http://www.pwcgov.org/documents/bocs/agendas/2008/0909/6-C.pdf, and September 16 report to Board of County Supervisors from Neighborhood Services, http://www.pwcgov.org/documents/bocs/agendas/2008/0916/9-A.pdf.

Anecdotal evidence and school enrollment figures also suggest that many Latinos have left the county (Shapira 2008).

Furthermore, the mandate for local police to identify and remove unauthorized immigrants has had mixed results. The policy bears an estimated five-year cost of $11.2 million. Yet evidence suggests a limited impact. Of the 636 suspected unauthorized immigrants questioned in the first six months of the program, 45 percent were released with no charges or with summonses, while 54 percent were arrested. Ten were determined to be legally present. Overall, fewer than 2 percent of all persons charged with crimes in the county were unauthorized immigrants.[33] In addition, it is unclear whether the new policy has had an impact on crime overall; the county's crime rate declined consistently from 2003 to 2007,[34] and comparable data for 2008 are not yet available.

In light of these consequences, it seems reasonable for Prince William County's leaders to consider the ramifications of their actions. Emerging fiscal realities may also force them to reconsider. The county has been hit hard by the economic downturn. It has the largest number of foreclosed homes of any county in the region, approximately one in every 103 housing units.[35] With home values sinking and unemployment on the rise, the county's tax revenues are sure to decline significantly. How well Prince William County weathers the downturn depends on its ability to attract and retain businesses, entice new home owners to settle, and hold onto area residents.[36] Once a beacon for new home owners in search of livable communities, Prince William County now has an opportunity, perhaps the necessity, to rebuild its reputation. A logical start would be to bring the public together on the immigration issue in ways that curb conflict rather than inflame it, empower all residents, old-timers and newcomers alike, and seek effective policies that successfully address long-term demographic change and challenges.

---

33. Based on data from police chief's report to Board of County Supervisors on September 9, 2008, http://www.pwcgov.org/docLibrary/PDF/008898.pdf. The police implemented the original policy on March 3, 2008. The Board revised it on April 29, after which police suspended enforcement for two months until the new version could be implemented, on July 1, 2008. Thus these data represent results of three different policies.

34. Prince William County Police Department, 2007 Crime Statistics report, http://www.pwcgov.org/docLibrary/PDF/007665.pdf.

35. According to RealtyTrac.com's July 2008 data.

36. As reported in a *Washington Post* article, prospective buyers on a recent "foreclosure bus tour" of Northern Virginia cited the extra commute, school quality, and political tensions over the county's policies toward illegal immigration as barriers to buying in Prince William County, despite lower home prices relative to other jurisdictions. See Miroff 2008.

WORKS CITED

Berube, Alan, Audrey Singer, Jill H. Wilson, and William H. Frey. 2006. "Finding Exurbia: America's Fast-Growing Communities at the Metropolitan Fringe." Washington, DC: Brookings Institution.

Cohn, D'Vera. 2004. "ESL Enrollment Slows in Inner Suburbs," *Washington Post*, December 20.

Constable, Pamela. 2007. "Klan Leaflets Denounced in Manassas," *Washington Post*, September 6.

Fortuny, Karina, Randy Capps, and Jeffrey S. Passel. 2007. "The Characteristics of Unauthorized Immigrants in California, Los Angeles County, and the United States." Washington, DC: Urban Institute.

Kumar, Anita. 2008. "Illegal Immigration Issues Attract Little Interest outside Northern Virginia," *Washington Post*, March 15.

Layton, Lyndsey, and Dan Keating. 2006. "Area Immigrants Top 1 Million," *Washington Post*, August 16.

Migration Policy Institute and New York University School of Law. 2007. "State Responses to Immigration: A Database of All State Legislation." www.migrationinformation.org/datahub/statelaws.cfm.

Miroff, Nick. 2008. "Real Estate Road Trips Scout Troubled Market; Foreclosure Tours Show Vacant Properties and Provide Advice," *Washington Post*, March 31.

Price, Marie, and Audrey Singer. 2008. "Edge Gateways: Immigrants, Suburbs, and the Politics of Reception in Metropolitan Washington." In *Twenty-First-Century Gateways: Immigrant Incorporation in Suburban America*, ed. Audrey Singer, Susan W. Hardwick, and Caroline B. Brettell. Washington, DC: Brookings Institution Press.

Shapira, Ian. 2008. "ESOL Enrollment Is Higher than Projected," *Washington Post*, October 12.

Singer, Audrey. 2007. "Latin American Immigrants in the Washington, DC Metropolitan Area." Paper prepared for "Latin American Immigrants: Civic and Political Participation in the Washington, D.C. Metro Area," Woodrow Wilson International Center for Scholars, November 1.

Turner, Margery Austin, G. Thomas Kingsley, Kathryn L. S. Petit, Mary Kopczynski Winkler, and Barika X. Williams. 2007. "Housing in the Nation's Capital, 2007." Washington, DC: Urban Institute. http://www.urban.org/publications/411575.html.

11 Local Immigration Policy and Global Ambitions in Vancouver and Phoenix

Doris Marie Provine

The decision of the U.S. Congress to devolve significant federal authority for enforcing immigration law to the state and local level—in tandem with a vigorous, racially charged, grassroots American movement to discourage settlement by unauthorized immigrants—has created a confusing and volatile political brew. Local legislative action and the political movement supporting it have drawn strength from the palpable inability or unwillingness of the federal government to deal effectively with unauthorized immigration, and from its failure to make an effective case for *legal* immigration as a key element for economic growth. A shift at the federal level toward more punitive policies has also helped the anti-immigrant movement gain support. These policies help to constitute citizen attitudes and thus shape further choices (Edelman 1964; McCann 2006). In a real sense, as Mettler and Soss argue, policies *make* citizens (2004, 64).

What evidence can be brought to support this perspective? Cities provide a fascinating and revealing vantage point for analysis. Mayors and other civic leaders in some large U.S. cities have stepped into the political void with their own statements connecting robust immigration to economic growth in their region. The mayor of Los Angeles, for example, met with Mexican President Felipe Calderón in February 2008; afterward he issued a statement arguing for the "need to build bridges, not walls" between the two nations (Risling 2008). Such arguments, unsurprisingly, face significant political opposition at the grassroots. Mayors and other local officials are not in a strong position to stem the anti-immigrant tide created by negativity at the federal level. Yet they are driven by economic and social realities to advocate a welcoming, cosmopolitan approach to urban governance. Cities that are ambitious for economic growth need to attract foreign investment and a large workforce that includes a significant foreign-born element, as Saskia Sassen and other scholars have noted (see, for example, Sassen 1996, 2001a, 3, 2001b, 2002, and 2005, 27). They must accept and support a diverse population with a transient element. They are also motivated by a sense that failure to act will have extremely negative consequences, having taken to heart Sassen's argument that some cities will become "nodes" in the global economy while others will be left behind.

The argument advanced here also requires a comparative dimension. Some highly developed nations, such as Canada, take a clear, positive position on the relationship between immigration and economic well-being. Growth-oriented elites in Canada can thus be expected to have a much easier time achieving their goals than their counterparts in U.S. cities. The positive spin at the national level helps to prevent anti-immigrant sentiment from gaining much political traction. By the same token, where the messages at the national level are garbled or negative, as in the United States, we would expect ambitious cities to encounter serious opposition, often from their own state governments, which reflect the uneasiness of the U.S. public with large-scale immigration, especially unauthorized immigration. This chapter tests these hypotheses by examining political rhetoric and policy in two cities that are in the throes of changes created by immigration: Phoenix, Arizona, and Vancouver, Canada.[1]

In each of these cities, civic leaders are deploying the rhetoric of the global city, tapping the self-interest and pride of residents to suggest a new significance for their city, a new independence, and growing power in the global marketplace. Leaders in these two cities believe that their municipalities are poised to become global cities, those "command posts in the world economy" that Sassen describes. They implicitly recognize that visas, residence permits, and passports are relics of an earlier age that can interfere with the push toward rapid development and cultural transformation. They oppose a harsh stance on unauthorized immigration because it would be incompatible with their image of the city as a cosmopolitan place that welcomes diversity. In light of the limitations of their constrained political position as city leaders,

1. I completed this research with the generous support of a Fulbright grant in North American Studies. This support, supplemented by a sabbatical from Arizona State University, allowed me to study local immigration policy on site in Vancouver during the fall of 2007. During this time I was able to interview local and national-level policy makers and activists regarding local and national policy related to unauthorized immigrants.

however, they seek to avoid, rather than confront, the issue of unauthorized immigrants if at all possible.

The civic leadership in Phoenix must navigate the dangerous waters of anti-immigrant activism from surrounding Maricopa County and the State of Arizona, with no reassuring signals from the federal level. Leaders in Vancouver sail in much calmer seas. Canadian cities benefit from immigrant-friendly policies at both the provincial and federal levels. The difference in political milieu has an impact, not only on what these two cities are able to accomplish as they seek to attract foreign investment and more accomplished foreign-born workers, but also on the political dialogue that circulates around issues of growth and development. At stake in this political dialogue is the future of the city in a globalizing economy, as well as the meaning of membership within that context. The struggle, at a broader level, is to define the city in global terms in a federal system that may be unprepared for a new urban assertiveness.

PHOENIX AND VANCOUVER IN COMPARATIVE PERSPECTIVE

These two western cities have much in common. Each of them is fast growing, far from the national capital, and close to an international border. Phoenix lies about 150 miles north of the border with Mexico. Vancouver, a port city on the Pacific Ocean, welcomes visitors from Asia and from the United States; it is only 45 miles north of Bellingham, Washington. Both cities have histories of severe racial/ethnic discrimination and hostility toward foreigners. Phoenix, located in territory that once was Mexican, depended in its early years on Mexican labor in agriculture and mining, exploiting these workers under a system that Ngai and others have described as "imported colonialism" (Ngai 2004, 13; L. Gordon 1999). Statehood in 1912 brought racial segregation that was rigidly enforced in public schools, recreation facilities, housing, and churches, and on job sites, where a lower "Mexican wage" prevailed. Legal segregation persisted until 1953, with lingering effects in residential and employment patterns (Gober 2006).

Vancouver has an equally regrettable racial history. Like Phoenix, Vancouver owes its early development in part to people it later excluded. First, indigenous populations were displaced. Later, Chinese and Sikh laborers built portions of the Canadian Pacific Railroad which links Vancouver to the rest of Canada (Papillon 2002, 6). When these laborers finished their work, they were discouraged, sometimes with extreme force, from making

Canada their permanent home (Greenwood and McDowell 1991). Perhaps the most violent single incident occurred shortly after the railroad's completion in 1907, when six thousand Anglo residents, including public officials, rioted against Vancouver's Chinese and Japanese residents, breaking all the windows in Vancouver's Chinatown and attempting to do the same in Japantown. During World War II, Vancouver sent its Japanese residents to internment camps, while camps near Phoenix housed Japanese Americans evacuated from the Pacific Coast.

Both cities have moved beyond these discriminatory histories, but the impact of this transformation has been more dramatic in Vancouver. In the 1960s, Vancouver was an overwhelmingly Anglo city with a British sensibility. The urban ambiance is now decidedly international (Papillon 2002; Wong and Ng 2002). In the 2001 census, nearly 18 percent of the city's population self-identified as Chinese, 7 percent as East Indian, and 3 percent as Filipino. The city also has tens of thousands of Japanese, Vietnamese, Iranians, Koreans, Russians, and East Europeans (Statistics Canada 2007). In all, about 40 percent of the city's population is foreign born, with the proportion in some suburbs exceeding 50 percent. Today the city celebrates its racial/ethnic diversity, with a strong boost from city leaders, who constantly proclaim the benefits of immigration and its connection to economic growth. Unauthorized immigration in Vancouver is significant, but it is treated as a management issue, not a cause for public concern.

Phoenix, with a smaller percentage of foreign-born residents, is awash in conflict over immigration. The 2006 census update indicates that 17.4 percent of the city's residents were born outside of the United States, mostly in Mexico. Of the nearly 3.8 million residents in surrounding Maricopa County, 29 percent identified themselves as Latino, with about half of this number born outside the United States. While unauthorized immigration is an important dimension of urban growth in both localities, local reaction to it in Phoenix could not be more different than what is seen in Vancouver. Phoenix and the State of Arizona have become transfixed with the issue. The state government has enacted a number of laws to discourage these immigrants from settling or remaining. Some originated as local initiatives adopted by huge popular margins. For many residents, there is no more salient political issue.

It is tempting to explain the difference in the salience of the unauthorized settlement issue in terms of the number and proportion of unauthorized immigrants in each place. The United States had an estimated 11.5 to 12 million unauthorized immigrants in 2006, between 370,000 and 432,000 of whom live in Arizona (Passel 2006; also see Pew Hispanic Center 2008). In Canada, estimates of the unauthorized population are less reliable and vary widely, from about 100,000 to as many as 500,000 (see, for example, Goldring, Bernstein, and Bernhard n.d.). Even taking into account Canada's much smaller population (33 million versus 300 million in the United States), the Canadian proportion of unauthorized immigrants to its total population is clearly much smaller. There are probably similar disproportions at the local level. Vancouver, with about two million residents, has a much smaller market for labor than Phoenix, which is more than twice as large. Still, the demand for workers had never been higher in Vancouver as the city prepared for the 2010 Olympic Winter Games. Unauthorized immigrants in Vancouver could eke out an existence in construction jobs, ethnic restaurants, and other occupations that operate on a cash basis, and many undoubtedly did and still do. Most local service providers interviewed in connection with this project believe that the number of unauthorized immigrants in Vancouver is increasing because of the local shortage of labor.

In my view, Vancouver is able to bypass the potentially volatile issue of unauthorized immigration for both demographic and political reasons. Immigrants without legal status are difficult to distinguish from the large number of foreign-born residents who live in the area legally. The political ambiance is perhaps even more significant in explaining why Vancouverites generally do not concern themselves with unauthorized immigration. National and local leaders constantly remind residents that immigration benefits the economy. Local leaders reinforce the message that foreign-born residents help make Vancouver a more dynamic and exciting place to live. The government claims to have a rational plan to manage immigration and to be responsive to changing economic trends. The issue is treated as a matter for expert judgment, minimizing the degree of political posturing involved. As Jeffrey Reitz noted in an overview of Canadian immigration policy: "It appears to be guided by the theme of nation-building and employs a managerial approach to support a perception that it serves national development interests" (2004, 98–99). In addition, a well-established policy to promote multiculturalism discourages racist or xenophobic rhetoric in the public sphere.

The urban leadership in Phoenix enjoys none of these advantages. Though federal policy has for some time favored robust immigration, there has been little effort to communicate with the American people about its value (Tichenor 2007; Martin 2004, 67). Nor has the federal government, until very recently, attempted to control unauthorized immigration (Hanson 2004, 88).

Political posturing and insider interests seem to dominate federal immigration policy making, which is constructed from deal making in Congress, without much input from immigration experts (Tichenor 2002). It is not surprising that Phoenix is a city divided, with urban elites determined to bypass the volatile immigration issue if possible and focus on enhancing the city's global significance, while the surrounding suburban and rural population remains unmoved or hostile to this vision and suspicious of the federal government's capacity to deal effectively with immigration issues.

PHOENIX AS A GLOBAL CITY

The political class in Phoenix enthusiastically embraces the image of the mythical phoenix that rises from the ashes to achieve greatness. The metaphor took hold early in the city's history, along with a commitment to fervid boosterism among city leaders. Phoenix began as a modest farming community in 1867 when a miner named Jack Swilling saw the potential for restoring canals dug centuries earlier by the indigenous peoples who once farmed there. When these channels were reopened, water flowed freely into long-abandoned fields and created bountiful harvests. The town grew slowly until residents persuaded the federal government to invest in a major dam to control periodic flooding (Gober 2006). President Theodore Roosevelt inaugurated Roosevelt Dam in 1911, and the city began to grow quickly at that point, reaching a population of 48,000 by 1930 and 106,000 by 1950.

Almost from its beginnings, Phoenix benefited from the enthusiastic descriptions of travel writers. At the turn of the century, when Phoenix was still struggling with rain, heat, and drought, John Black described it as "one of the handsomest towns in the Southwest," and James McClintock deemed it the "center of farming paradise," with a social life "comparable with the best of that of many cities far older and larger" (Buchanan 1978, 77, 83). A 1934 article in the local newspaper described Phoenix as "perfection in the sun" and "the perfect home" (Buchanan 1978, 115). For city leaders, the goal was to encourage settlement in order to compete with more established western cities like Denver in amenities and wealth (Luckingham 1993). The economy at that time was largely based on agriculture.

With the invention of air-conditioning and the advent of a leisure economy, Phoenix boomed. City boosters began to stress the city's attractiveness as a winter tourist destination, a Mecca for the ailing, and a location for "clean" business. The metro area reached 3.1 million in 2000. Phoenix was the fastest-growing city in the United States in 2006, with 96,000 migrants from within the United States, 65,000 from outside, and 40,000 more births than deaths. The U.S. Census Bureau projects that Phoenix will have seven million residents by 2040.

Aspiring to Be a Global City

The city's current political leaders and Arizona's governor now stress a more international image, one based on the city's attractions to a global audience. This spirit was captured well by Phoenix Mayor Phil Gordon in his May 15, 2007, State of the City speech:

> Think about the acknowledged great cities of the world: New York, Paris, London. All these cities first achieved their greatness in centuries gone by. But this is a brand new Century and Phoenix Arizona IS emerging—and is being recognized—as the first great City of the 21st Century.

The "brand-newness" of the city is a frequent theme. Michael Crow, the local university's president, described Phoenix as "the last 'unmade place' . . . the last place that you can build exactly what you want." The mayor quoted him in his State of the City speech.

What these leaders want is a global city, but without any of its inherent problems. Along with enthusiastic speeches by city officials before the Chamber of Commerce and other groups, there are frequent reports from business leaders on the city's global potential. The same pattern can be seen at the state level. Periodic "Town Hall" reports from annual meetings of Arizona's leading figures in business and government illustrate the mind-set, as evidenced in various report titles, such as "Arizona as a Border State–Competing in the Global Economy" (Arizona Town Hall 2005) and "Moving All of Arizona into the 21st Century Economy" (Arizona Town Hall 2001).

The political obstacles that lie in the way of achieving this vision arise, ironically, out of the area's success in attracting people who are looking for a new start in their personal lives, not an urban renaissance. Patricia Gober, who has chronicled the city's culture, observes that Phoenicians tend to focus on their immediate surroundings, not on the larger life of the city or its fragile relationship with the natural environment; she criticizes residents for their tendency to "live big and think small" (2006, 201–208). The phenomenal growth on the urban fringe reflects that preference. The city has annexed vast territory in an attempt to keep the suburbs from dominating the center, but this has not created the sense of urbanity needed for a strong, internationally attractive urban infrastructure. Phoenix is now the nation's fifth-largest city in population and the second-largest in geographical size, but it has a less developed urban core than any major U.S. city.

Legal Populism

The pervasive enthusiasm of civic leaders for growth in a desert city threatened by heat islands, increasing congestion, and a growing strain on the local water supply suggests the extent to which boosterism can avoid unpleasant realities. But even the most determined city enthusiasts cannot fail to have noted the rise of a strong grassroots anti-immigrant movement in Arizona. Citizen initiatives to discourage unauthorized immigrants from settling or staying in Phoenix appear regularly and pass by overwhelming margins. In 2004, voters approved restrictions on undocumented residents' access to social services and stricter identification requirements to prevent noncitizen voting. In 2006, a citizens' initiative eliminated in-state tuition for noncitizen residents by a margin of nearly three to one.[2]

The state legislature took up the cause in 2006 with a law that the district attorney has interpreted as making persons who hire someone to help them immigrate as equally criminally liable as is the smuggler. In 2007 the legislature limited the availability of bail for unauthorized immigrants accused of serious crimes. Arizona gained national attention with another law, which took effect in January 2008, that punishes employers who knowingly hire undocumented workers with a temporary suspension of their business licenses. On a second offense, they face permanent revocation of their licenses. No employer has yet been sanctioned under the law, but investigations of some are under way.

Laws already in effect have created hardships for the resident population of unauthorized settlers, particularly young people brought to the state as children. Nearly five thousand of those who sought higher education during the 2007 academic year were denied in-state tuition, financial aid, and

---

2. For an overview of Arizona ballot propositions, their contents, and their outcomes, see http://en.wikipedia.org/wiki/List_of_Arizona_Ballot_Propositions. For the complete text of Proposition 300, the ballot proposition that required citizenship for in-state tuition and various other social services, see http://www.azsos.gov/election/2006/info/PubPamphlet/english/Prop300.htm.

adult education classes. About two-thirds of this total are college students (Wingett and Benson 2007).

Policing Immigration

The conflict between the urban and suburban/rural factions is currently playing out in the ranks of law enforcement in Phoenix and surrounding Maricopa County. The federal government set the stage for such conflicts when it adopted the 1996 Illegal Immigration Reform and Immigrant Responsibility Act. This law provides funding for federal training of local police for immigration enforcement. The difference between the response of the county Sheriff's Office and that of the Phoenix Police Department is instructive.

The Sheriff's Office was among the first to take advantage of the federal government's offer to share responsibility for enforcement of immigration laws. Sheriff Joseph Arpaio put 160 of his personnel through this training, about a third of the total that trained under this federal program (Stables 2007). Within the first eight months of their training, sheriff's deputies arrested 450 unauthorized immigrants. The sheriff has also offered to station members of the department on the border with Mexico, well outside his countywide jurisdiction. The office maintains a "migrant hotline" to allow any member of the community to report information about suspected undocumented immigrants.

The leadership of the Phoenix Police Department has taken a different course, asking officers not to inquire about immigration status in routine policing, a policy that has drawn intense fire at the county and state levels, and it appears to be changing under that pressure. In an apparent effort to deflect public criticism, city police have embedded a few federal immigration agents in their operations—but only, it is claimed, to assist with gang-related violence and drug smuggling. City police maintain a confidential hotline to encourage undocumented residents to report crime and other problems. Officers meet regularly with groups from the Latino community to solicit their concerns.

Phoenix boosters avoid the topic of illegal immigration as much as possible. If pressed, they attempt to finesse local hostility to unauthorized Mexican immigration by laying the blame on the federal government (see, for example, Arizona Town Hall 2005, xvi–xvii). It seems obvious, however, that their vision of a global city will be difficult to achieve in a state so hostile to immigrants of Hispanic origin. The legislature has made English the state's official language, and it currently risks a contempt citation for defying a court order to increase spending on education for Spanish-speaking students. Legislators angrily rejected a proposal to support an international baccalaureate program in the state's public high schools as "un-American." The state legislature is prepared, in short, to contest any globally oriented initiatives coming from Phoenix or the Governor's Office that infringe upon its own more traditional vision.

In his seminal study of the rise of nationalism, Benedict Anderson suggested that communities be distinguished by "the style in which they are imagined" (1991, 6). Metropolitan Phoenix and the State of Arizona are divided over whether a more ethnically and racially diverse, cosmopolitan, international metropolitan area is desirable. The city is therefore divided over how to address unauthorized immigration.

VANCOUVER AS A GLOBAL CITY

Vancouver factors immigration into its own rather grandiose vision of itself as a globally significant place. Economic growth and "densification" of the resident population are key elements of its urban strategy. Image is also an issue, as evidenced by the way city leaders talk about the 2010 Olympic Winter Games, which Vancouver hosted. The Olympic Games not only added significant federal investment to the area infrastructure, they also made Vancouver more visible to the world. Mayor Sam Sullivan marked this mood in his first State of the City address in January 2007: "As we move closer to 2010, Vancouver is emerging on the world stage as a City of the Future."

It is easy to see how Vancouver has developed such high expectations for itself. It is one of North America's most livable cities because of its climate and its location on the Pacific Coast. Its late arrival on the urban landscape and its beautiful setting nestled near the Pacific Ocean tend to inspire the imagination. Lance Berelowitz, author of a book about Vancouver as "dream city," describes the city as "unmade" (2005, 263), in tones reminiscent of Phoenix boosters. Like Mayor Sullivan, Berelowitz sees in Vancouver an ambition to be a global city:

> Vancouver has always been a seductress, a city of desire. It is now consciously selling itself as such on the global marketplace of cities. And many are buying. In the process, Vancouver is reinventing itself in hyper-real time. (259)

Vancouver, unlike Phoenix, would shrink if it were not for new foreign residents. The municipal government is well aware that retaining them is a

priority, and has invested accordingly. The city supports a "multicultural social planner," an active economic opportunity office, comprehensive diversity training for government and the private sector, and a grants program that
targets immigrant and ethno-cultural minority community organizations
(Good 2005, 270). The policy has been described as "sustainable diversity"
that involves "creating the best possible conditions for ethnic and cultural
diversity to become a great asset in the new economy" (Papillon 2002, 26).
Most significantly for this discussion, local policy and national policy are in
alignment on the importance of attracting and retaining immigrants.

Canadian Immigration Policy

Canada assiduously courts growth through recruitment of educated populations from all over the world. Immigration now accounts for over half of the
nation's annual 1.4 percent population growth. Canada is tenth in the world
in the proportion of migrants to total population (Migration Policy Institute
2007a, 2007b). The demographic effects have been dramatic, particularly in
the nation's three major cities: Toronto, Montreal, and Vancouver. In Toronto,
over 50 percent of residents are foreign born; in Vancouver, as noted earlier,
the proportion is 40 percent. Asian migration has been particularly heavy in
Vancouver and, in the estimation of most observers, beneficial for its economy
and cosmopolitan image (Wong and Ng 2002, 509).[3]

The Canadian government's approach to immigration is straightforward
and well known to most residents. Most legal immigrants (approximately
250,000 per year) enter via a point system based on various measures of human and social capital. Multiyear temporary worker permits accounted for an
additional 100,000 in 2005, with another 15,000 coming as seasonal agricultural
workers. The persistent need for these workers has encouraged a change of
policy that permits some temporary workers to obtain permanent residency.
Canada also supports a provincial nominee program that admits about 15,000
people per year. This is a vehicle for employers to hire skilled foreign workers
that they have identified. Putting the program at the provincial level allows for
regional variation and promotes buy-in from employers by offering flexibility
and convenience. The emphasis in all of these programs falls upon economic
growth and development. Family reunification accounts for only 24 percent of
legal admissions, in sharp contrast to 63 percent in the United States.

---

3. Between 1996 and 1998, business immigrant entrepreneurs invested a total of Can$831.5
   million in Canada, much of which came from Asia (Wong and Ng 2002).

The parameters of the immigration system are frequently criticized by Canadians seeking to make it function more humanely and with greater justice in individual cases. The policy debate is robust in part because the federal government is clear about its goals. The Ministry of Citizenship and Immigration reports annually to Parliament on immigration patterns and plans for the future. In contrast, when George W. Bush became president, he closed the U.S. Department of Labor's Division of Immigration Policy and Research. The two nations also differ in their support for scholarly research on immigration. Canada participates in the global Metropolis project, which provides support for research on urban growth and integration of newcomers; it also sponsors annual conferences on immigration-related topics. The United States does not support the Metropolis project or any other program to encourage critical scholarly review of its immigration policies.

Canada also appears to spend proportionately more on integrating immigrants than does the United States. Canada's federal contribution in 2006 was $398 million, with significant additions at the provincial and municipal levels. The United States, on the other hand, works through block grants for education and housing that have no separate allocation for immigrants. Canada also differs from the United States in formally vesting some authority for immigrant assimilation at the provincial level and supervising the process. The provinces are invited to develop plans and to invest some of their own resources for this purpose. Cities have also been invited to move aggressively into this arena (Papillon 2002, 16; see also Bradford 2002). Significantly, none of these programs is controversial in Canada.

Unauthorized Immigration in Vancouver

Not everyone who arrives in Vancouver comes through legal channels. The 2010 Olympics almost certainly increased the rate of unauthorized immigration into Vancouver, and probably into other cities with a high demand for manual labor. Vancouver also has visa overstayers and failed refugee claimants among its residents. It is an accepted fact that construction sites are hiring unauthorized workers and paying them on a cash basis. Employers have little to fear; the enforcement apparatus is not directed toward them. The drug trade also depends heavily on unauthorized immigrant labor, with drug bosses often arranging for entry and accommodations.

Vancouver adopts a two-pronged approach to unauthorized immigration. One prong is enforcement. Local police have authority to detain immigrants until immigration authorities can pick them up for removal. Some municipal police officers exercise this authority with enthusiasm. A noise complaint, for example, can result in a document check, detention, and removal. There is no policy against seeking identification from victims of crime or anyone else with whom the municipal police come into contact. Any unauthorized resident caught committing any type of crime will be deported. Overstayers caught in routine traffic stops can often be located through the electronically maintained system that displays warrants for their appearance.

The population of unauthorized residents is further reduced by relatively generous policies concerning regularization. Students can earn the right to stay permanently, for example, by obtaining work and graduating from college. Recent changes in the law give some students up to three years to find employment. Marrying a Canadian is a sure route to legality. Another route to legal status is refugee status. About twenty thousand people per year apply for refugee status *from inside* Canada. There is no one-year time limit on inland applications, as there is in the United States. About 40 percent of these applicants are successful. Successful applications for humanitarian and compassionate exception to the removal laws allow another 10 to 20 percent to enter. This is a last resort for failed refugee applicants. The lengthy appeal process in refugee cases can also enhance opportunities for entry. Even if all these efforts fail, an applicant may be able to convince authorities that it would be too dangerous to return to their home country. In addition, Canada has occasionally provided regularization to specific groups. There have been eight such targeted "amnesties" since 1960.

CONCLUSION

Canada's relatively liberal immigration policy, its enthusiasm for immigration as an engine for growth, and its long-standing multiculturalism policy all help Vancouver—and Canada—avoid the eruption of white racism, the sleeping giant in both Canada and the United States. This is not to say that racism is absent in contemporary Canada. National data on the significantly lower employment rates and lower pay for immigrants and persistent accounts of job discrimination against them all indicate otherwise. But national immigration policy does not seem to be encouraging racism in Canada, while the same cannot be confidently asserted for the United States. The Southern Poverty Law Center reports that the number of hate groups in the United States has risen 48 percent since 2000, to 888 organized groups, many of which are connected to long-standing white nationalist organizations and many of which are exploiting the issue of immigration. The Anti-Defamation League reports that the Ku Klux Klan, which a few years ago had seemed moribund, has rebounded with the exploitation of immigration (2007).

The Canadian government avoids the issue of unauthorized immigration by refusing to notice it or to estimate its extent. The government seems willing to risk a certain lack of "legibility" in its knowledge of who is and who is not legally in the country in order to avoid dealing directly with this potentially volatile issue (Scott 1998). The implicit message is that unauthorized residence is an unavoidable, but reasonably controllable, by-product of an aggressive legal immigration policy. This no-ask policy has practical advantages. It allows Vancouver to ease the tightest labor market it has had in three decades by giving employers free rein to hire unauthorized workers on a cash basis. Employers in Vancouver can do this knowing that they will not be targeted for immigration enforcement.

There is, clearly, a hard edge to this policy of tolerance for unauthorized workers. The workers themselves are at constant risk of discovery and deportation. Exploitation of unauthorized workers is common, and lack of public services for these immigrants and their families is a significant problem. But because their existence is not a fully acknowledged part of the urban scene, these matters receive little public discussion and debate. In this ambiguous situation, schools and social services agencies are forced to chart their own course. Municipal and transit police are left with little guidance in how to weigh immigration enforcement against other values. Racial profiling is a result, and police cannot be entirely sure how to treat witnesses and victims of crimes. Thus, while there is a lively debate about whether Canada—and Vancouver—are sufficiently welcoming of their legal immigrants and about the situation of foreign-born residents in general, there is little talk about how those who fall outside the limits of law survive (Hanley 2007, 1; Goldring, Bernstein, and Bernhard n.d.; Bernhard, Goldring, and Young 2007).

Vancouver thus receives mixed signals from its national leaders and laws regarding the role of unauthorized immigrants: as immigrants they are very welcome, but as unauthorized residents they are deportable. In Phoenix, the framing message from the national level is much less supportive of immigration in general and is actively hostile toward those who come without authorization. Local leaders eager to frame Phoenix as a more cosmopolitan, global city are thus in a difficult position. Phoenix, with perhaps more natural assets than Vancouver in terms of size, wealth, and job opportunities, may be in a poorer position than Vancouver to attract and retain immigrant talent.

The mass media in each nation, Abu-Laban and Garber suggest, tend to exacerbate this situation (2005). These authors studied news reports from each nation in order to determine how the national media frame the immigration issue. Their findings indicate that the U.S. media tend to describe the devolution of immigration enforcement to the states and municipalities in individualistic and local terms, as if localities are free to chart their own course with regard to unauthorized residents. Rarely is the federal role in controlling immigration discussed. The Canadian media take a much different tack, tending to focus on debates at the national level and keeping the issue firmly in that venue. Canadian news sources thus give local officials a degree of "cover" that U.S. urban leaders do not enjoy. Abu-Laban and Garber's analysis helpfully indicates how national media participate in the elite-dominated effort to frame the immigration debate, but their methodology does not allow the authors to determine the extent to which political leaders are able to shape what the media covers.

The tide of anti-immigrant activism runs particularly strong in a politically conservative state like Arizona, often frustrating the efforts of civic leaders to maintain their vision of a transnational global city. The tragedy here is not that these leaders are unable to achieve their goal of a wealthy, open, cosmopolitan society based on neoliberal economic principles of light regulation and entrepreneurial opportunity. The tragedy is that opportunities are few for reasonable, searching, and empathetic dialogue about the situation of the city's large number of unauthorized residents. The Phoenix Police Department remains stuck on the horns of a terrible dilemma in fashioning a role for itself. The case for a more humane approach can hardly be heard.

Vancouver is in a better position for positive dialogue about residents who lack legal status, but it is hampered in how far it can go as a city when Canada lacks a permanent regularization program and a commitment to legalizing the status of as many residents as possible. Living in the shadow of the law is usually a better option than risking deportation for otherwise law-abiding residents. The likelihood of a forward-looking dialogue is low, in other words, as long as both Canada and the United States cling to the idea that they can, and should, control the terms of local residence through national policy.

WORKS CITED

Abu-Laban, Yasmeen, and Judith Garber. 2005. "The Construction of the Geography of Immigration as a Policy Problem: The United States and Canada Compared," *Urban Affairs Review* 40, no. 4 (March): 520–61.

Anderson, Benedict. 1991. *Imagined Communities: Reflections on the Origin and Spread of Nationalism.* 2d ed. New York: Verso.

Anti-Defamation League. 2007. "Ku Klux Klan Rebounds with New Focus on Immigration." Press release. http://www.adl.org/PresRele/Extremism_72/4973_72.htm.

Arizona Town Hall. 2001. *Moving All of Arizona into the 21st Century Economy.* Tucson, AZ: University of Arizona.

———. 2005. *Arizona as a Border State–Competing in the Global Economy.* Tucson, AZ: University of Arizona.

Berelowitz, Lance. 2005. *Dream City: Vancouver and the Global Imagination.* Vancouver: Douglas and McIntyre.

Bernhard, Judith K., Luin Goldring, and Julie Young. 2007. "Living with Precarious Legal Status in Canada: Implications for the Wellbeing of Children and Families," *Refuge.* http://goliath.ecnext.com/coms2/summary_0199-7796211_ITM.

Bradford, Neil. 2002. "Why Cities Matter: Policy Research Perspectives for Canada." Discussion Paper No. F/23. Ottawa: Canadian Policy Research Networks.

Buchanan, James E. 1978. *Phoenix: A Chronological and Documentary History.* Dobbs Ferry, NY: Oceana Publications.

Edelman, Murray. 1964. *The Symbolic Uses of Politics.* Urbana, IL: University of Illinois Press.

———. 1988. *Constructing the Public Spectacle.* Chicago, IL: University of Chicago Press.

Gober, Patricia. 2006. *Metropolitan Phoenix: Place Making and Community Building in the Desert.* Philadelphia, PA: University of Pennsylvania Press.

Goldring, Luin, Carolina Bernstein, and Judith Bernard. n.d. "Institutionalizing Precarious Immigration Status in Canada," *Citizenship Studies.* Forthcoming.

Good, Kristin. 2005. "Patterns of Politics in Canada's Immigrant-Receiving Cities and Suburbs: How Immigrant Settlement Patterns Shape the Municipal Role in Multiculturalism Policy," *Policy Studies* 26, nos. 3/4: 261–89.

Gordon, Linda. 1999. *The Great Arizona Orphan Abduction*. Cambridge, MA: Harvard University Press.

Gordon, Philip. 2007. "State of the City." http://216.197.100.172/news/view.cfm?id=1179265859.

Greenwood, J. M., and J. M. McDowell. 1991. "Differential Economic Opportunity, Transferability of Skills and Immigration to the United States and Canada," *Review of Economics and Statistics* 73, no. 4: 612–13.

Hanley, Wayne. 2007. "The Status of Migrant Farm Workers in Canada, 2006–2007." Report by the UFCW (United Food and Commercial Workers) Union.

Hanson, Gordon H. 2004. "Commentary." In *Controlling Immigration: A Global Perspective*, ed. Wayne A. Cornelius, Philip L. Martin, and James F. Hollifield. 2d ed. Stanford, CA: Stanford University Press.

Luckingham, Bradford. 1993. "The Promotion of Phoenix." In *Phoenix in the Twentieth Century: Essays in Community History*, ed. Wesley Johnson. Norman, OK: University of Oklahoma Press.

Martin, Philip L. 2004. "The United States: The Continuing Immigration Debate." In *Controlling Immigration: A Global Perspective*, ed. Wayne A. Cornelius, Philip L. Martin, and James F. Hollifield. 2d ed. Stanford, CA: Stanford University Press.

McCann, Michael. 2006. "Preface." In *The New Civil Rights Research: A Constitutive Approach*, ed. Benjamin Fleury-Steiner and Laura Beth Nielsen. London: Ashgate.

Mettler, Suzanne, and Joe Soss. 2004. "The Consequences of Public Policy for Democratic Citizenship: Bridging Policy Studies and Mass Politics," *Perspectives on Politics* 2, no. 1: 55–73.

Migration Policy Institute. 2007a. "Size of the Foreign-Born Population and Foreign Born as a Percentage of the Total Population, for the United States: 1850 to 2006." http://www.migrationinformation.org/datahub/charts/final.fb.shtml.

———. 2007b. "Top Ten Countries with the Highest Share of Migrants in the Total Population." http://www.migrationinformation.org/datahub/charts/6.2.shtml.

Ngai, Mae M. 2004. *Impossible Subjects: Illegal Aliens and the Making of Modern America*. Princeton, NJ: Princeton University Press.

Papillon, Martin. 2002. "Immigration, Diversity, and Social Inclusion in Canada's Cities." Discussion Paper F/27. Ottawa: Canadian Policy Research Networks.

Passel, Jeffrey. 2006. "The Size and Characteristics of the Unauthorized Migrant Population in the U.S.: Estimates Based on the March 2005 Current Population Survey." Pew Hispanic Center, March 7. http://pewhispanic.org/files/reports/61.pdf.

Pew Hispanic Center. 2008. "Arizona's Population Growth Parallels America's," January 24. http://pewhispanic.org/pubs/702/arizona-population.

Pham, Huyen. 2007. "The Privatization of Immigration Law Enforcement." http://works.bepress.com/huyen_pham/1/.

Reitz, Jeffrey R. 2004. "Canada: Immigration and Nation-Building in the Transition to a Knowledge Economy." In *Controlling Immigration: A Global Perspective*, ed. Wayne A. Cornelius, Philip L. Martin, and James F. Hollifield. 2d ed. Stanford, CA: Stanford University Press.

Risling, Greg. 2008. "Calderon Meets with Mayor of L.A.," *Oakland Tribune*, February 15. http://findarticles.com/p/articles/mi_qn4176/is_/ai_n24314868.

Sassen, Saskia. 1996. "The Global City." In *Readings in Urban Theory*, ed. Susan S. Fainstein and Scott Campbell. Oxford: Blackwell.

———. 2001a. *The Global City: New York, London, Tokyo.* 2d ed. Princeton, NJ: Princeton University Press.

———. 2001b. "The Global City: Strategic Site/New Frontier." http://www.india-seminar.com/2001/503/503%20saskia%20sassen.htm.

———, ed. 2002. *Global Networks, Linked Cities.* New York: Routledge.

———. 2005. "The Global City: Introducing a Concept," *Brown Journal of World Affairs* 11, no. 2 (Spring): 27–43.

Scott, James C. 1998. *Seeing Like the State: How Certain Schemes to Improve the Human Condition Have Failed.* New Haven, CT: Yale University Press.

Stables, Eleanor. 2007. "State, Local Police Slowly Warming to Immigration Enforcement," *CQ Politics: Homeland Security–Immigration,* November 7. http://cqpolitics.com/frame-templates/print_template.html.

Statistics Canada. 2007. "Population by Selected Ethnic Origins, by Census Metropolitan Areas (2001 Census) (Vancouver)." http://www40.statcan.ca/l01/cst01/demo27x-eng.htm.

Tichenor, Daniel J. 2002. *Dividing Lines: The Politics of Immigration Control in America.* Princeton, NJ: Princeton University Press.

———. 2007. "Testimony of Daniel J. Tichenor before the House of Representatives Committee on the Judiciary Subcommittee on Immigration, Citizenship, Refugees Border Security, and International Law," March 30.

Wingett, Yvonne, and Matthew Benson. 2007. "Migrant Law Blocks Benefits: Prop. 300 Denying College Aid, Child Care," *Arizona Republic*, August 2. http://azbilingualed.org/NEWS_2007/migrant_law_blocks_benefits.htm.

Wong, Lloyd L., and Michele Ng. 2002. "The Emergence of Small Transnational Enterprise in Vancouver: The Case of Chinese Entrepreneur Immigrants," *International Journal of Urban and Regional Research* 26, no. 3: 508–30.

SECTION FOUR

Exploring Tensions at the Local Scale

12 All Immigration Politics Is Local: The Day Labor Ordinance in Vista, California

Michael S. Danielson

On a warm August day in 2007, between fifteen and twenty men and teenage boys gathered in the parking lot of the Vons supermarket at the corner of Escondido Avenue and South Santa Fe Avenue in Vista, a city in North San Diego County, California. Some of the men clustered in patches of shade; others stood exposed to the hot sun in hopes of being better positioned when potential employers drove into the parking lot looking for day laborers to move furniture or work on a construction site. One of the men was an undocumented indigenous immigrant from a rural village in Puebla, Mexico. He first left his home village several years earlier and spent a few months in Tijuana, earning enough money to pay a *coyote* (people smuggler) to help him cross the heavily fortified U.S. border. He now worked in construction and landscaping in Vista and elsewhere in San Diego's affluent North County, and regularly sent part of his earnings to his wife and four children in Mexico. He noted, though, that over the course of the previous year, opportunities for day labor jobs had dwindled significantly.

The earnings of migrant day laborers in communities across the United States help sustain families and entire communities throughout Mexico and elsewhere in Latin America and the developing world.[1] In June 2006,

I am grateful to Todd Eisenstadt for invaluable guidance in the development of this study, and to the students in his spring 2008 American University course, "Mexican Politics in the Age of NAFTA," for their intelligent comments and suggestions. I also thank the many individuals I interviewed for sharing their experiences, insights, interpretations, and time. This research was made possible by a 2007 American University Dean of Academic Affairs grant to Dr. Eisenstadt.

1. In 2007, Mexicans living abroad sent home US$24 billion (Inter-American Development Bank 2008), nearly three times the amount remitted in 2001. The importance of these transfers to families and communities in sending areas is difficult to overstate, with 73

the Vista City Council debated and unanimously passed Ordinance 2006-9, known as the "day labor ordinance." Vista's day laborers, along with their remittance-dependent family members in Mexico and other sending locations, were among the most important stakeholders in the public policy debate that surrounded the ordinance and riveted the attention of the Vista community in 2006 and 2007. However, because most day laborers and many of their family members and allies are noncitizens, and thus lack full political rights, they became subjects in a local political drama in which they could not play an active role.

In this case study, I argue that the introduction, passage, and subsequent legal struggles surrounding Vista's day labor ordinance were driven by a convergence of demographic and political factors at both the national and the local level. Vista is a traditional immigrant-receiving community, where newcomers, most from Mexico, have been settling for several decades. During this period, Vista has gone from being a small, mostly white town to a city that is nearly half Latino.[2]

National political factors and their local manifestations were important as well: the failure of the Bush administration and Congress to enact comprehensive federal immigration reform contributed to a nationwide push by state and local governments to enter the realm of immigration policy.[3] In the months prior to the passage of Vista's day labor ordinance, millions of immigrants and their allies took to the streets in a wave of marches culminating in the May 1, 2006, "Day Without an Immigrant" in hopes of influencing the reform debate in Congress (Archibold 2006). The mobilizations were particularly intense in Vista, where upwards of two hundred police officers were ultimately called in from around the county to clear some eight hundred to twelve hundred people from the streets after a reported riot (Repard and Davis 2006).

The Vista mobilizations and the increased salience of the immigration issue more generally helped generate a significant counter-wave of nativist activism in Vista, reflecting what was happening across the country. The convergence of these political and demographic factors shaped the environment in which Mayor Morris Vance and the Vista City Council unanimously

---

percent of the estimated ten to twelve million Mexican immigrant adults living in the United States sending an average of $2,250 each year (Watson 2007, 2).

2. Esbenshade et al. (2007) have shown that local initiatives like the Vista day labor ordinance were more likely to be introduced and passed in locales where the "increase in the Latino or immigrant population" has been greatest.

3. Wayne A. Cornelius, interview by the author, July 30, 2007.

passed Ordinance 2006-9 in June 2006. The fact that the mayor and two of the four Council members were up for reelection the following November made these actors especially motivated to respond to public pressure to address the problem of undocumented immigration generally and the day labor issue specifically.[4]

VISTA'S DAY LABOR ORDINANCE: PLAYERS IN THE DEBATE

Ordinance 2006-9 is relatively limited in its content. It requires employers to obtain a registration certificate from the city to hire day laborers and to provide workers with a sheet detailing the terms of employment. Employers were subject to a $100 fine if they failed to register under the ordinance (Kauffman 2006). Although the underlying intent of the ordinance remains a point of contention, a central objective was to limit "off-the-street" hiring at the city's ad hoc day labor site. Mayor Vance identified as a primary purpose of the ordinance to "bring some order to the shopping center."[5] His office had received numerous complaints that shoppers pulling into the parking lot were being "swarmed" by day laborers. In public comments before the City Council, one Vista resident noted that his wife now "refuses to shop [at the shopping center where the day labor site is located] because of all the people that are hanging around there, that look seedy and shady." Local business owners had also stated that the day labor hiring site was damaging to business.

Mayor Vance noted that pro-immigrant activists had also been voicing concerns, asserting that employers frequently violated these workers' labor rights. Accordingly, as the city attorney clarified moments before final passage of the ordinance, "the whole thrust of the ordinance is to address a series of problems that have occurred that were documented in the national studies . . . and try to minimize those abuses here in the City of Vista." Nevertheless, pro-immigrant activists like migrant rights attorney Claudia Smith of California Rural Legal Assistance (CRLA) reject this assertion as disingenuous. Rather than being concerned with the rights of the day laborers,

---

4. I conducted over twenty open-ended interviews about the ordinance with key actors and decision makers in Vista and San Diego County, including the mayor of Vista and three of the four City Council members. I complemented information gathered during the interviews with transcripts from the two City Council meetings at which the day labor ordinance was discussed, press coverage in the *San Diego Union-Tribune* and *North County Times*, and an analysis of demographic data from the U.S. Census Bureau. Unless otherwise noted, quoted material in this chapter is drawn from verbatim transcripts of City Council meetings referenced above.

5. Mayor Morris Vance, interview by the author, August 7, 2007.

Smith said, "what the ordinance would do is shut down day-labor sites" and deny these workers their livelihoods (Tenbroeck 2006).

Tina Jillings, a candidate to the Vista City Council in 2006 and cofounder of the Coalition for Justice, Peace and Dignity, similarly argued that the Council was not interested in protecting day laborers, but rather wanted to pacify the increasingly aggressive and politically active San Diego Minutemen chapter and Vista Citizens Brigade, who often clash with day laborers and their supporters at the day labor site.[6] In comments before the Council, Jillings reaffirmed this point:

> We all know that if the protection of the day laborers was really the motivating factor of this ordinance, we would be discussing a job center rather than an ordinance. A job center where they would be protected—the laborers would be protected from the elements, such as the cold winter mornings, the hot sun in the summer. Where they would have access to a bathroom and water and, most of all, protection from the verbal abuse [from the Minutemen] that they have been having to take over the last few weeks and months.

Legal Director David Blair-Loy of the American Civil Liberties Union of San Diego and Imperial Counties echoed Jillings's assessment, arguing that the day labor ordinance was motivated by Minutemen demands that the City Council "do something" about illegal immigration in the community. Moreover, the fact that the Minutemen "claimed it as a victory" suggests that the ordinance had more to do with curtailing day labor in the city and "cracking down" on illegal immigration than protecting the workers.[7]

Indeed, Stuart Hurlbert, a Minuteman and secretary on the Board of Directors of Californians for Population Stabilization, notes that "Minutemen groups have always been strong supporters of different ordinances to get control of towns," and they had put pressure on Vista and other cities to act on the immigration issue by regularly attending City Council meetings.[8] Vista Councilman Steve Gronke confirmed that the Minutemen frequently send e-mails to Council members and regularly attend Council meetings.[9]

---

6. Tina Jillings, interview by the author, August 7, 2007.

7. David Blair-Loy, interview by the author, July 25, 2007.

8. Stuart Hurlbert, interview by the author, August 2, 2007.

9. Steve Gronke, interview by the author, August 7, 2007.

The San Diego Minutemen chapter was founded by ex-marine Jeff Schwilk in 2005, and the Vista Citizens Brigade was founded in 2006. These groups, as well as the Minutemen Project and Minutemen Civil Defense,[10] originally focused their efforts on the U.S.-Mexico border. Minutemen activists would camp in the mountains of eastern San Diego County and attempt to catch illegal border crossers, thereby "supporting" the efforts of the Border Patrol. According to Hurlbert, some Minutemen groups have been camped near Campo, California, for two years, conducting "border vigilance." More recently, however, the San Diego Minutemen shifted attention to the communities where immigrants settle and work, to day labor sites, and to migrant camps.[11]

According to Hurlbert, although the Minutemen are officially pacifist, the leaders "don't necessarily control everyone who shows up at an event." Most are ex-military or former police, and Hurlbert characterized the typical Minuteman as "wild and woolly."[12] With some five hundred to six hundred supporters in San Diego County, the Minutemen have succeeded in drawing attention to the illegal immigration issue. Furthermore, their rallies and surveillance of day labor sites "draw out opposition supporters, and the police and sheriff show up, which has an impact because they get paid overtime wages."[13] Minutemen groups are best known for their vigilante tactics, such as attempting to apprehend migrants at the border and harassing migrants and potential employers at day labor sites. In addition to these extra-institutional tactics, though, Minutemen regularly attend City Council meetings, and it can be argued that they have been instrumental in pushing the issue of day labor and undocumented immigration to the top of the local policy agenda in Vista and other communities around the country.

---

10. Speaking about the Minutemen, Carl Braun, California leader of the Minutemen Civil Defense Corps, noted, "they don't abide by our rules, our SOP [standard operating procedure], and would not be considered Minutemen" (Sanchez 2007). According to Sanchez (2007, 1), the San Diego Minutemen have become too militant "even for these hard-line groups."

11. A recent example of alleged Minutemen vigilante action was the vandalism of the McGonigle Canyon shantytown, a migrant camp nestled between two affluent North San Diego County suburban developments. San Diego Minutemen founder Jeff Schwilk and followers remain under scrutiny by the San Diego police for their alleged role in the January 2007 vandalism, in which migrants' makeshift shelters, sleeping bags, and clothing were cut to shreds (Sanchez 2007, 4).

12. A retired San Diego State University biology professor, Dr. Hurlbert is anything but a typical Minuteman. Rather, his main concern is that immigration, in providing a safety valve for overpopulation in Mexico, places an enormous strain on the environment.

13. Hurlbert, author interview.

THE LETTER OF THE LAW VERSUS THE SUBTEXT

Despite the official justifications for the day labor ordinance—to protect the rights of day laborers and "bring some order" to the hiring site in Vista—there is substantial evidence that the ordinance had the effect (whether intended or not) of relieving the intense pressure that the Minutemen and their allies were bringing to bear, at least in the short term. Yet at the time of my research (a year after the ordinance's passage and two ACLU lawsuits attempting to overturn it),[14] neither the Minutemen nor the pro-immigrant activists seemed particularly satisfied. Frustrated by the situation and the limited tools available to the city government to effectively address the issue, Councilman Gronke lamented in an interview with the author that "it's difficult to be moderate locally."

It appears that underlying anxieties about undocumented immigration and the city's growing Latino population, exacerbated by the high visibility of day laborers in Vista's public spaces, turned day labor into a flashpoint issue whose political significance extends far beyond its direct economic or social impacts (see Varsanyi, chap. 7, this volume). Vista's Latino-origin population rose from 17 percent to 47 percent between 1980 and 2007 (Sauer 2006),[15] and in 2007, 29.2 percent of Vista's 98,000 residents were foreign born. When considering questions of political representation in Vista, it is important to note that though almost half of the city's residents are Latinos, because the majority of the foreign born have not naturalized, this group makes up only 24.5 percent of potential voters—that is, citizens eighteen years and older. Mayor Vance emphasized that he represents all of the city's residents, but the fact that such a large portion of Vista's adult population lacks formal political representation signals an important public policy problem and generates significant tension within the community.

Although it is clear that Vista's U.S.-born population is advantaged with respect to formal political representation, for the Minutemen, similar groups, and like-minded residents, demographic changes associated with in-migration constitute an invasion from the South. Hurlbert argues that "the objective of many in the opposition is to recover the Southwest [for Mexico]."[16] Hurlbert recalls hearing pro-immigrant activists from the opposing camp shouting, "Go

---

14. The ordinance was drafted such that the City of Vista was able to avoid the legal problems that have confronted many other U.S. cities that attempted to regulate illegal immigration.

15. Vista's experience is not unique. According to census data, the Latino population nationwide increased from 6.4 percent in 1980 to 15.1 percent in 2007.

16. Hurlbert, author interview.

back to Europe, pilgrim." Graffiti on the wall of the men's restroom of the Vons supermarket at the day labor site highlights the racial tensions and territorial struggle ongoing in Vista: Someone has scrawled "Beaners, go home," and beneath this someone has written in reply, "We are home" (Kauffman 2006).

Because Vista has long been an immigrant-receiving community, such tensions between the city's non-Latino white population and its immigrant and U.S.-born Latino population are not new (Eisenstadt and Thorup 1994). However, tensions heightened when millions of immigrants and their supporters rallied in cities across the United States in spring 2006 in support of national immigration reform and immigrant rights. And they reached a boiling point following the shooting deaths of six unarmed Latino men by white police officers in Vista in 2005 and 2006. The San Diego District Attorney's Office concluded that there was no evidence of criminal conduct in five of the six shootings.[17] Even so, Vista resident Tina Jillings decided to become involved in local politics when the "Vista sheriff started shooting Latinos."[18] In combination, the growing salience of immigration nationwide, the massive mobilization of Latinos, immigrants, and allies in spring 2006, and the equally passionate counter-mobilizations of anti-immigrant groups had created a highly polarized political environment as the City of Vista took up the day labor issue.

Although most actors involved in the debate acknowledge that immigration is supposed to be a federal issue, the Minutemen and their allies believed that it was up to them, through their citizen vigilance and activism in local politics, to "get control of towns" in the absence of federal reform.[19] Their statements at City Council meetings leading up to the passage of Vista's day labor ordinance reveal their deep-felt concern about illegal immigration (Schwilk 2007). Along similar lines, consider the words of Eric Wallace, a Vista contractor who refuses to hire undocumented labor:

> Citizens of Vista and cities across the United States, if you're okay with the illegal aliens living in utter squalor in canyons just below your beloved homes, do nothing. If saving a little money on vegetables or getting some illegal guy to mow your lawn . . . is more important to you, continue to look the

---

17. The ACLU, acting on behalf of two local citizen groups, requested a review by the state attorney general, who did not challenge the decision of the district attorney (ACLU 2007a).
18. Jillings, author interview.
19. Hurlbert, author interview.

other way. But if you're thick-skinned enough to stand up to
the modern-day slave trade and brush off false accusations
of being a racist, support the rule of law in your country.

On the other side of the debate, many speakers before the Council represented groups that advocate for the rights of immigrants, both documented
and undocumented, and view the Minutemen's harassment of day laborers
and the ordinance itself as a discriminatory and racist attack on the city's
Latino population. As Enrique Morones, founder of the Border Angels human rights group, commented at a City Council meeting, "This legislation,
in reality, targets only one community, just as the Minutemen have targeted
only one community [Latinos]." The Minutemen have described Morones as
their "public enemy number one."[20]

Broader anxieties about demographic change and illegal immigration fueled a slew of passionate public comments at the City Council meetings in
which the ordinance was introduced and passed, even though the mayor
reiterated that the ordinance was not directed toward issues of illegal immigration and had nothing to do with race or Latino ethnicity. The city attorney and mayor were dismayed that people did not seem to understand
what the ordinance was about. As City Attorney Darold Pieper clarified with
subtle sarcasm after a heated period of public comments: "The ordinance
does not purport in any way to regulate day laborers, illegal immigrants,
immigration status at all, right to work, or any of the other issues that have
been addressed so eloquently here today." Yet whatever the letter and force
of the law, few failed to recognize that in political and symbolic terms the
ordinance had *everything* to do with Latino immigration.

DAY LABOR IN CALIFORNIA AND THE NATION: CONFLICTING
SOLUTIONS TO AN UNACCEPTABLE STATUS QUO

The 2004 National Day Labor Survey (NDLS), the first systematic and nationally representative study of the day labor market, found that 97 percent
of day laborers in California and 94 percent in other states are born outside
of the United States. Further, 80 percent of day laborers in California are
undocumented, and 68 percent are from Mexico (Gonzalez 2007, 6).[21] In

---

20. Enrique Morones, interview by the author, July 31, 2007.
21. Only 3 percent of the undocumented workers in California are day laborers
    (Gonzalez 2007, 1). Yet, even though day labor constitutes such a small portion of
    the California labor market, the sector's recent growth, its emergence as a national

addition, as noted in Vista's ordinance and emphasized by Mayor Vance and others, the day labor sector is characterized by widespread abuse of workers (Government Accounting Office 2002; Valenzuela et al. 2006, i). The most commonly cited abuses include failure to pay (or pay the correct amount) and failure to transport the worker back to the pickup spot.

According to NDLS data, "Almost half of all day laborers experienced at least one instance of wage theft in the two months prior to being surveyed," and more than half of day laborers who were injured on the job did not receive medical care (Valenzuela et al. 2006, ii). In addition, though a large majority of day laborers rely on this work as their sole source of income, employment is unstable and, because pay in the aggregate is very poor, day laborers' earnings are meager—ranging from a median of $1,400 in "good" months to $500 in "bad" months (Valenzuela et al. 2006, ii). Day labor employment in general is also risky given that employers typically do not have workers compensation insurance. Addressing the widespread labor violations and low pay that characterize the sector were listed among the stated objectives of the Vista ordinance.

The status quo at informal day labor sites is unpalatable to both defenders of immigrant rights and anti-immigration advocates, albeit for dramatically different reasons. The varied reasons underlying the opposition to informal day labor sites in Vista led representatives on both sides to promote wildly different solutions. Supporters of immigration and immigrant rights argued for city-sponsored, official day labor sites. These work centers, they argued, could help limit violations of laborers' rights. Furthermore, formal work centers could be expected to reduce workers' reliance on the unregulated and often publicly disruptive informal day labor sites.

Immigration's opponents posit that ordinances like the one passed in Vista, as well as direct anti-solicitation bans, are better solutions to the "problem" of immigration generally and day labor specifically. The Minutemen and their allies aim to limit the presence of undocumented immigrants "with or without the help of federal or local agents." Through their direct operations and activities such as border and day labor site vigilance, San Diego Minutemen activists and allied "local citizen brigades" aim to "clean up [their] own neighborhoods" by making the situation so inhospitable and difficult that undocumented immigrants will "self-deport" (Schwilk 2007).

---

phenomenon, its status as an important source of flexible, short-term labor for home owners and construction contractors, and its high visibility make day labor highly salient in local politics.

Though Stuart Hurlbert thinks it unwise to focus too much attention on encouraging day laborers to self-deport, he confirms that this should be the broad strategy of the Minutemen and other groups opposed to "amnesty."[22]

> I think everyone who is not in favor of amnesties [pathways to legalization] is in favor of self-deportation as the primary way to deal with the problem. At least I know of no individuals or organizations who think it is feasible, desirable or cost-effective to try to round up all the millions of illegals who are here now, the third alternative. . . . So virtually everything [that law enforcement agencies, Minutemen, and Californians for Population Stabilization do] . . . should work to discourage more illegal immigration and encourage self-deportation of illegals here now.

Mayor Vance seems to find himself caught somewhere in the middle. After passage of the day labor ordinance, he identified it as just a first step. The second step would be to:

> explore and find a hiring site that we can utilize. One that has restroom facilities, it has water, and that it provides a safe environment for legal day laborers. And I think that the site that we've had thus far is not an appropriate site. We've received a number of inquiries in the city as to why the major intersection of the city is being used for that, there in the Vons shopping center. But, I really do believe that the next step is to find, in conjunction with a nonprofit organization that can run it, that we do find a day labor site that will be for this area.

Just over a year later, however, Mayor Vance recalled in an interview with the author how he was "crucified" by the conservative host of a KFMB San Diego talk-radio program for even suggesting a hiring center. Opponents of this solution in Vista and neighboring communities argued that the local government should not be spending tax dollars on work centers, which were likely to attract even more undocumented immigrants to their communities. The most prevalent argument against establishing a hiring center, Vance noted, is

22. Correspondence with the author, 2008. It should be noted that these are Dr. Hurlbert's views, and to his knowledge "there is no official strategy of the San Diego Minutemen . . . principles, yes."

that "all of the illegal immigrants in the area would come to Vista." Councilman Gronke, for one, remains cynical about the impact that local governments can have on an issue of such magnitude as undocumented immigration. Efforts to respond at the local level, he said, "are going to [continue happening] because the Feds aren't going to do anything." Nevertheless, local ordinances are likely to simply create a "balloon effect," pitting neighboring cities against each other as immigrants relocate locally rather than "self-deporting" to their countries of origin.[23] Given the City Council's lack of support for a hiring center, Mayor Vance ultimately stopped pressing for this solution.

LEGAL CHALLENGES TO VISTA'S DAY LABOR ORDINANCE

Opponents of the Vista ordinance include pro-immigrant and human rights activists and civil libertarians. Challenging the assertions of Vista's mayor and City Council members, the ACLU and CRLA argued that the day labor ordinance was discriminatory in that it specifically targeted Latinos.

To prevent the ordinance from going into effect, these groups filed a lawsuit against the City of Vista on July 17, 2006, on behalf of two day laborers and one employer of day laborers. In the complaint, *Hernandez et al. v. City of Vista*, the plaintiffs argued that the ordinance unjustifiably imposes a restraint on employers' right to free speech by requiring that they obtain a permit before engaging in free speech—hiring a day laborer. Additionally, the lawsuit claimed that the ordinance violates the Equal Protection Clause of the Fourteenth Amendment in that it discriminates on the basis of race and ethnicity, and that the ordinance unconstitutionally targets day laborers because of their Latino origin (ACLU 2006). As David Blair-Loy put it when interviewed, the ordinance was a "pretext for unlawful discrimination."

The ACLU and the City of Vista reached a settlement almost a year later, on June 26, 2007. The settlement altered the enforcement of the day labor ordinance such that employers would be permitted to register "on the spot" rather than automatically being cited and fined if they attempted to hire a day laborer without a permit. There was no acknowledgment or rectification of the ordinance's alleged discriminatory motivation and impact. Blair-Loy noted that it is very difficult to prove intent to discriminate, given that immigrants are not considered a "suspect class" for a discrimination challenge under the Equal Protection Clause. Accordingly, it would have been necessary to prove that the ordinance targeted individuals based on their Latino ethnicity;

---

23. Gronke, author interview.

it would have been insufficient to demonstrate that they were targeted because of their immigration status.

In addition to making the ordinance less punitive by allowing employers to register on the spot, the City of Vista agreed to not "automatically" release the personal information of employers who registered to hire day laborers, as had been stipulated in the original ordinance. Rather, the settlement provided that when a request for public records is received, employers are to be given time to seek a court order to prevent the release of their personal information (ACLU 2007b).[24] When Vista passed its day labor ordinance, the Minutemen and other outspoken opponents of immigration felt it did not go far enough, and, according to Blair-Loy, this contingent was particularly upset about the settlement with the ACLU.[25] As San Diego Minutemen founder Jeff Schwilk lamented, the ordinance "does not forbid anybody from hiring illegal aliens. All it does is, basically, in a way, condone the behavior it was meant to deter" (Kauffman 2006).

Perhaps to express his displeasure with terms of the settlement that "weakened" the ordinance, Vista resident and leader of the San Diego Minutemen and Vista Citizens Brigade Michael Spencer sparked a "second-generation" lawsuit by making a public records request for the names, telephone numbers, and addresses of those who had registered with the city as day labor employers (*John Doe et al. v. City of Vista*, 2007). On July 5, 2007, the ACLU filed a class action privacy complaint seeking a temporary restraining order on the release of the private information "pending adjudication of the legal issues involved in the proper balance between personal privacy and public disclosure."

The narrowly tailored argument that the ACLU advanced was that the privacy rights of these individuals outweigh any public interest that would be served by the release of their personal information.[26] Though the City of Vista did not take a position on the matter, several media outlets— including the *North County Times*, *San Diego Union-Tribune*, and *Los Angeles Times*—advocated for public disclosure over privacy rights. After granting a temporary restraining order on September 20, 2007, to prevent release of the information, a San Diego County Superior Court judge ultimately barred the City of Vista from releasing the information (ACLU 2007b). Thus, although

---

24. Though city officials agreed to this provision, they believe that they are required by state law to allow public access to these records.

25. Blair-Loy, author interview.

26. Spencer and other day labor opponents had threatened to publicize the names and other personal information of registered employers.

the ACLU and its allies scored some moderate successes in modifying or limiting the scope of Vista's day labor ordinance, the ordinance remains in force in the city.[27]

CONCLUSION

According to Mayor Vance's assessment, the day labor ordinance has been moderately successful in limiting the exploitation of day laborers while simultaneously putting a damper on day labor hiring in the city. The ordinance's success in limiting day labor activity in the Vons shopping center is consistent with the experience of a day laborer from Puebla, Mexico, with whom I spoke at the day labor site one year after the ordinance went into effect. He and other workers had noted a drying up in day labor jobs since the passage of the ordinance, and he believes that employers are now less likely to look for workers at the shopping center because of the persistent vigilance of Minutemen activists, who have taken it upon themselves to enforce the day labor ordinance, intimidating both potential employers and day laborers.

While the ordinance and vigilance by the Minutemen may help explain the perceived decrease in day labor opportunities in the area, the steep decline in the San Diego housing market and the more general economic slowdown since 2006 are probably far more important factors.[28] This alternate explanation is supported by recent estimates by Vista's assistant city manager that indicate that the number of day laborers congregating at the site has not decreased. In fact, the average number of day laborers waiting daily at the site for potential employers had increased to fifty as of January 2008, up from a pre-ordinance estimate of between twenty-eight and thirty-four (Rodriguez and Davis 2008). Thus, despite the perception that day labor employment has become scarcer, it is evident that the day labor ordinance has failed to achieve its objective of "bringing some order to the shopping center."

---

27. Vista is not alone in its effort to address the growing visibility of informal day labor hiring. Almost sixty California cities have passed some form of day labor ordinance to limit or prohibit employer and/or worker solicitation within their local jurisdictions. But in numerous challenges, federal courts have ruled that bans on solicitation amount to unconstitutional limits on the right to free speech (Gonzalez 2007, 13). In addition, many ordinances have been challenged as discriminatory under the Equal Protection Clause of the Fourteenth Amendment.

28. This is consistent with the interpretation of the Inter-American Development Bank (2008) that the deceleration of remittance flows to Mexico between 2006 and 2007 is related to the slowing of the U.S. economy.

Regardless of the inner motivations of Vista's mayor and City Council members, the day labor ordinance demonstrated to the community that the local government was addressing the issue. Furthermore, the ordinance's nuanced design also satisfied a political function—the mayor and two incumbent Council members were reelected in November 2006—without subjecting the city to costly lawsuits to the same extent seen elsewhere in San Diego County and around the country.

The case of Vista's day labor ordinance is emblematic of the deep social divisions in hundreds of communities across the United States that are experiencing marked demographic and cultural changes but see no signs of comprehensive immigration reform coming from the federal level. As Mayor Vance put it, "we are going through a 'Latino-ization' of the country, and this is scary to people."[29] With respect to Vista, Vance attributes much of the controversy to "growing pains": "A lot of times people here wish Vista could again be as it used to be: a small, country town" (Sauer 2006). Tina Jillings makes a similar point, though with a slightly sharper tone: "Some seem to think they can get rid of all the Mexicans and get their white, homogeneous community back" (Sauer 2006). In a city that has gone from 17 percent Latino in 1980 to 47 percent in 2007, this would indeed be a false hope.

WORKS CITED

ACLU (American Civil Liberties Union). 2006. "ACLU Sues to Stop Vista Day Labor Ordinance: Ordinance Violates First Amendment," July 18. http://www.aclusandiego.org/news_item.php?article_id=000121.

———. 2007a. "ACLU Statement on CA Attorney General Review of Vista Officer-Involved Shootings: ACLU Troubled by Report's Rationales," July 13. http://www.aclusandiego.org/news_item.php?cat_id_sel=002&sub_cat_id_sel=000014&article_id=000274.

———. 2007b. "Victory in Vista Privacy Rights Case: Personal Information of Private Individuals Will Not Be Released," September 20. http://www.aclusandiego.org/news_item.php?article_id=000307.

Archibold, Randal C. 2006. "Immigrants Take to U.S. Streets in Show of Strength," *New York Times*, May 2.

Eisenstadt, Todd A., and Cathryn L. Thorup. 1994. *Caring Capacity versus Carrying Capacity: Community Responses to Mexican Immigration in San Diego's North County.* Monograph No. 39. La Jolla, CA: Center for U.S.-Mexican Studies, University of California, San Diego.

---

29. Vance, author interview.

Esbenshade, Jill, Barbara Obrzut, Benjamin Wright, Soo Mee Kim, Jessica Thompson, and Edward O'Conner. 2007. "Division and Dislocation: Regulating Immigration through Local Housing Ordinances." Washington, DC: Immigration Policy Center, American Immigration Law Foundation.

Gonzalez, Arturo. 2007. "Day Labor in the Golden State," *California Economic Policy* 3, no. 3 (July).

Government Accounting Office. 2002. "Worker Protection: Labor's Efforts to Enforce Protections for Day Laborers Could Benefit from Better Data and Guidance." GAO-02-925. Washington, DC: GAO, September.

Inter-American Development Bank, Multilateral Investment Fund. 2008. "Remittances to Latin America and the Caribbean 2007 (US$ millions)." http://www.iadb.org/mif/remesas_map.cfm?language=English&parid=5.

Kauffman, Bruce. 2006. "Day Labor and the Law," *San Diego Reader,* December 21. http://www.sandiegoreader.com/news/2006/dec/21/day-labor-and-law/.

Repard, Pauline, and Kristina Davis. 2006. "200 Officers Clear Streets in Vista after Reported Riot," *San Diego Union-Tribune,* May 2. http://justfixit.uniontrib.com/news/northcounty/20060502-9999-7m2vista.html.

Rodriguez, Mathew, and Kristina Davis. 2008. "Day-Labor Controversy Simmers on Back Burner," *San Diego Union-Tribune,* February 17. http://www.signonsandiego.com/uniontrib/20080217/news_lz1mc17labor.html.

Sanchez, Casey. 2007. "Blunt Force: San Diego Nativist Group Faces Troubles." Southern Poverty Law Center Intelligence Report. Reprinted by Coalition for Peace, Justice and Dignity, North San Diego County, California.

Sauer, Mark. 2006. "Vista at a Crossroads: City Again in Spotlight, This Time over Day Laborers," *San Diego Union-Tribune,* July 23.

Schwilk, Jeff. 2007. "DL Report: Illegal Day Labor Sites in San Diego County," October 29. http://sandiegominutemen.com.

Tenbroeck, Craig. 2006. "Vista Considers Day-Laborer Ordinance," *North County Times,* June 11.

Valenzuela, Abel, Jr., Nik Theodore, Edwin Meléndez, and Ana Luz González. 2006. "On the Corner: Day Labor in the United States, The National Day Labor Study." Los Angeles, CA: Center for the Study of Urban Poverty, University of California, Los Angeles. http://www.uic.edu/cuppa/uicued/.

Watson, Gregory Francis. 2007. "Investment of Migrant Resources: Remittances and Development." Mexico, DF: Inter-American Development Bank, Multilateral Investment Fund, February 2. http://idbdocs.iadb.org/wsdocs/getdocument.aspx?docnum=986640.

13 The "Law-and-Order" Foundation of Local Ordinances: A Four-Locale Study of Hazleton, PA, Escondido, CA, Farmers Branch, TX, and Prince William County, VA

JILL ESBENSHADE, BENJAMIN WRIGHT, PAUL CORTOPASSI, ARTHUR REED, AND JERRY FLORES

Over the past few years, a new phenomenon of local immigration regulation has swept the country as a growing number of city and county governments have passed or considered regulation aimed at ridding their communities of undocumented immigrants. This local-level regulation has taken various forms but has frequently consisted of ordinances banning landlords from renting to, or employers from hiring, undocumented immigrants, along with provisions to prohibit day labor and restrict the use of languages other than English in official city business. Together, these provisions constitute what are often referred to as Illegal Immigration Relief Acts (IIRAs). A number of ordinances across the country have been embroiled in legal battles and have been found unconstitutional. Because of the dubious legal position of such ordinances, many cities have put their ordinances on hold or adopted alternative measures. In all, at least 131 cities and counties in thirty states considered at least one, and often multiple, regulations between May 2006 and September 2007.[1]

In this chapter, we utilize discourse analysis to elucidate the justifications used for such policies and to delineate the bases on which local residents and city officials support the ordinances. Knowing the ways in which

---

1. Our list of 131 localities was obtained by cross-referencing a list compiled by the Fair Immigration Reform Movement with a similar list presented by the Puerto Rican Legal Defense and Education Fund and then checking any discrepancies against news reports.

supporters define the nature of the "problem" may lead to a clearer under-standing of the impetus for local immigration regulation. Although we cata-logued the statements of ordinance opponents, we focus exclusively on pro-ponents' arguments in this chapter.

This study is based on a review of more than forty-five hours of audio- and videotapes of city council and county supervisor meetings in which local or-dinances or policies targeting undocumented immigrants were debated. The analysis includes over seven hundred testimonies, primarily of local residents.[2] The meetings we reviewed took place in four locales: Escondido, California; Farmers Branch, Texas; Prince William County, Virginia; and Hazleton, Pennsylvania.[3] These four locales were chosen for study because of their prom-inence in the debate over local ordinances and for their geographical diversity, with representation from the West, Southwest, South, and Northeast.

These debates offer a unique opportunity to explore the rhetoric indi-viduals employ in the debate around immigration. Although a number of studies have looked at the presentation of immigration issues in the media and official documents, this study allows us to explore how these frames are reflected in the discourse of city residents. The most-often-cited reasons for these ordinances, including those outlined in the ordinances themselves, are the economic costs and deterioration in quality of life (crime, overcrowding, and disease) attributed to undocumented immigrants. However, we found that in both citizen and official testimony, the more ideological concept of "law and order" was the argument most commonly advanced in support of the ordinances. The focus was on "illegality" itself, rather than material im-pacts of the presence of undocumented immigrants.

Researchers have interrogated the social construction of "illegality" through various means, particularly for the Mexican population. Both De Genova (2004) and Massey (2003) show how unfair and often illogical im-migration legislation and policy, rather than individuals' criminal acts, have produced "the illegal Mexican." Inda (2006) makes a similar point through

---

2. In the meetings, local residents, residents from neighboring areas, and organizational representatives spoke from the floor to argue for or against the proposed ordinance or resolution. We refer to these people as "speakers." City council members and county supervisors also spoke for or against, as well as asking questions of city or county staff. In all, there were 64 testimonies from 26 officials and 765 testimonies from speakers. Of those, we were able to record a position and an actual argument for 59 of the officials' testimonies and 672 of the speakers' testimonies. Multiple uses of arguments by any speaker or official on a given day are only counted once in any category or subtheme.

3. For more on Prince William County, see Wilson, Singer, and DeRenzis and Waslin, this volume. For more on Hazleton, see Fleury-Steiner and Longazel, this volume.

an analysis of government reporting and enumeration. The militarization of the United States' southern border has also been an integral part of underscoring the association between illegality and Mexican immigrants (Andreas 1998–1999; Nevins 2002).

Transmission of the "illegal" framework to the public happens most directly through the media. As Chavez (2001) points out in his study of national magazine coverage of immigration, it is unclear to what extent the media incite or simply reflect anxiety over immigration. Nevertheless, the emphasis on "illegality" in media discourse on immigration has been clearly documented by several researchers. Nevins (2002) found illegality to be the most common theme in coverage of California's Proposition 187. Nevins traces this theme to the 1950s, when the term "wetback" predominated. Ono and Sloop (2002), who also analyzed national media coverage of Proposition 187, found economic issues to be the most common arguments used on both sides of the debate, followed by the concepts of criminality and morality—similar to our "law-and-order" arguments. Keogan (2002) found geographical variations in coverage, with the portrayal of immigrants in the *Los Angeles Times* focusing much more heavily than the *New York Times* on legal status and negative impacts. Coutin and Chock (1995) also found more nuanced coverage, with journalists creating paradoxical and sometimes subversive images of "illegal immigrants" gaining upward mobility to citizenship through the amnesty program. They also found, however, that the image of those who remained "illegal" constituting a threat to social stability was not significantly altered. Discourse analysis on immigration has largely focused on national media (Chavez 2001; Ono and Sloop 2002) and on media outlets in big cities like Los Angeles and New York (Coutin and Chock 1995), which are often immigrant strongholds (Nevins 2002; Keogan 2002; Ono and Sloop 2002). Our study shows that the language of illegality has been widely adopted by average citizens in smaller cities and suburbs that are undergoing demographic and economic shifts.

We begin the chapter with a brief history of each of our four communities in order to capture the flavor of the regulations in their respective contexts and thereby provide a better sense of the ordinance movement.[4] We then review the arguments used in support of the regulations and compare them to the official justifications. Finally, we delineate the contours of the "law-and-order" arguments and conclude with an analysis of the contradictions involved in this paradigm.

---

4. For more on the overall ordinance movement and the legal, logistical, and economic challenges it faces, see Esbenshade and Obrzut 2007–2008.

DEVELOPMENT OF THE ORDINANCE ISSUE IN FOUR CITIES

Hazleton, Pennsylvania

Hazleton is located in northeastern Pennsylvania and in 2000 had a population of 23,246.[5] At that time, only 1.7 percent of its population was foreign born, and only 4.9 percent was Latino. Although official census data are not available, the numbers of Latino and foreign born rose as people, particularly Latino immigrants, fled New York City for Hazleton in the aftermath of the terrorist attacks of September 11, 2001.

On June 15, 2006, Mayor Lou Barletta proposed an IIRA, copied nearly verbatim from a proposal considered the previous autumn in San Bernardino, California. In San Bernardino, Joseph Turner, the founder of Save Our State, an avowed anti-immigrant and blatantly racist organization, had unsuccessfully petitioned for a citywide vote on the proposal. In Hazleton, in contrast, Barletta's prominent position in local government and his more sophisticated rhetoric quickly made him the national spokesperson for these ordinances.

There was very limited debate in Hazleton on the ordinances. Council members were mainly concerned about the effect on landlords and the enforceability of the housing regulations. Many fewer residents spoke to the issue than in other locales. Speakers were not encouraged and were even intimidated. The president of the City Council, Joe Yannuzzi, repeatedly reprimanded, "this is not a discussion" and "this is not up for debate." When one Latino resident testified that he now felt unwelcome in Hazleton, Mayor Barletta replied, "I just have one question, and it's the point that I'm trying to make. Are you here legally or illegally?" (June 15, 2006). Within a month the city passed its first version of the ordinance and was promptly sued by the ACLU and others.

In March 2007, the Hazleton case went to a full trial. An article in the *Pittsburgh Gazette* described the testimony:

> During five hours on the witness stand, Mr. Barletta said Hazleton is being ruined by violent crime, crowded schools and a clogged emergency room at the city's private hospital. He attributed many of the problems to what he called "illegal aliens," even though he admitted he had no idea how many such immigrants are in his city. (Simonich 2007)

---

5. Hazleton had reached its peak population in the 1940s during its coal-mining boom.

In a 200-page decision, U.S. District Court Judge James Munley found the employment and rental prohibitions in Hazleton unconstitutional because they were preempted by federal law and violated due process rights guaranteed under the Fourteenth Amendment.

The Hazleton case, more than any other, brought national attention to these ordinances. The case has been covered by a variety of media outlets but received particular attention from Lou Dobbs on CNN. On October 25, 2006, Dobbs even went to Hazleton for a special "town hall" edition of his show, titled "CNN America Votes 2006 Special: Broken Borders." Dobbs also solicited money for Hazleton's defense numerous times on his program. The Hazleton case is now pending in the Third Circuit Court of Appeals.

Escondido, California

Escondido, California, lies about thirty miles north of San Diego. The local economy, once based in agriculture, now relies on a mix of agriculture, tourism, services, and high-tech industries. As of 2006, Escondido had a population of approximately 133,510, which is 49 people *fewer* than in 2000. Although Escondido has not grown in this decade, there has been a shift in its population, with foreign-born residents rising from 25.5 percent of the population to 31.1 percent and the Latino population increasing from 38.7 to 44.3 percent.

Though opponents filed lawsuits on August 15, 2006, against similar ordinances in Hazleton, Pennsylvania, and Riverside, New Jersey, the following day the Escondido City Council, purportedly aiming to address overcrowding, proposed an ordinance to sanction landlords who rent to undocumented immigrants. An October 4, 2006, meeting to discuss the ordinance drew large crowds, with the council chambers filled to capacity and another four hundred people outside. An October 18 meeting had fewer demonstrators, but it still required forty police officers to keep the crowds on each side of the issue separate. As described in the local paper:

> What started as a crowd of about 30 people before the meeting then grew into two raucous crowds totaling about 100 people. One was predominantly Latino, carrying religious symbols and picket signs. The other was predominantly white, carrying American flags and photos of officers the group said were killed by illegal immigrants. (Eakins and Sifuentes 2006)

Despite the fact that almost twice as many people testified against the ordinance as for it, the City Council passed the measure on October 18 by a three-to-two vote.

On November 16, 2006, U.S. District Court Judge John Houston, responding to constitutional challenges that opponents of the legislation had raised, granted a temporary restraining order to prevent enforcement. The City of Escondido subsequently decided not to pursue the matter in court because of cost concerns,[6] and it agreed to a permanent injunction against enforcement.

Yet, despite the city's decision to abandon the measure, during the January 2007 City Council meeting, Council Member Marie Waldron introduced her "New Year Resolution," a recommitment of the city to deal with illegal immigration. During the emotional discussion that followed, the majority of council members committed to proposing another ordinance as soon as the legal challenges were resolved. Seeking other strategies, the city is now using periodic driver's license checkpoints to deter illegal immigration. In the meantime, Escondido's ordinance spurred the California legislature to adopt, and Governor Schwarzenegger to sign in October 2007, AB 976, which *prohibits* cities from enacting laws requiring landlords to check the legal status of tenants and even bars landlords from voluntarily conducting such checks.

Farmers Branch, Texas

Farmers Branch is a suburb north of Dallas with a population of 27,508, over a third of whom are Latinos. On November 13, 2006, the Farmers Branch City Council passed Ordinance 2892, prohibiting landlords from renting to undocumented immigrants. Simultaneously, the city adopted an English-only measure and authorized the police to enter into a 287(g) agreement with Immigration and Customs Enforcement (ICE) to collaborate in the removal of undocumented immigrants.[7] The Council also considered, but rejected, a prohibition on employment of undocumented workers. As in the other locales, the City Council meeting included a long debate inside chambers and protests outside. Also as in the other locales, Ordinance 2892 was challenged in court. However, unlike in the other cities, opponents submitted hundreds of petitions to have the housing prohibition withdrawn or brought before city voters.

---

6. On only the injunction phase and subsequent settlement, Escondido has spent some $200,000 to $250,000, a combination of its own legal fees and the legal fees of the plaintiffs' counsel (ACLU 2006).

7. For more on 287(g) agreements, see the chapters by Waslin and Rodríguez, Chishti, and Northman, this volume.

City residents voted on Ordinance 2903, a revised version of 2892, on May 12, 2007. The issue was so contentious that Mayor Bob Phelps, who opposed the initiative, fled town during the vote. As the *Dallas Morning News* reported:

> Federal agents, sent to investigate the second act of vandalism at the mayor's house since the furor over illegal immigrants erupted, candidly told the Phelpses that out of town was perhaps the best place for them to be [during the elections]. "These last few months have been the worst time—I don't know, maybe of my life," Mr. Phelps said. (Floyd 2007)

Over two-thirds of city voters cast their ballots in favor of the regulation. After the vote, Council Member Tim O'Hare, the originator of the ordinances and now mayor, swore that if the city was to be sued again, he would take the issue all the way to the Supreme Court. The city immediately found itself embroiled in a second lawsuit. Judge Sam A. Lindsay of the U.S. District Court for the Northern District of Texas issued temporary restraining orders on both ordinances before either was implemented.

In response, five days after the second temporary restraining order, the City Council passed a third ordinance (2952) to address legal concerns raised in the lawsuits. The new ordinance shifts responsibility for checking renters' documents from individual landlords to the city and expands the regulation to include rental of single-family homes. The city has now decided to drop its defense of the first two ordinances after spending almost $1 million on its own legal team and being billed nearly another million dollars by plaintiffs' lawyers. Farmers Branch continues defending the third ordinance (Trejo and Sandoval 2008).

Prince William County, Virginia

Prince William County is located in northern Virginia, roughly thirty-five miles south of the District of Columbia. According to U.S. census data, the county's population increased approximately 27 percent between 2000 and 2006, from 280,813 to 357,503 inhabitants. This increase comprised a dramatic rise in the foreign-born and Latino populations, both of which nearly doubled as a percentage of population, to about 20 percent each. In response, Prince William County took a different tack than that adopted by the locales described above. It established a 287(g) agreement and limited the provision of services, rather than housing and employment opportunities.

In January 2007, the Board of County Supervisors directed county staff to study the possibility of reducing undocumented immigrants' access to services and collaborating with ICE to remove any undocumented immigrants arrested for crimes. In July 2007, the staff made a presentation to the supervisors about possible services reductions, including in libraries, public swimming pools, and even education. Supervisor Wally Covington went so far as to suggest challenging the constitutional protection of the right of undocumented minors to attend school, saying, "With this new Supreme Court, we have a real opportunity to overturn *Plyler v. Doe*" (Miroff 2007).[8] Because of the draconian nature of these suggested restrictions, the debate sparked substantial media coverage and controversy. County staff then determined which services were already disallowed by federal law, which were protected from limitation, and which fell into a middle category that could be considered for restriction.

On October 16, 2007, the Prince William Board of County Supervisors adopted Resolution 07-894. Although the resolution does not challenge the right of undocumented children to use educational facilities or library books, it does restrict services to undocumented elderly immigrants and those with disabilities, and it limits access to some drug prevention programs. It also requires verification of legal status to acquire a business license. In addition, the Board of Supervisors decided to expand its 287(g) program to cover the juvenile detention facility.

The Board's meetings attracted activists, both pro and con, from across the capital area. The debate preceding the Board's October 16 vote lasted more than twelve hours. During this time, more than 268 people spoke from the floor, and over a thousand gathered outside the building. So far the resolution seems more resistant to legal challenge than housing and/or employment ordinances in other cities have proved to be. Judge James C. Cacheris of the U.S. District Court in Alexandria dismissed a suit by the Puerto Rican Legal Defense and Education Fund for lack of standing on November 1, 2007 (McLaughlin 2007). However, in December the immigration subcommittee of the Virginia State Advisory Panel to the U.S. Commission on Civil Rights, headed by Linda Chavez (former director of the Commission under Reagan), conducted a hearing to investigate potential violations of anti-discrimination laws.

---

8. In a five-to-four decision in *Plyler v. Doe* (457 US 202 (1982)) the U.S. Supreme Court decided that undocumented children are entitled to K–12 public education.

OVERVIEW OF ARGUMENTS

In reviewing the city and county meetings discussed above, our first finding is that in three of the four locales many more people spoke against than in favor of the ordinances. In Hazleton, 24 spoke against and only 6 in favor; in Prince William County, it was 247 against and 147 in favor; and in Escondido, 104 against and 59 in favor. Only in Farmers Branch did the speakers in favor of the ordinance (118) outnumber those against (60). Yet the regulations were approved in every city. In Prince William County and Farmers Branch, officials voted unanimously in favor of the proposals, and there was only one defector in Hazleton, whose concerns were limited to technical questions. There was more dissent in Escondido, where the City Council voted three to two in favor and the mayor expressed opposition.

In reviewing the audio- and videotapes of local government meetings, we categorized supporting arguments into nineteen specific themes and then grouped those into five larger categories. The percentage of speakers from the floor who mentioned each type of argument at least once is displayed in figure 13.1.

Figure 13.1 Arguments in Favor of Regulations, by Percentage of Speakers

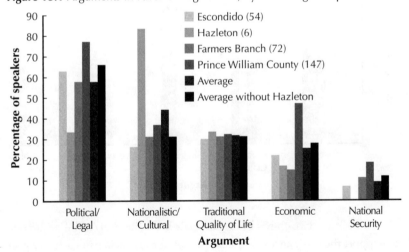

Political/Legal arguments were by far the most common, with an average of 58 percent of speakers advancing these types of considerations, versus 44 percent for Nationalist/Cultural worries, 32 percent for Traditional Quality of Life issues, 25 percent for Economic Costs, and only 9 percent for National

Security concerns. In fact, if we remove Hazleton, where there were only six speakers in favor of the measure, the numbers are even more dramatic, with Political/Legal rising to 66 percent and Nationalist/Cultural falling to 31 percent, making Political/Legal more than twice as prevalent as any other category. The most notable of the Political/Legal arguments was the "law-and-order" subtheme. In Hazleton, 50 percent of those who made Political/Legal arguments relied on law-and-order notions, but this was only one of two speakers. In each of the other three cities, approximately 80 percent of speakers (162) articulated the law-and-order subtheme. This means that virtually half (49 percent) of *all* ordinance supporters used a law-and-order argument.

City and county officials' arguments reflected a similar—though less dramatic—pattern. Political/Legal arguments were the most used, with "law and order" the most common theme in the arguments in this category. Figure 13.2 shows the breakdown of arguments by city officials.

Figure 13.2 Arguments in Favor of Regulations, by Percentage of City Officials

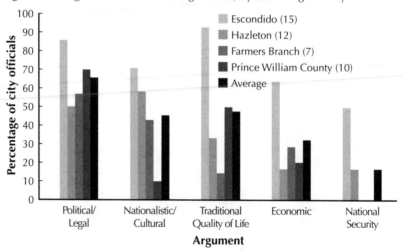

On average, two-thirds of city officials used Political/Legal arguments to support the ordinances, and at least half of the officials in each city used these arguments. On average, between 17 and 48 percent of city officials used the other categories. No other category of arguments was employed by half the official speakers in more than two cities. Within the Political/Legal category, the "law-and-order" theme again accounted for the majority of arguments: between 50 and 75 percent in each city.

ARGUMENTS COMPARED TO OFFICIAL JUSTIFICATION

Our findings show that for Hazleton and Farmers Branch the *original* justifications for their ordinances, as stated in the ordinances themselves, were not the primary focus of the arguments made by either City Council members or citizens. However, in Escondido and Prince William County, the preamble more closely resembles the rhetoric of those in favor, with Escondido presenting a somewhat more mixed picture.

The preamble of the Hazleton ordinance, borrowed verbatim from San Bernardino and then copied from Hazleton by dozens of cities across the country, begins with the deterioration of quality of life due to "illegal" immigration:

> The People of the City of Hazleton find and declare . . . that
> illegal immigration leads to higher crime rates, contributes
> to overcrowded classrooms and failing schools, subjects our
> hospitals to fiscal hardship and legal residents to substan-
> dard quality of care, and destroys our neighborhoods and
> diminishes our overall quality of life.

These preambles (and the Prince William County resolution) go on to mention the economic burden that "illegal" immigration imposes on the community. In Escondido the idea of an ordinance was first discussed under a section of the agenda entitled, "Discussion Regarding the City's Regulation of Overcrowding in Residential Neighborhoods and Related Issues" (August 16, 2006). The preamble to the Escondido ordinance discusses both traditional quality-of-life issues—particularly crime, overcrowding, and deteriorating housing conditions—and the economic burden these cause.

The preamble to the original Farmers Branch ordinance (2892) began with the justification of safeguarding the community against terrorism:

> Whereas, in response to the widespread concern of future
> terrorist attacks following the events of September 11, 2001,
> landlords and property managers throughout the country
> have been developing new security procedures to protect
> their buildings and residents . . .

Although this section of the preamble was deleted from the final version of the ordinance, the threat of potential terrorism was the *only* impetus given in the first two versions of the law (2892 and 2903). The Farmers Branch ordinance was then modified in response to two lawsuits filed against the city.

The preambles to the *final* Farmers Branch ordinance, the original Escondido ordinance, and the original Prince William County directive include notions of law and order as justifications. The Prince William County preamble did this implicitly, and the Escondido and final Farmers Branch ordinances did so explicitly:

> Whereas, the Prince William Board of County Supervisors believes that illegal immigration is causing economic hardship and *lawlessness* in this County... (Res. 07-609, July 10, 2007; italics added)

> The people of Escondido find and declare
> 1. Federal law requires that certain conditions be met before an alien may be authorized to be a lawful permanent resident, or be lawfully present, in the United States. Those conditions are found principally at the United States Code Title 8, section 1101 et seq.
> 2. Illegal aliens, as defined by federal law, do not normally meet such conditions as a matter of law when present in the City.

The final version of the Farmers Branch resolution is nearly identical to the two paragraphs from the Escondido preamble presented above. Prince William County ends its Resolution 07-894 (a later version) by thanking its staff "on the tremendous work done in the interest of maintaining the rule of law in Prince William County."

In two of the four cities, Traditional Quality of Life issues, Economic Costs, and National Security were the *only* original motivations given for the ordinances. In Escondido, while Rule of Law was primary in the preamble, Traditional Quality of Life issues actually framed the original City Council discussion and call for an ordinance. Only in Prince William County was Rule of Law clearly the central concern. As shown by our analysis of the testimony of both officials and citizens, arguments based on Rule of Law were much more common than these other categories. The exception was Hazleton, where Nationalist/Cultural arguments dominated among both speakers and officials, a concern not mentioned in the ordinance at all.

LAW AND ORDER

The most common arguments made by proponents of the ordinances were those involving "law and order." These arguments fell into three main contentions: "order versus chaos," "illegal is illegal," and "we, the legal, versus them, the illegal." Each of these arguments was present in all four locales.

Order versus Chaos

The idea that "illegals" are creating chaos found expression in every locale. As Penny Magnotto of Escondido said, "I simply want order in my city." This sentiment referred as much to disruptions to the nature of society as to possible disruptions of the peace (as portrayed in Lou Barletta's images of rampant crime, disease, and general societal deterioration). As Joe Yannuzzi, Hazleton council member, expressed it, "Ordinances are put on the books to keep people civil. That's the difference between civilization and uncivilized people" (June 15, 2006).

Order was not only seen as an important facet of civilization in general but of American civilization in particular. As with other themes, there was an element of nationalism embedded in the concept of order. This emphasis on rule of law as a foundation of U.S. society was made by officials and citizens alike. John T. Stirrup, Jr., the county supervisor who first proposed the new policies in Prince William County, framed his underlying motivation as follows: "I think the Board has reemphasized that this is about the rule of law. It's what our American civilization is all about; this is the basis of it" (July 10, 2007). The specter of disaster that ensues after allowing "illegals" to break the law was also a common theme, as Patricia Bennett, a resident of Escondido, observed: "America is a country of laws. . . . If we break down our laws, this country will fall into ruin" (October 18, 2006). Moreover, the law and order of the United States was sometimes implicitly or even explicitly counterposed to lawless Mexico: "Not to implement the law is . . . to create anarchy. . . . That is Mexico" (Escondido resident Francisca Galván, October 18, 2006).

Illegal Is Illegal

This mantra emerged in all four case studies and clearly stood for the idea that someone who breaks the law in order to enter the country is de facto a criminal. Again with a nationalist flavor, Charles Berger, resident of Prince William County, insisted on this point: "It's real simple; when you cross the border illegally, you compromise the sovereignty of the country. And despite what everybody else has told you, if you're here illegally, if you cross the border illegally, you are a criminal! Don't keep saying, 'I'm not a criminal. I'm not a criminal.' You're a criminal!" (October 16, 2007). In addition to being a de facto criminal, the "illegal" also breeds more criminality, as Susie Hall of Escondido contends: "Once a human being has broken the law, he has an easier step . . . to break more laws" (October 18, 2006).

It is not only the illegal but also those who defend him who are to blame for the spiral of criminal activity. As Hazleton Mayor Lou Barletta explained, "When you start justifying one criminal act, it becomes easier and easier to justify more. Illegal is illegal, period!" (July 13, 2006). Moreover, the city itself was seen as complicit in this illegality, as Evelyn Miller of Escondido warned: "This council can be a lawless [council] by allowing violation of federal law or be a law-abiding city council by not aiding and abetting" (October 18, 2006).

The idea of the illegal as criminal is important because it justifies punishment and, consequently, the punitive ordinances. It is the individual illegal who is responsible for his actions. On January 22, 2007, Tom Bohmier of Farmers Branch expressed one version of this pervasive idea:

> Our laws are written in black and white and should not be interpreted in shades of grey. . . . As far as legal, if a resident consciously continues to drive under the influence of alcohol and is jailed for ten years, then their spouse and their family suffer as a direct result of their decision. When an illegal crosses into the border and obtains fake documents, they have broken two laws, one of which is a felony. Yes, their families may suffer as a result of their deportations, but they made the decision to break our laws.

Legal versus Illegal

Not only were undocumented immigrants consistently referred to as lawbreakers, they were also contrasted to legal residents. "Illegals" were often presented as an affront to the legal residents and, even further, as privileged over legal residents. Donna Widowski, of Prince William County, asserted: "What I witnessed was a direct slap in the face to all hardworking, law-abiding citizens of this country. . . . Our elected officials need to reprioritize the concerns of our law-abiding, legal residents over those who are operating lawless in our country" (October 2, 2007). For many of the speakers, there is a clear sense of direct conflict between "us" and "them." For instance, Anita Helinihi, nineteen-year resident of Escondido, spoke about the spring 2006 pro-immigrant protests: "The illegal aliens need to protest in their own country and cities, not ours. We do not want them here. There are too many. We are being invaded and need to take back what's ours" (October 18, 2006).

Undocumented immigrants were not only contrasted to the residents but also to the residents' ancestors, who were *legal immigrants* "doing things the right way," that is, entering legally and assimilating. Prince William County Supervisor Maureen S. Caddigan articulated this sentiment:

> My parents were born in Ireland, so I am from immigrant parents. But they came here over seventy years ago with the Italians, the Polish, the Germans. And they came here and they did it the right way, and that is all that we are asking. We are not against immigration, because that is what this county, this country, was built on, but they came here as citizens. They saluted our flag, they held our flag, and they conformed to the way of the American people. And it is a great country. And that is all that we are saying today. The word is "illegal," against the law, "illegal," and I am supporting this motion. (July 10, 2007)

These statements served to connect the speakers to an immigrant background and simultaneously to contrast them to the "illegal" immigrants. Moreover, such assertions function to justify the current residents' ownership of the United States. As Mayor Barletta of Hazleton expressed, "This country was built on the backs of legal immigrants. My own great-grandparents came to this country seeking a better life" (June 15, 2006). It is not only current residents who are violated by the presence of "illegal" immigrants; their ancestors are equally posited as victims of these intruders. Even in Texas, formerly Mexican territory, Sue Bucy claimed that the ancestors of the area's current residents' are violated by the presence of these immigrants, whom she later clarifies are Mexican. "So, please, if you are going to be here in our country, be here legally, and don't take advantage of what *our* ancestors have worked hard for" (November 13, 2006).

In fact, ordinance supporters constantly defended the ordinances as race neutral. For the most part, government officials and even speakers in Prince

William County and Hazleton were careful not to allude to specific racial or national groups. However, much of the rhetoric in Farmers Branch and Escondido focused on Latinos, and references were made in every city to statistics or incidents involving Latinos. Moreover, in every city Latinos reported a rise in racial hostility following the introduction of the regulations into public debate.

CONCLUSION: "LAW AND ORDER" AND LOCAL ORDINANCES

Our analysis of testimony from city council and county supervisor hearings reveals that while formal justifications for the ordinances largely revolve around issues legitimately under the purview of local governments (local criminal activity, overcrowded hospitals, rising education budgets), the principal driver of public support is not concern over these traditional quality-of-life or economic issues. In fact, in none of the four locales did even a third of supporters mention any quality-of-life issue. And in three locales, fewer than a quarter of all speakers mentioned economic issues, and in the fourth (Prince William County) the number was still under 50 percent. Rather, the greatest portion of citizens is concerned with the more amorphous idea of "illegality." Illegality at the level of being present in the country illegally, however, is not a crime over which local police or governments generally have jurisdiction (except in the limited case of 287(g) agreements). Illegal presence is clearly a federal matter. Yet it is illegal presence itself that seems to be of most concern to the public and even to local officials, rather than the supposed quality-of-life and economic ramifications of illegal presence that politicians and pundits so often invoke.

The irony is that these ordinances do not address the concerns that surround illegality. In fact, the ordinances may exacerbate them. For instance, the desire to create order and promote "civilization" may be undermined given that efforts to deal with national problems on a local level can generate disorder. Even if local measures are successful, they merely push undocumented immigrants from one community to another. Officials in all of the four locales we examined acknowledged that the point of their ordinance was to deter "illegals" from coming to *their* city. As Mayor Barletta argued at a City Council meeting, "If we pass this [ordinance] we're going to send a clear message that if illegal immigrants are going to go somewhere in the United States, I don't think I'd choose Hazleton, Pennsylvania" (June 15, 2006). In this way, the issue is not resolved but is only passed along. Furthermore,

Prince William County has specifically reduced access to programs whose purpose is to create order (drug treatment and prevention, and homeless intervention) and to provide for civilized treatment of vulnerable populations (the elderly and people with disabilities).

Moreover, three of the four communities have made no effort to reduce local demand for immigrant labor. Immigrants in these three communities are told, in effect, that they must live elsewhere even though their productive power is utilized in the ordinance locale. In the fourth community, Prince William County, the message is more blatant. There seems to be an attempt to rid the locale of any nonproductive members on the one hand—the elderly, homeless people, and people with disabilities—and, on the other, of members who are too economically independent—business owners. Only the hardworking employees are left alone.

Ordinance supporters also espouse a concern over respect for the law of the land, privileging this concern over legality per se. This is expressed most clearly in their definition of "illegals" as criminals. However, the "crime" of arriving in the country or remaining "illegally" is a violation not of local but of federal law. The ordinances are, in effect, an end run around the U.S. legal system and the recognition of such fundamental pillars of that system as proper jurisdiction, the legislative process, and constitutional protections. Instead, the ordinances attempt to add new crimes, either by immigrants themselves or by landlords or employers, to the framework.

The climate these debates created has had unmistakable and profound effects on Latinos in all of these communities. Though supporters of the ordinances try to make clear distinctions between "illegal" and "legal" residents, Latinos, regardless of status, have reported increased tensions (Esbenshade and Obrzut 2007–2008). Latino resident after Latino resident spoke of a growing sense of being under attack. Ana Reyes described the effect of this heightened hostility in Farmers Branch:

> I am overwhelmed by the hatred that has filled this community and has been directed at the Hispanic residents. After experiencing a lifetime of friendly smiles and hellos, I am now greeted with complete disregard and angry glares. I want to stand and tell you I am not for illegal immigration, but it has been very clear that the destructive division that has been created in this community is due in part to the fear in changing demographics, with the growing number of

> Hispanic residents. Without bringing forth any statistical in-
> formation about the number of undocumented immigrants
> in this city, you have targeted all of us. You see our children
> coming out of school, you see our families coming out of
> the grocery stores or the post office, and you assume "illegal
> immigrants." You hear us interact with one another in our
> native language, and you say, "They don't speak English."
> And when a young Hispanic man stands at the steps of this
> building that presumably stands for justice to tell you about
> his pride serving in the armed forces, we heard those shouts,
> "Does he have papers?" (January 22, 2007)

Clearly, the "us-versus-them" attitude that ordinance supporters have demonstrated creates its own reality, something that many observers describe as "now-divided communities." The emphasis on "illegality" underscores this division as other terms—undocumented, unauthorized, irregular migrant—do not. It places these individuals beyond the pale of civilized society and thus identifies them as deserving of exclusion from such basic rights as the right to shelter.

There is no denying that there is a racial element to these policies, and many sociologists have argued that "illegality" is the color-blind code, as Bonilla-Silva would phrase it, for "Latino" (2006). The great majority of those affected by the laws are Latinos, who make up over 80 percent of the undocumented population in the United States (Passel 2005). These regulations appear to be both a result of racism and a catalyst for increased racism. As retired San Diego County Assistant Sheriff and Escondido resident Bill Flores argued, "What this resolution wants to say is that there are too many brown faces in Escondido" (January 10, 2007). Simultaneously, as Ana Arias contended regarding the ordinance in Hazleton, "It is very divisive, and it is creating hatred and racism in the community" (July 13, 2006).

This brings us to a final internal contradiction in these ordinances. George Sánchez has noted that nativism and racism, while related, "often lead in different directions" (1997, 1013), and, as René Galindo and Jami Vigil point out, racial nativism involves the opposing goals of assimilation and exclusion (2006). Nativism, the preference for native-born persons over foreigners, often presents itself through an insistence that immigrants learn English and relinquish their previous loyalties and identities. And though such sentiments were certainly in evidence during these ordinance debates, most strongly in Hazleton, the ordinances are in fact directed toward the more racist goal of exclusion. However, not only have the ordinances been unsuccessful at expelling undocumented immigrants, their vulnerability to legal challenges has meant that the ordinances have also undermined the goal of assimilation. What the ordinances *have* achieved is the further alienation and marginalization of Latinos in general within these communities, potentially converting the accusation of non-assimilation into a self-fulfilling prophecy.

WORKS CITED

ACLU (American Civil Liberties Union). 2006. "Anti-Immigrant Ordinances: Escondido, California." http://www.aclu.org/immigrants-rights/anti-immigrant-ordinances-escondido-calif.

Andreas, Peter. 1998–1999. "The Escalation of U.S. Immigration Control in the Post-NAFTA Era," *Political Science Quarterly* 113, no. 4: 591–615.

Bonilla-Silva, Eduardo. 2006. *Racism without Racists: Color-Blind Racism and the Persistence of Racial Inequality in the United States.* Lanham, MD: Rowman and Littlefield.

Chavez, Leo R. 2001. *Covering Immigration: Popular Images and the Politics of the Nation.* Berkeley, CA: University of California Press.

Coutin, Susan Bibler, and Phyllis Chock. 1995. "'Your Friend, the Illegal': Definition and Paradox in Newspaper Accounts of US Immigration Reform," *Identities* 2, nos. 1–2: 123–48.

De Genova, Nicholas. 2004. "The Legal Production of Mexican/Migrant 'Illegality,'" *Latino Studies* 2: 160–85.

Eakins, Paul, and Edward Sifuentes. 2006. "Rental Ban Divides Escondido Protesters; Crowds Erupt in Shouting Match after Vote," *North County Times,* October 18.

Esbenshade, Jill, and Barbara Obrzut. 2007–2008. "Local Immigration Regulation: A Problematic Trend in Public Policy," *Harvard Journal of Hispanic Policy* 20: 33–48.

Floyd, Jacquielynn. 2007. "Mayor: No Real Winners in This Vote," *Dallas Morning News,* May 13.

Galindo, René, and Jami Vigil. 2006. "Are Anti-Immigrant Statements Racist or Nativist? What Difference Does It Make?" *Latino Studies* 4: 419–47.

Inda, Jonathan Xavier. 2006. *Targeting Immigrants: Government, Technology and Ethics.* Malden, MA: Blackwell.

Keogan, Kevin. 2002. "A Sense of Place: The Politics of Immigration and the Symbolic Construction of Identity in Southern California and the New York Metropolitan Area," *Sociological Forum* 17, no. 2: 223–53.

Massey, Douglas. 2003. "Closed Door Policy," *American Prospect* 14, no. 7 (July 3).

McLaughlin, Seth. 2007. "Illegals-Law Challenge Rebuffed: Sanctions Stand in Prince William," *Washington Times*, December 1.

Miroff, Nick. 2007. "Prince William Passes Resolution Targeting Illegal Immigration: Stricter Aspects of Original Plan Are Softened," *Washington Post*, July 12.

Nevins, Joseph. 2002. *Operation Gatekeeper: The Rise of the "Illegal Alien" and the Making of the U.S.-Mexico Boundary.* New York: Routledge.

Ono, Kent, and John Sloop. 2002. *Shifting Borders: Rhetoric, Immigration and California's Proposition 187.* Philadelphia, PA: Temple University Press.

Passel, Jeffrey. 2005. "Estimates of the Size and Characteristics of the Undocumented Population." Pew Hispanic Center Report. Washington, DC, March 21.

Sánchez, George. 1997. "Face the Nation: Race, Immigration and the Rise of Nativism in Late Twentieth Century America," *International Migration Review* 31, no. 4: 1009–30.

Simonich, Milan. 2007. "Hazleton Mayor, ACLU Square Off over Immigration," *Pittsburgh Post-Gazette*, March 15.

Trejo, Frank, and Stephanie Sandoval. 2008. "Farmers Branch Won't Pursue Legal Battle on Immigrant Rental Ban Ruled Unconstitutional," *Dallas Morning News*, September 29.

14 "Tired of Illegals": Immigrant Driver's Licenses, Constituent Letters, and Shifting Restrictionist Discourse in California

Hinda Seif

In the fall of 2003, two California laws that weighed heavily on immigrant communities were dramatically reversed, then reinstated. A decade earlier the California legislature had passed laws that for the first time required a Social Security number and proof of lawful immigration status to get a driver's license, ultimately preventing up to two million California drivers from obtaining or renewing their licenses (Office of Senate Floor Analyses 2003). In 2003 State Senator Gil Cedillo authored a bill that would remove these restrictions. Governor Gray Davis signed the bill into law in September 2003 at a rally in the parking lot of the Department of Motor Vehicles in East Los Angeles. In so doing, he put the final nail in the coffin of his governorship. A month later, Davis became the first California governor recalled from office. His successor was bodybuilder and movie star Arnold Schwarzenegger, one of whose first acts in office was to overturn Davis's action and "terminate" the new driver's license legislation.

Though few states required driver's license holders to have lawful immigration status prior to September 11, 2001, forty-two states now require license applicants to be lawfully present in the United States, and all states instruct them to provide their Social Security number (NILC 2009). Further, the federal

This research was conducted with the support of the University of California's Center for Comparative Immigration Studies and Institute for Labor and Employment, UC ACCORD, and the College of Liberal Arts and Sciences at the University of Illinois at Springfield. Although all who made this chapter possible are too numerous to mention, special thanks to the offices of Senator Gil Cedillo and former Assemblyman Marco Firebaugh, Wayne Cornelius, Bianet Castellanos, Roger Rouse, Julie Cottle, Travis DuBry, Heather Dell, Jennifer Manthei, Jonathan Isler, and Monica Varsanyi.

government's 2005 REAL ID Act imposed related licensing regulations on state motor vehicle authorities.[1] Clearly, immigration-related driver's license restrictions are a significant policy trend across the country. California accounted for 24 percent of the undocumented immigrants present in the United States in 2008 (Passel and Cohn 2009),[2] and the case of the California driver's license is key to understanding the changing context of immigration politics.

What was the tone of political discourse that drove the stunning political turnabout regarding driver's licenses for the undocumented? Most analyses of anti-immigrant rhetoric focus on the mass media, a crucial arena for shaping public opinion (Chavez 2001; Ono and Sloop 2002; Santa Ana 2002; Akdenizli et al. 2008; Vélez et al. 2008). However, transformations of media and communications and the changing political context since 9/11 demand new analyses of restrictionist discourse. This includes the grassroots political pressure directed at state and local politicians at a time when immigrant policy is increasingly devolving to the subnational level (see Esbenshade et al., this volume). In this chapter, I analyze ninety-eight pieces of correspondence sent to Senator Cedillo's office between 2004 and 2005 regarding his legislative efforts to restore driver's license privileges to immigrants in California regardless of their ability to prove lawful presence in the United States. Constituents' letters offer insight into the arguments of the individuals who attempt to pressure elected officials regarding immigration policy. We begin to see how vocal advocates for restricting the rights of the undocumented envision the United States as a nation and how they view its relationship to Mexico, Mexican immigrants, and U.S. citizens of Mexican ancestry. The letter writers, who as a group tend to be older, whiter, and more male than the average Californian, appear to be influenced by the messages of a transforming (and sometimes misinforming) mass media. They use its increasingly dehumanizing immigration rhetoric in the same letters in which they assert that they are not racist. Rather than addressing the specifics of the proposed driver's license bill, most writers highlight perceived criminal, economic, political, and cultural threats posed by Mexico, Mexican immigration, or the "Mexicanization" of California and the nation.

---

1. The REAL ID Act was enacted as part of the Emergency Supplemental Appropriations Act for Defense, the Global War on Terror, and Tsunami Relief (Public Law No. 109-13). It requires an applicant to present proof of lawful U.S. presence and a Social Security number in order for a driver's license to be accepted as federal identification. However, the act also provides for the issuance of licenses that do not qualify as federal identification. Many states have obtained extensions until 2011 to comply with this act, and various bills have been introduced in Congress to amend or repeal it.

2. California's share of the undocumented population has been declining as Mexican immigrants settle across the country (Zúñiga and Hernández-León 2005).

SHIFTING IMMIGRATION POLICY DISCOURSE

Immigration-related discourse opens a window on the ways in which governments and their citizenry imagine the nation. Because rhetoric and reality are mutually constituted, the words we use to describe immigration shape law, policy, and immigrants' daily lives. The United States is a country of immigration, so related images and metaphors are central to our self-definition. There are administrative and popular discourses of immigration, and each has changed over time. For example, the colloquial term "alien" calls to mind Martians when used in everyday speech, yet in U.S. statutes it references any noncitizen. Although government authorities and citizens now commonly refer to unauthorized immigrants as "illegals," the judicial use of the term dates from as recently as 1950 (Neuman 1996).

In 1994, California's passage of Proposition 187 signaled a new phase of immigrant policy and discourse. Grassroots activists expressed their frustration with the federal government's failure to stop illegal immigration and resolved to take enforcement into their own hands. Although most provisions of this voter initiative were voided in the courts, had it stood, it would have denied a host of state benefits and services—including K–12 education—to persons who lacked proof of federal lawful presence. By using the state's referendum system, restrictionists brought their struggle to the subnational level, bypassing the legislative process to write their own law aimed at driving the undocumented out of California.

Many scholars have identified racism in the Prop. 187 debates (Hondagneu-Sotelo 1995; Inda 2000; K. Johnson 1995; Ono and Sloop 2002; Santa Ana 2002). For example, in his analysis of depictions of California's voter initiatives in the *Los Angeles Times*, sociolinguist Santa Ana (2002) examined the use of negative metaphors—immigrants as animals—that represented Latin American immigrants as less than fully human. Despite Mexican immigrants' long-standing relationship to the Southwest—an area wrested from Mexico through war in the mid-nineteenth century—they were depicted in the popular media as parasites on the U.S. body. The discourse of Mexicans invading a homogenous European-American house blurred the distinction between illegal immigrants, lawful residents, and citizens of Latin American ancestry. In these ways, the news media and law constructed Latinos as outsiders or illegals in relation to the nation-state (Santa Ana 2002).

The changing contexts of communications and politics since the passage of Proposition 187 require new examinations of immigrant politics and policy discourse (Akdenizli et al. 2008; Padín and Smith 2004; Sohoni 2006).

The revolution in information technologies is transforming media and grass-roots networking, communications, and activism. These changes, along with Latino organizing against political restrictionism, have altered the forms and scope of immigrant and anti-immigrant activism. Labor unions, immigrant rights organizations, and Latino politicians have made some headway toward reframing Latino immigrants from parasites (Inda 2000) and hyper-fertile breeders (Gutiérrez 2008) to crucial workers for the U.S. economy (Milkman 2006; Seif 2008). The 2006 marches in support of immigration reform, largely mobilized through an expanding and varied Spanish-language news media, replaced images of passive illegal immigrants hiding in the shadows with visible political subjects (Suro, in Akdenizli et al. 2008). On the other hand, since the tragedy of 9/11, restrictionists have portrayed unauthorized mi-gration as a national security menace as well as an economic threat. The con-centration of media ownership means that consent is manufactured with an unprecedented intensity. Yet while traditional print newspapers contract and consolidate, sensationalist Web logs (blogs) multiply. Cable has transformed network television, which increasingly relies on relatively inexpensive real-ity shows such as ABC's short-running *Homeland Security, USA*. The formerly sober evening news hour, meanwhile, finds it must entertain to stay on the air, and news programs often turn to divisive immigrant debates to draw an audience. Driver's license policies in California and across the country are affected by these changes in public discourse.

THE DRIVER'S LICENSE ISSUE IN A LOS ANGELES IMMIGRANT DISTRICT

Driver's license restrictions crystallize the challenges facing immigrant neighborhoods like those in California Assembly District 46. Before it was reapportioned in 2000, Assembly District 46 in downtown Los Angeles comprised Koreatown, Japantown, Chinatown, and Pico Union, the largest and increasingly settled Central American community in the United States (Coutin 2003; Hamilton and Chinchilla 2001). It was home to immigrants who cleaned the office buildings and cared for the aging parents of the global city's corporate executives. It was also the hub for numerous organi-zations that served and mobilized Latin American workers and their fami-lies: the Los Angeles County Federation of Labor; the Service Employees International Union (SEIU) Local 1877 (Justice for Janitors); the Coalition for Humane Immigrant Rights of Los Angeles (CHIRLA); and the Central American Resource Center (CARECEN). Although we have no accurate count of the district's undocumented population, the area's residents were the least likely to have health insurance in California, and 36 percent of its children were uninsured (Brown et al. 2001, 68). In 2000, less than 20 percent of district residents were registered to vote, also the smallest proportion in the state, and further, although the great majority of district residents were of Latin American ancestry, less than 44 percent of the district's registered voters were Latino (Institute of Governmental Studies 2000). Poverty, low levels of formal education, and lack of citizenship were all barriers to electoral participation.

Gil Cedillo, Assembly District 46's representative from 1998 to 2002, was raised in East Los Angeles and served as general manager of SEIU Local 660 from 1991 to 1996.[3] Following the passage of Proposition 187, he led the United Food and Commercial Workers Union's Campaign for Dignity and Civic Participation, one of the numerous citizenship and voter registration efforts aimed at Latino workers that helped usher candidates sympathetic to immigrant workers into office. During his 1998 primary campaign, Cedillo walked door to door through District 46 to hear of the residents' needs, and one common theme was the need to reverse recent restrictions on driver's licenses.[4] Members of the Pico Union Housing Neighborhood Network were dismayed that police were seizing the cars of immigrants who had been denied a license. Without cars, how were residents to get to work at construction sites at the edge of sprawling suburbs and to their off-hour jobs in janitorial and food services and health care? The driver's license laws also overwhelmed local law enforcement and justice administration. Hours that police spent trying to identify unlicensed drivers meant less time to fight crime, and court dockets were filled with related misdemeanors. Cedillo pledged that, if elected, he would fight for restoration of driver's license privileges for California's immigrant workers. His electoral success was part of a broader political trend in which a half-million Latino Californians became U.S. citizens (H. Johnson et al. 1999, 59). The 1.1 million Latinos who registered to vote during the 1990s (Baldassare 2002, 161) helped elect a new generation of Latino and pro-immigrant politicians (Frank and Wong 2004; Milkman 2006; Seif 2008).

When he arrived in Sacramento, freshman legislator Cedillo and likeminded individuals in law enforcement, local government, business, and labor unions believed that restoring driver's license access to immigrants

---

3. Cedillo has represented the district as state senator since 2002.
4. David Galaviz, interview by the author, April 19, 2001.

was good policy for the state. Some argued that the California Department of Motor Vehicles needed to focus on its mission of road and highway safety and leave immigration law enforcement to the federal government. Because a license is required to register a car and purchase auto insurance in California, restoring driving privileges to more immigrants would yield more registered cars and insured drivers. Despite warnings from political veterans who cautioned him about the political dangers of trying to change the license laws,[5] Cedillo kept his campaign promise and soon introduced related legislation. Governor Davis vetoed Cedillo's first three attempts to pass driver's license bills. After his fourth driver's license bill was signed and enacted but then repealed in 2003, Cedillo introduced Senate Bill (SB) 1160 in February 2004 and SB 60 in January 2005, which elicited the letters analyzed in this chapter.

Both bills, designed as compromises with the newly seated Governor Schwarzenegger, would have incorporated strict standards for undocumented applicants, including mandatory criminal background checks. SB 60 also aimed to place California in compliance with the federal REAL ID Act by issuing a special driver's license to persons who could not meet the requirements for a Social Security number and proof of lawful presence. Caught between claims from some immigrant and civil rights advocates that the new legislative proposals were discriminatory, reverberations from the recent recall and repeal of related laws, and ongoing anti-license campaigning, SB 1160 never reached the Senate floor and SB 60 was vetoed by Governor Schwarzenegger.

ANALYZING CONSTITUENT LETTERS: PITFALLS AND PROMISE

By 2003, California's legislative offices were fielding an onslaught of calls and correspondence opposing Cedillo's driver's license bills.[6] Rather than signaling a vibrant informed and democratic debate, many phone calls and constituent letters were deeply disturbing.

To complement my prior research on immigrant legislative advocacy (Seif 2004, 2008, 2010), I analyzed letters, postcards, and other ephemera sent to Senator Cedillo in 2004 and 2005 in opposition to the proposed driver's license legislation. We examined the gender balance of the letter writers

5. Ibid.
6. California is not the only state where constituent opposition was significant on this issue. A Tennessee law (2004) and an executive order issued in New York by Governor Eliot Spitzer in 2007 extending driver's license access to state drivers regardless of their federal immigration status were rescinded due to restrictionist campaigns and heavy constituent communications (Confessore 2007; New York Immigration Coalition 2007; Tennessee Immigrant and Refugee Rights Coalition 2005).

and whether they represented California's diverse population. How did the authors refer to immigrants who lacked lawful immigration status, and how did they invoke race? We looked at the arguments the authors offered against restoring driver's license privileges and the ways that 9/11 may have affected their line of reasoning. Is there any evidence of the influence of media and restrictionist groups on their language and contentions? Finally, we were interested in what these letters suggest about the state of democratic deliberations on immigrant issues and, more broadly, the vision the writers hold of California and our nation.

With the help of graduate assistant Becky Buhl, I coded the letters and included ephemera (envelopes, copies of news articles, graphics) in hopes of answering these questions. There are many limitations to the use of constituent correspondence for academic research. Because letters were not stored for the purpose of scholarly analysis, the set of letters in the file is probably incomplete. Few voters contact their elected representatives, and letters are only one form of constituent communication. For example, much voter contact now occurs via e-mail, a form that is even less likely than paper to be stored and saved. Further, various demographic groups may favor one communication format over the others. The rhetoric of written letters may be distinct from e-mail correspondence sent by younger, more educated, affluent, and computer-savvy constituents with ready Internet access. Thus we cannot assume that Cedillo's letter writers are typical of Californians, California voters, or even Californians who oppose allowing undocumented immigrants to obtain driver's licenses. Despite these caveats, analyzing constituent correspondence is an underutilized way to shed light on vocal restrictionists, their beliefs, and especially the intense pressure placed on legislators to torpedo recent immigrant-friendly legislation. Though the letters are modest in number, their messages are magnified because legislative staff considers each individually composed constituent letter to represent the position of numerous voters.[7]

---

7. In a study of written communication, the researcher must grapple with missing or inconclusive data. For example, it is impossible to accurately determine the sex and race of letter writers. I use their self-identifications and infer probable demographic information (such as their sex) from their names. Pseudonyms are used here and identifying information is changed to protect confidentiality. Because some writers mailed multiple letters, the identification of each letter writer is counted only once for coding purposes. For all other coding categories, I enumerate whether a word or phrase was used at least one time per letter. Thus, if an author referred to immigrants without lawful status as "illegal aliens" and "illegals" in one letter, each is counted once. If he sends a new letter and uses the terms again, each category is counted again.

BRING IT BACK TO WHAT IT WAS BEFORE: WRITER DEMOGRAPHICS AND IDENTIFICATION

> *I fought war in Europe, Pacific, Korea and Vietnam and you people are letting the USA GO TO HELL? Bring it back to what it was before and act in the best interests of the People and country. Bring back patriotism and proud of country.*[8]

Like Arthur, who penned the preceding words in a shaky hand, the individuals who corresponded with Cedillo in these letters do not reflect the demographic diversity of his district, California voters, or Californians in general. Based on an analysis of names, it appears that there is a strong male bias among the letter writers, with forty-two male and twenty-two female authors. Men are more likely to be repeat correspondents and to use overtly hostile language, which raises questions about the gendered nature of nativist politics. Although the vast majority of the letters to Senator Cedillo's office have California addresses, none was sent from a zip code within his district. Cedillo represents a majority Latino district, yet only seven writers identify themselves as non-European American. Although it is not possible to determine the race or ethnicity of writers who do not self-identify, one refers to himself as "Hispanic," another calls himself a "Latino who was born and raised and has an allegiance to the USA," and two others have Spanish surnames. One writer identifies himself as black and another as Filipino-American. There are no other Spanish or Asian surnames among the writers, and people of color appear to be significantly underrepresented.[9]

Six writers refer to their personal history of immigration or family relationships to immigrants. These identifications appear to be offered as evidence that the writers do not discriminate based on race or are supportive of lawful immigration. Two women co-authors state, "Janice is married to an immigrant and it took them 3 years of arduous paperwork to legalize his entry into this country." Margaret writes, "I was married to a Latino for 50 years and enjoyed his family and relatives. But they came here legally." While six writers share that they are seniors or retired, an analysis of word choice and penmanship

---

8. All letter quotes are exact. The author did not alter the letter writers' spelling, grammar, or punctuation.

9. In California, Democrats, voters under age twenty-three, Latinos, nonvoters, and noncitizens are more likely to support expanding the pool of immigrants eligible for a driver's license than are Republicans, seniors, non-Latinos, and voters (DiCamillo and Field 2005).

suggests that additional letter writers were of advanced age, which accords with empirical findings that seniors ranked immigration as a greater concern than did other demographic groups during the 2007 reform debates (Dionne, in Akdenizli et al. 2008).[10] Most of the letters contain numerous spelling and grammatical errors. This suggests that the majority of letter writers are not highly educated, an inference that supports research conclusions that greater formal educational attainment correlates with more positive attitudes toward immigration (Dionne, in Akdenizli et al. 2008; Scheve and Slaughter 2001).

Aside from basic demographic information, the most common self-identification among the writers is "citizen" (twelve) or "American" (nine), an expression of pride and association with the United States and a claim to a legitimate political voice. Similarly, when writers proclaim that they are "voters" (three) or "taxpayers" (two), they assert membership and political power in California and implicitly contrast themselves with immigrants who cannot vote and whom they perceive as public burdens. Six writers self-identify as veterans, including three men who served in World War II. This suggests a link between military service and concern about the national threat posed by unlawful border crossings and unlawful presence. Perhaps because the writers were older than average, they were most likely to refer to traditional regional newspapers (sixteen) such as the *Los Angeles Daily News*. However, seven writers referenced restrictionist organizations and Web sites, four forwarded anti-immigrant e-mails, three corresponded after seeing Lou Dobbs interview Senator Cedillo on CNN, three sent copies of articles that appear to come from restrictionist writers or organizations, two referenced Fox News, and another two used the logos of conservative talk radio shows. These varied information sources suggest the influence of transforming news media on constituents' correspondence. Writers frequently used multiple exclamation points, capital letters, bold typeface, and underlining in their letters, akin to shouting on paper. These writers are angry, and they feel that Senator Cedillo and other elected representatives do not hear them.

CHANGING MEDIA THEMES AND IMMIGRANT CHARACTERIZATIONS

Restrictionist activists have shaped the driver's license debates by campaigning in the media, testifying at legislative hearings, advising lawmakers, and instigating floods of voter communication (Anti-Defamation League

---

10. U.S. seniors are most likely to be trained in traditional writing systems, and their handwriting may be affected by the aging process (Koppenhaver 2002).

2007). According to the Anti-Defamation League, organizational spokespersons with racist and nativist institutional links currently advise and lobby elected officials. Representatives of organizations such as the Federation for American Immigration Reform (FAIR) are welcomed as immigration experts and represent the restrictionist perspective on talk radio and in major media outlets such as National Public Radio, the *New York Times*, the *Los Angeles Times*, and the *Chicago Tribune*.[11]

This power of restrictionists in contemporary journalism is demonstrated by a comprehensive study of the new media's impact on immigration debates through 2007. Pundits on television news, the Internet, and talk radio have used a narrative of immigration as controversy and crisis to mobilize segments of the population against all policy proposals that might improve the lives of the undocumented. This has made it harder to achieve political compromise on immigration policy (Akdenizli et al. 2008). A study of the new rhetoric of anti-immigrant advocacy organizations, politicians, and media figures found that subtle forms of hate speech against immigrants and Latinos are commonplace in today's immigration debates (NCLR 2008a). By uniting dehumanizing terms and stereotypes with racial or ethnic appeals, these sources cultivate a hostile environment for immigration. Persons of Latin American ancestry are accused of presenting socioeconomic, criminal, and military threats, though these assertions are inadequately substantiated. Mexico and illegal immigrants are accused of plotting the reconquest of California and the Southwest, with the support of Chicano activists (NCLR 2008b). These themes also run through the letters sent to Senator Cedillo.

This shifting context of immigration discourse appears to have influenced the ways that letter writers on the driver's license issue define the undocumented. Unauthorized, undocumented, illegal—all terms used to describe persons lacking lawful immigration status represent a political choice, and none is truly neutral. Ngai (2004) reminds us that the words commonly used to name this population have shifted over time. Decades after "wetback" was largely replaced by the less overtly racist yet more criminalizing "illegal immigrant" and "illegal alien" in popular discourse, the new usage became dominant in federal immigration law, as in the 1996 Illegal Immigration Reform and Immigrant Responsibility Act. Immigrant advocates, Latino activists and journalists, and scholars have decried the use of "illegal alien," a

---

11. In December 2007 the Southern Poverty Law Center classified FAIR as a hate group because of its ties to organizations and individuals that promote white supremacy and eugenics (Beirich 2007).

term that conjures up images of lawbreakers from outer space (K. Johnson 1996–1997; National Association of Hispanic Journalists 2006).

An analysis of the driver's license letters suggests that restrictionist discourse may be shifting. The most common characterization of persons lacking lawful status is still some variation of "illegal" (ninety-seven). However, "illegal aliens" (thirty-five) and "illegals" (thirty-six) are used at similar rates and more often than "illegal immigrant" (twenty-six). This parallels the growing media use of the designation "illegals," which dehumanizes as it denies its subjects even a negatively modified identity as "immigrants" or "aliens" (National Association of Hispanic Journalists 2006). As "illegal" morphs from adjective to noun, it becomes the defining feature of its subject. Numerous letter writers explain their terminology selection and deliberately reject the idea that "illegals" are "immigrants" or merely "undocumented": "California still strong enough to resist driving licenses to illegal aliens—and that is the correct term."

Related to this illegalization process (De Genova 2002) is another dominant refrain—the immigrant as criminal or lawbreaker (thirty-two). Jerry writes, "The attitude is, I'm Mexican, I don't have to obey American laws." Andrew refers to "Mexican immigrants who broke our laws by breaking into our country ILLEGALLY." Despite empirical evidence that immigrants are less likely than citizens to commit crimes (Rumbaut and Ewing 2007), the undocumented are depicted as people who steal, rob, or cheat (six), as rapists (four), murderers (three), gangbangers (two), and drug dealers (one). In the letters, they are trespassers (two) and fugitives (one). More directly related to the driver's license issue, they are called illegal drivers (one) and hit-and-run motorists (one). Although government justifications for denying driver's licenses to the undocumented center on national security and terrorism, potential drivers are rarely labeled terrorists in the letters (six). More often, they are assumed to be Mexicans (fifteen). Although numerous writers assert that their opposition to the legislation is not racist or about race, they occasionally use racialized pejoratives such as "wetback" (five) and employ mock Spanish (such as "EST STOOPIDO!").

NEW ISSUE, OLD RHETORIC

Rather than addressing the specifics of the proposed driver's license legislation, almost all arguments against it highlight the threats—criminal, economic, political, military, cultural, and environmental—that undocumented immigrants allegedly pose to California. Themes of terrorism or security surface in only fifteen letters, as in the following examples. "Doesn't this undermine the efforts of Dept of Homeland Security?" "You recklessly ignore our laws and put the security of our state and nation in danger." Most justifications for driver's license restrictions echo those offered during the Proposition 187 debates.

The most common are that licensing will promote or reward criminal behaviors unrelated to terrorism (forty-one) and that illegal immigrants are a burden for taxpayers and public infrastructure (twenty-seven). Rather than a violation of civil immigration law, writers associate unlawful presence with criminality. "Right now you are encouraging them to steal are you not?" "He comes to take that which does not belong to him, perhaps to commit a crime like working here illegally, dealing in drugs, robbery, rape, theft, or just plain taking another person's Social Security number and converting it to his own benefit." Writers maintain that because immigrants are here without legal authorization, they should not be granted any privileges. "You said there is no reason, not to give illegal aliens a drivers license. . . . How about the fact that they have sneaked into the country, disregarding our laws and have no business being here?" Others believe that granting licenses would be rewarding illegal behavior. "Why do you insist on rewarding illegal aliens with a drivers' license?" Many feel that license access would provide an incentive for border crossings and other illegal acts. "Mostly, [licensing] is just more silent encouragement for people to disregard our laws and come here illegally."

Although the empirical evidence is less than clear (Card 2005; Porter 2006), the second-most-popular argument (twenty-seven) is that the presence of undocumented immigrants hurts U.S. citizens economically. "We don't need anymore burden on California taxpayers due to the constant flood of illegal aliens." In fact, many letters begin with a primary argument about the perils of rewarding illegal behavior and then decry the costs related to the presence of the unauthorized immigrant population. In some letters, the undocumented are accused of getting public assistance for which they are categorically ineligible. "Illegals ruining California. Want welfare. Free health and hospital care. Food stamps. Free Rent." Other writers refer to the strain that immigrant families place on schools, hospitals, prisons, and public infrastructure, a more limited and accurate picture of the services they may use. "Our schools and hospitals are inundated with illegals and what do you do?" Perhaps related to the number of writers who are retirees, only eight express concern about unauthorized employment. A rare writer who describes himself as Mexican

American poignantly connects the disappearance of skilled blue-collar jobs to competition with undocumented workers. "How about the construction jobs, the plumbing jobs, the carpet laying jobs, and the factory jobs that not too long ago paid a decent wage until we started getting undercut by the illegals."

Writers express other concerns about illegal immigration and the expansion of driver's license access. These are often offered after the writers have expressed their primary concerns about immigrants as criminals or financial liabilities. Another eight express concern that "illegals" will vote in U.S. elections, a fear promoted by restrictionist spokespersons and media (NCLR 2008a). Some writers argue that because the 1993 "motor voter" law enables persons to register to vote when they apply for a license, Cedillo's bill would enfranchise the undocumented.[12] Such illegal voting is largely understood to help the Democratic Party, a boost that the letter writers see as a political threat. "I can see all kinds of problems coming when 'illegals' have a 'drivers License.' When they go the polls to vote (Democratic) they will say—'see I have a license—I can vote. Check my license—I can do whatever.'" "You see with a valid driver's license, they will be able to vote and completely change the laws of our state." Eight letter writers also accuse Cedillo ("does the word illegal mean anything to you except a way to get illegals to vote"), Latinos ("Latinos want to flood this country with illegals to create a voting bloc"), and Democrats ("the drivers license is merely a way to provide democratic party with more votes") of conspiring to illegally influence California politics. Though there is a robust history of lawful noncitizen voting in the United States (Hayduk 2006; Varsanyi 2005) and new citizen voters are affecting state politics (Ramakrishnan 2005), all individuals must swear or affirm that they are citizens when they register to vote. Despite rumors and accusations of illegal noncitizen voting, there is very little evidence of this crime. Intimidation and harassment to obstruct voting is far more common than noncitizen voter fraud (Minnite and Callahan 2003).

Along with the threat of illegal Mexican voters, Mexico is a recurring theme in seventeen letters. Four authors depict Mexicans as criminals who can escape punishment by returning across the border. "The Mexican can cause mayhem and celebrate their holidays, stop traffic and disrupt areas of the city, and kill and maim people and than flee to Mexico and have

---

12. The National Voter Registration Act of 1993 requires states to provide citizens with the opportunity to register to vote when they apply for or seek to renew a driver's license. The Help America Vote Act of 2002 mandates that in order to vote, registrants must provide either a driver's license number, a state ID number, or the last four digits of their Social Security number.

no fear of extradition." Two writers object to the Mexican government's efforts to prevent the execution of its citizens, although Mexican law and international human rights norms support this stance. "If illegals get drivers license they will immigrate to U.S. and kill someone only to run back across the border." In seven letters, writers assert that licensing these immigrants would be a step toward making California more like, or even part of, Mexico. "SB 1160 etc., is the Mexicanization of California—(is unacceptable, must not become Law)." This includes charges that Mexico is trying to reconquer the southwestern United States, a farfetched yet popular refrain of anti-immigrant organizations and some right-wing media pundits (Anti-Defamation League 2007; NCLR 2008b). "Tired of hearing Mexicans say they are going to take back California." Four assert that the United States should treat illegal immigrants as poorly as Mexico treats those who cross its southern border, and two believe that the poverty that causes Mexicans to illegally enter and work in the United States needs to be addressed by Mexico, not by the United States.

Other letter writers offer less inflammatory arguments, the most common (fourteen) being that California's voters oppose letting undocumented immigrants drive. Jerry asks, "Senator, are you again getting into just what the majority of us in California are not wanting?" Nine writers make environmental claims that licensing immigrants will contribute to overpopulation ("too many here now") and pollution ("illegal aliens would clog our already crowded freeways and produce smog"). For three writers, because immigrants lack knowledge of the English language and U.S. laws and customs, they should not be allowed to drive. Josephine, from Southern California, writes, "Most of them do not speak English. You really want them driving without being able to read signs or whatever?" If it prevailed, this position would prevent many legal immigrants and foreign students from driving. The theme of language surfaces in nine letters and includes complaints that immigrants do not learn English, that Spanish use is prevalent in the state, and that translation services cost the taxpayers. A doctor writes, "Many are too lazy to learn English so, again at the taxpayers expense, we provide translators and have documents printed in Spanish, thus encouraging their indolence."

A small minority of authors directly address substantive issues in Cedillo's legislative proposal. Seven fear that when undocumented drivers obtain licenses, few will purchase insurance and premiums will rise.[13] Curtis

---

13. In fact, after the undocumented were permitted to drive legally in New Mexico and Utah, rates of uninsured motorists declined by over 50 percent (NILC 2008).

followed the bill and was concerned with amendments: "Your bill is too watered down and will not do a thing to fix the problem." Jason discusses federal preemption ("Federal law supersedes state law. You cannot give a legal document to an illegal citizen"). Yet most writers seem to be venting general concerns about "illegal" immigrants, especially those from Mexico, who are seen as threats to person and property, to political power and national sovereignty, and to order. They are understood as dangers to the economy, environment, language, and culture of California and the nation. For many, this perception of menace extends to the Mexican nation, legal immigrants from Mexico, U.S. citizens of Mexican ancestry, and other Latinos. For example, four writers criticize or attack the Chicano student organization MEChA (Movimiento Estudiantil Chicano de Aztlán) and its members. ("Do not vote for Cruz Bustamante because he was in MECHa will in college"). In one inflammatory postcard, a writer calls for the death of Mexican immigrants and all persons of Hispanic descent ("I Hope the terrorists nuke California and kill every filthy Spic in the state").

CONCLUSION: RESTORING DEMOCRATIC DEBATE IN STATE IMMIGRANT POLICY

The letters in opposition to Cedillo's driver's license proposals appear to be disproportionately written by white males and seniors from outside his district and do not reflect the diversity of California. The angry tone and use of racialized discourse in numerous letters suggest that these voices may not reflect the state majority or even the majority of those opposed to restoring driving privileges to more of California's immigrants. Although fear of immigrants in times of economic, social, and political change may resonate historically, the restrictionist rhetoric analyzed here also departs significantly from that of the past. Because of popular constructions emerging over the twentieth century that identified much Mexican and Latin American immigration as "illegal," the undocumented are one of the last groups in the United States that may be freely attacked with social approbation. Yet numerous letter writers assert that they are not racist, even as they may subtly or overtly impugn persons of Latin American ancestry. Because of demographic and legal changes, Gil Cedillo and other representatives of California's immigrant districts must either bow to the pressures of largely white voters outside of their districts or take up the highly controversial cause of improving the lives of the people in their districts regardless of their immigration status.

The changing media and political contexts also make California's driver's license struggle distinct from legislative battles of the past, driving Cedillo's bills to defeat and fueling the rapid spread of similar restrictions throughout the country. Perhaps as important as the security concerns used to justify restricting the rights of immigrants after 9/11 is the increased capacity for restrictionist activists to disseminate their message and organize through transformed news media and information technologies. Letter writers' repetition of the language of nativist or hate groups, including the dehumanizing term "illegals," hints at the reach of activists' messages. Themes such as the Mexican as criminal invader and illegal voter and the reconquest of the Southwest by Mexico generate ambivalence toward or rejection of Latinos as part of the nation. According to the Federal Bureau of Investigation, reports of hate crimes against Latinos increased by approximately one-third between 2003 and 2006 (Mock 2007), at a time when anti-immigrant organizing and rhetoric escalated. What can be done to encourage healthy, democratic debate on the merits of state-level immigrant policy proposals? Scholars and civil rights organizations must continue to examine the impacts of the recent wave of restrictionist activism on traditional news media and newer forms of information dissemination. News outlets should resist the temptation to entertain at the expense of our society's newest members. Journalists and elected officials should be vigilant of immigration "experts" who spread misinformation and hatred, and elected officials should be careful about assuming that the correspondence they receive about immigrants reflects the beliefs of their constituents or the voting public.

WORKS CITED

Akdenizli, Banu, E. J. Dionne, Jr., Martin Kaplan, Tom Rosensteil, and Roberto Suro. 2008. "Democracy in the Age of New Media: A Report on the Media and the Immigration Debate." Washington, DC: Brookings Institution.

Anti-Defamation League. 2007. "Immigrants Targeted: Extremist Rhetoric Moves into the Mainstream." http://www.adl.org/civil_rights/anti_immigrant/.

Baldassare, Mark. 2002. *A California State of Mind: The Conflicted Voter in a Changing World*. Berkeley, CA: University of California Press.

Beirich, Heidi. 2007. "The Teflon Nativists: FAIR Marked by Ties to White Supremacy." Intelligence Report. Montgomery, AL: Southern Poverty Law Center.

Brown, E. Richard, Ying-Ying Meng, Carolyn A. Mendez, and Hongjian Yu. 2001. "Uninsured Californians in Assembly and Senate Districts, 2000." Los Angeles, CA: Center for Health Policy Research, University of California, Los Angeles.

Card, David E. 2005. "Is the New Immigration Really So Bad?" *Economic Journal* 115, no. 507: 300–23.

Chavez, Leo R. 2001. *Covering Immigration: Popular Images and the Politics of the Nation.* Berkeley, CA: University of California Press.

Confessore, Nicholas. 2007. "Spitzer Drops Bid to Offer Licenses More Widely," *New York Times,* November 14.

Coutin, Susan Bibler. 2000. *Legalizing Moves: Salvadoran Immigrants' Struggle for U.S. Residency.* Ann Arbor, MI: University of Michigan Press.

De Genova, Nicholas P. 2002. "Migrant 'Illegality' and Deportability in Everyday Life," *Annual Review of Anthropology* 31: 419–47.

DiCamillo, Mark, and Mervin Field. 2005. "Californians Oppose Issuing Driver's Licenses to Undocumented Immigrants." San Francisco, CA: Field Research Corporation.

Frank, Larry, and Kent Wong. 2004. "Dynamic Political Mobilization: The Los Angeles County Federation of Labor," *Working USA* 8: 155–81.

Gutiérrez, Elena R. 2008. *Fertile Matters: The Politics of Mexican-Origin Women's Reproduction.* Austin, TX: University of Texas Press.

Hamilton, Nora, and Norma Stoltz Chinchilla. 2001. *Seeking Community in a Global City: Guatemalans and Salvadorans in Los Angeles.* Philadelphia, PA: Temple University Press.

Hayduk, Ron. 2006. *Democracy for All: Restoring Immigrant Voting Rights in the United States.* New York: Routledge.

Hondagneu-Sotelo, Pierrette. 1995. "Women and Children First: New Directions in Anti-Immigrant Politics," *Socialist Review* 25, no. 1: 169–91.

Inda, Jonathan. 2000. "'Foreign Bodies': Migrants, Parasites, and the Pathological Nation," *Discourse: Journal for Theoretical Studies in Media and Culture* 22, no. 3: 46–62.

Institute of Governmental Studies. 2000. "Report on Minority Registration from the 2000 General Election." Statewide Database. Berkeley, CA: University of California, Berkeley.

———. 2001. "Census 2000 (Latino/Non-Latino) Race Variables by 1991 Districts." Berkeley, CA: University of California, Berkeley.

Johnson, Hans P., Belinda Reyes, Laura Mameesh, and Elisa Barbour. 1999. "Taking the Oath: An Analysis of Naturalization in California and the United States." San Francisco, CA: Public Policy Institute of California.

Johnson, Kevin R. 1995. "An Essay on Immigration Politics, Popular Democracy, and California's Proposition 187: The Political Relevance and Legal Irrelevance of Race," *Washington Law Review* 70: 629–73.

———. 1996–1997. "Aliens and the U.S. Immigration Laws: The Social and Legal Construction of Nonpersons," *University of Miami Inter-American Law Review* 28, no. 2: 263–92.

Koppenhaver, Katherine. 2002. *Attorney's Guide to Document Examination*. Westport, CT: Greenwood Press.

Milkman, Ruth. 2006. *L.A. Story: Immigrant Workers and the Future of the Labor Movement*. New York: Russell Sage Foundation.

Minnite, Lori, and David Callahan. 2003. "Securing the Vote: An Analysis of Election Fraud." New York: Demos.

Mock, Brentin. 2007. "Immigration Backlash: Hate Crimes against Latinos Flourish." Montgomery, AL: Southern Poverty Law Center.

National Association of Hispanic Journalists. 2006. "NAHJ Urges News Media to Stop Using Dehumanizing Terms When Covering Immigration," *PRNewswire*, March 28.

NCLR (National Council of La Raza). 2008a. "NCLR Challenges Distortions Made about Minority Communities, Washington, D.C." Press release, October 16. http://www.nclr.org/content/news/detail/54376/.

———. 2008b. "Fact Sheet: Code Words in the Debate." Washington, DC: NCLR.

Neuman, Gerald L. 1996. *Strangers to the Constitution: Immigrants, Borders, and Fundamental Law*. Princeton, NJ: Princeton University Press.

New York Immigration Coalition. 2007. "'F.A.I.R. Hearings': An Analysis of the Intimate Connections between 'Experts' Testifying against the New York State DMV Policy and the Anti-Immigrant, Nativist Group - F.A.I.R." http://www.thenyic.org/images/uploads/FAIR_Hearings_Report.pdf.

Ngai, Mae M. 2004. *Impossible Subjects: Illegal Aliens and the Making of Modern America*. Princeton, NJ: Princeton University Press.

NILC (National Immigration Law Center). 2008. "Why Denying Driver's Licenses to Undocumented Immigrants Harms Public Safety and Makes Our Communities Less Secure." Fact Sheet. http://www.nilc.org/immspbs/dls/FactSheet_dls_2008-01-16.pdf.

———. 2009. "Overview of States' Driver's License Requirements." http://www.nilc.org/immspbs/dls/state_dl_rqrmts_ovrvw_2009-04-27.pdf.

Office of Senate Floor Analyses. 2003. "SB 60: Drivers License Eligibility: Undocumented Immigrants." Sacramento, CA: California State Senate Rules Committee.

Ono, Kent, and John M. Sloop. 2002. *Shifting Borders: Rhetoric, Immigration, and California's Proposition 187*. Philadelphia, PA: Temple University Press.

Padín, José, and Shelley Smith. 2004. "Death of a Nation: Conservative Talk Radio's Immigration and Race Curriculum." In *Censored 2005*, ed. P. Phillips. New York: Seven Stories Press.

Passel, Jeffrey, and D'Vera Cohn. 2009. "A Portrait of Undocumented Immigrants in the United States." Report. Washington, DC: Pew Hispanic Center. http://pewhispanic.org/files/reports/107.pdf.

Porter, Eduardo. 2006. "Cost of Illegal Immigration May Be Less than Meets the Eye," *New York Times*, April 16.

Ramakrishnan, S. Karthick. 2005. *Democracy in Immigrant America: Changing Demographics and Political Participation*. Palo Alto, CA: Stanford University Press.

Rumbaut, Rubén, and Walter Ewing. 2007. "The Myth of Immigrant Criminality and the Paradox of Assimilation: Incarceration Rates among Native and Foreign-Born Men." Washington, DC: Immigration Policy Center, American Immigration Law Foundation.

Santa Ana, Otto. 2002. *Brown Tide Rising: Metaphors of Latinos in Contemporary American Public Discourse*. Austin, TX: University of Texas Press.

Scheve, Kenneth, and Matthew Slaughter. 2001. "Labor-Market Competition and Individual Preferences over Immigration Policy," *Review of Economics and Statistics* 83, no. 1: 133–45.

Seif, Hinda. 2004. "'Wise Up!' Undocumented Latino Youth, Mexican-American Legislators, and the Struggle for Higher Education Access," *Latino Studies* 2, no. 2: 210–30.

———. 2008. "Wearing Union T-Shirts: Undocumented Women Farm Workers and Gendered Circuits of Political Power," *Latin American Perspectives* 35, no. 1: 78–98.

———. 2010. "The Civic Life of Latina/o Immigrant Youth: Challenging Boundaries and Creating Safe Spaces." In *Handbook of Research on Civic Engagement in Youth*, ed. L. Sherrod, J. Torney-Purta, and C. Flanagan. Hoboken, NJ: John Wiley and Sons.

Sohoni, Deenesh. 2006. "The 'Immigrant Problem': Modern-Day Nativism on the Web," *Current Sociology* 54, no. 6: 827–50.

Tennessee Immigrant and Refugee Rights Coalition. 2005. "The Tennessee Driving Certificate: Background, Pitfalls, and Lessons Learned." http://www.nilc.org/immspbs/dls/TN_cert_lessons_learned_0605.pdf.

Varsanyi, Monica. 2005. "The Rise and Fall (and Rise?) of Noncitizen Voting: Immigration and the Shifting Scales of Citizenship and Suffrage in the United States," *Space and Polity* 9, no. 2: 113–34.

Vélez, Veronica, Linsay Perez Huber, Corina Benavides Lopez, Ariana de la Luz, and Daniel G. Solorzano. 2008. "Battling for Human Rights and Social Justice: A Latina/o Critical Race Media Analysis of Latina/o Student Youth Activism in the Wake of 2006 Anti-Immigrant Sentiment," *Social Justice* 35, no. 1: 7–27.

Zúñiga, Víctor, and Rubén Hernández-León, eds. 2005. *New Destinations: Mexican Immigration in the United States.* New York: Russell Sage Foundation.